12

DATE DUE

very 11/4/13	
OCLC 11/21	
OCLC 8/3/23	

GAYLORD   PRINTED IN U.S.A.

Vera K. Fast is a historian and archivist. She holds a PhD from the University of Manitoba and, until her retirement, worked as an archivist in the Provincial Archives of Manitoba.

'This is a thoroughly engaging and moving history of events which until now have been treated only partially, superficially, or largely biographically. It is a comprehensive historical overview and analysis of a remarkable, early chapter in the history of the Holocaust.'

Lionel Steiman,
Professor (retd) and Senior Scholar,
University of Manitoba

'Vera K. Fast presents a well-rounded account of the Kindertransport movement. Her extensive research in British archival sources ensures that her views are solidly grounded and her substantial use of first-person accounts by Kindertransport participants gives the reader a good understanding of what it felt like to be uprooted. Particularly noteworthy is the author's discussion of the different viewpoints within the rescue community and the Jewish community that enriched but also complicated the task of rescuing the children from the Continent. Her account of the personal experiences of the Kindertransport children are fascinating for themselves and for their relevance to the twenty-first century world in which there are many child refugees.'

Daniel Stone,
Professor Emeritus of History,
University of Winnipeg and
President of the
Jewish Heritage Centre of Western Canada

'As a Jewish child being persecuted by the Nazi government in Germany in the 1930s, I was fortunate that my parents put me on a Kindertransport to Great Britain. Vera K. Fast has written a comprehensive and well researched book leading up to and chronicling this historical rescue mission. I highly recommend it as serious reading of another aspect of the history of the Holocaust.'

Margaret Heller Goldberger,
Chair of the Speakers Bureau of the Kindertransport Association
and Member of the Board of Governors
of B'nai B'rith International

CHILDREN'S EXODUS

A History of the Kindertransport

VERA K. FAST

I.B. TAURIS

LONDON · NEW YORK

Published and reprinted in 2011 by I.B.Tauris & Co Ltd
6 Salem Road, London W2 4BU
175 Fifth Avenue, New York NY 10010
www.ibtauris.com

Distributed in the United States and Canada Exclusively by Palgrave Macmillan,
175 Fifth Avenue, New York, NY 10010

ISBN: 978 1 84885 537 3

A full CIP record for this book is available from the British Library
A full CIP record for this book is available from the Library of Congress

Library of Congress catalog card: available

Camera-ready copy edited and supplied by
Oxford Publishing Services, Oxford
Printed and bound in Great Britain by
CPI Antony Rowe, Chippenham

MIX
Paper from
responsible sources
FSC
www.fsc.org
FSC® C013604

For my children and grandchildren

Jane and David
Adrian and Andrew

With deep gratitude that they have been spared
the trauma of the children whose stories are related
in the following pages

CONTENTS

vii

ILLUSTRATIONS

ABBREVIATIONS

AJR	Association of Jewish Refugees
ATS	Army Transport Service
BCRC	British Committee for Refugees from Czechoslovakia
CBC	Canadian Broadcasting Corporation
CBF	Central British Fund for German Jewry
CCCC	Committee for the Care of Children from the Camps
CRREC	Chief Rabbi's Religious Emergency Council
FHLA	Friends' House Library/Archives, London
HCD	House of Commons Debates
HL	Hartley Library/Archives, University of Southampton
HM	His Majesty's
IOM	Isle of Man
IWM	Imperial War Museum
JRC	Jewish Refugees Committee
LMA	London Metropolitan Archives
LPL	Lambeth Palace Library, London
NV	Naamloze Venootschap
ORT	*Obshestvo Remeslenofo zemledelcheskofo Truda* (Society for Trades and Agricultural Labour)
OSE	Oeuvre de Secours aux Enfants
RAF	Royal Air Force
RCM	Refugee Children's Movement
SPSL	Society for the Preservation of Science and Learning
SS	Schutzstaffel (Defence Corps)
UNRRA	United Nations Relief and Rehabilitation Administration
WIZO	Women's International Zionist Organization

GLOSSARY

Berochoth	heartfelt thanks
Din Torah	judgement according to the Torah
Erev	eve of
Goy/goyim	non-Jew/non-Jews (pejorative)
Habonim	Jewish socialist Zionist youth movement
Halacha/Halakah	Jewish laws, supplementing written laws or custom
Kaddish	prayer for the dead
kashrut	Jewish dietary laws
Mischlinge	people of mixed (Aryan/Jewish) descent; non-Aryan Christians
Mitzvah	commandment
Quakerspeisung	Quaker meals
Sabbath	weekly reunion
shikse	derogative Yiddish term for a non-Jewish female
Streifendienst	Hitler Youth secret police force
Tefilla	song of nearness to the Almighty
Tefillin	(also called phylacteries) are a set of small, black leather boxes containing scrolls inscribed with verses from the *Torah*, worn by observant Jews during weekday morning prayers.
Torah	Jewish written law
Wiedergutmachung	to make good again
Yad Vashem	Israel's official memorial to the Jewish victims of the Holocaust
Yeshiva	seminary
Yom Kippur	Day of Atonement

ACKNOWLEDGEMENTS

IT is with pleasure and gratitude that I acknowledge those individuals whose stories I have used and those institutions and archives that allowed me access to information. I wish especially to thank David Lewinski and the late Hugh Schramm (always referred to as 'Hughie' by friends and family), who first introduced me to the Kindertransport story, and who remained friends long after our first interviews. Also to Nora and Pat who extended such generous hospitality.

Bertha Leverton opened many doors. Her energy and helpfulness were a source of inspiration, as were her positive attitude, organizing ability (the first Kindertransport reunion was her brainchild) and her part in collecting and keeping alive the amazing stories of other *Kinder* like herself.

Michael Gelb refused to let this project die. His faith in the story, his patient encouragement and valuable suggestions mark him as a true altruist.

Without the Schonfeld Family's permission to access the papers and photographs of their father, Rabbi Doctor Solomon Schonfeld, the refugee children's story would be sadly incomplete. Many thanks for your generosity and helpfulness.

The Hartley Library's conferral of a Visiting Fellowship at the University of Southampton, and the guidance of Dr Chris Woolgar, made possible much of the research and writing of this study. I am deeply indebted for this assistance and the continuing interest and support of Dr Woolgar and his staff.

The staff at the Lambeth Palace Library, the Wiener Library, the Bodleian Library in Oxford, the British Library, and the London

Metropolitan Archives were always helpful. I acknowledge with thanks permission to access the records of the Board of Deputies and those of the Central British Fund (now World Jewish Relief), as well as the tapes and transcripts of interviews made available by the Imperial War Museum. This is a unique and valuable resource. At the United States Holocaust Memorial Museum Caroline Waddell of the Photo Archive provided helpful assistance, as did Kurt Goldberger, President of the Kindertransport Association of North America (KTA). Special thanks to Margaret Goldberger for reading and commenting on the manuscript; as a *Kind* she provided information not found in any archives, and did it so promptly! She has been the soul of helpfulness.

I also wish to acknowledge the many *Kinder* who agreed to be interviewed and those who are mentioned in the pages of this book. Not all are identified by their full name. Some asked that only their given names be used, a few requests to use a full name were not acknowledged, while some, as in Dr Schonfeld's papers, are identified by only one name in the primary documents. Whatever the reason, all those whose stories have been used, are hereby gratefully acknowledged.

Heartfelt thanks also to Dr Lionel Steiman and Dr Daniel Stone for the many hours of time they gave so generously to reading and critiquing this manuscript and to their helpful suggestions. Their encouragement and comments certainly made this a better and more accurate historical work.

Selina and Jason Cohen of Oxford Publishing Services expertly provided the essential technical and indexing support required. Joanna Godfrey at I.B.Tauris has been most helpful and encouraging and so swift to bring this project to fruition. We need more editors like you, Joanna. Thank you. Thanking you also to Jayne Ansell, production editor at I.B.Tauris, for tying together all the bits and pieces and making them come out right.

Finally I wish heartily to thank my husband, Peter, for his unfailing support and patience. Sharing a spouse with thousands of *Kinder* for ten or more years is not always what one expects from marriage, and it takes a kind heart and an open mind to endure gracefully. Bless you, Peter!

PREFACE

'MY father was a musician. He was often away, travelling to play in concerts and sometimes he would take me with him, but he was an "Aryan", and my mother was Jewish, a "non-Aryan". After the Nuremberg laws of 1935, when marriage to a non-Aryan became a crime against the state, my father's family and his colleagues persuaded (forced?) him to leave my mother, my two brothers and me. We never saw him again, though we looked for him after the war.'

These recollections of Hugh (Horst) Schramm constituted my introduction to the Kindertransport movement. As I listened to the stories of Hugh and later of David Lewinski (both of whom had been fostered by an Anglican Church worker in northern Canada), and as my interest broadened to include other *Kinder*, I realized that their stories were part of a much larger whole, a lesser-known aspect of Holocaust history. Therefore children's stories – whether about the Kindertransport, life in hiding, or survival in the camps – form the fabric of the tapestry presented in the following pages.

My book surveys Jewish child refugee immigration to Great Britain, from the first Kindertransport in 1938 to the arrival of the last displaced persons in 1948. I rely heavily on rarely used primary sources to shed light not only on the story as a whole, but on its lesser-known aspects. The first chapter is a brief survey of the political background of Nazism and the Holocaust, while the subsequent early chapters examine the organizations that undertook to evacuate Jewish children and place them in homes throughout Britain; they detail the youngsters' experiences, starting with separation from their parents

xiii

through arrival in the receiving camps and, finally, placement in foster care. All the refugee children in London and other sensitive locations were evacuated to the countryside when the Second World War was declared, often to villages where no one had ever seen a Jewish person. Older teens faced internment as 'enemy aliens' – a few were actually sent to Canada or Australia as 'prisoners of war'!

Portions of this history are reasonably well known, recounted in numerous memoirs. Yet a memoir can offer the reader no more than one individual's experience of larger phenomena. The present study synthesizes many published and unpublished accounts of the children's lives in wartime and postwar Britain. The reader will learn that many of the children's experiences were deeply painful; earlier religious upbringing often influenced how difficult a placement might be and how easily a child might adjust. The unique situations of Orthodox Jewish children and of Jewish Christian children in particular – hitherto little studied – will receive special attention.

Its focus on published *Kinder* memoirs notwithstanding, my book relies heavily on unpublished material found in the Wiener Library in London, the archives of the Society of Friends (Quakers) in London, the records of the Society for the Protection of Science and Learning in the Bodleian Library at Oxford University, and the records of the Jewish Board of Deputies in the London Metropolitan Archives, among others. The most significant troves, however, are the newly-available papers of Rabbi Dr Solomon Schonfeld in the Hartley Library of the University of Southampton, and the papers of George Bell, Bishop of Chichester, in the Lambeth Palace Library, London.

Bishop Bell's papers document in particular the Judeo–Christian experience – Jewish converts to Christianity. Helen Bentwich, active in Jewish refugee work, first drew the bishop's attention to the plight of the non-Aryan Christians in Germany in 1933, noting, 'The Jews belong to a community ... but these "non-Aryans" are veritable pariahs and belong to no corporate body which unites them.'[1] The Bell papers trace the increasing involvement of British Christians in the refugee movement, along with ever expanding Jewish efforts, in the amelioration of the suffering of their German–Jewish coreligionists, culminating in the formation of several organizations to assist child refugees. They also document the growing Christian concern for all Jewish children. Bishop Bell's papers, to my knowledge, have not previously been used in works related to the Kindertransports. They shed light on aspects of the movement hitherto seldom inspected.

The Kindertransport story might well have ended with the arrival of the last children from the Netherlands except for the subsequent career of Rabbi Dr Solomon Schonfeld, animating spirit of the Chief Rabbi's Religious Emergency Council (CRREC). Schonfeld extended the term 'children's transports' to describe the evacuation of several hundred children who had survived the Holocaust in hiding or even in concentration camps. Schonfeld's extensive collection has yet to be thoroughly mined, but it opens windows onto many subjects. Of particular interest in the present work is its material on the Orthodox Jewish response to the Holocaust. Together with the Chief Rabbi of the United Hebrew Congregations of the British Empire, Dr Joseph Hertz, Rabbi Schonfeld helped form the CRREC in 1938, as the specifically Orthodox arm of the Kindertransport movement. Dr Schonfeld proved to be a courageous, energetic and charismatic leader, but also one whose individualistic methods often caused friction with other refugee organizations. One source of tension was his commitment to saving not merely the lives of the children but also their Jewish identity – as Dr Schonfeld himself, and from his point of view no one else, defined it. In contrast to these convictions, most other relief agencies focused on physically bringing the children to safety and only then addressing their spiritual needs. This friction is well documented both in the Schonfeld papers and – from an opposing point of view – in the records of the Central British Fund (now the World Jewish Relief) and of the Board of Deputies of British Jews. These sources permit a new understanding of tensions that at times threatened to bring all rescue efforts to a halt.

Dr Schonfeld also organized the postwar rescue of hundreds of children who had been hidden or who had survived internment in concentration camps. His papers record the search for these children in postwar Europe and the sometimes dramatic methods used to bring them to England. Documents in the collection prove definitively that postwar ransoms were paid for some children, a point of previous debate among some historians. A profoundly dramatic story in itself, this second wave of child refugees was in many respects directly connected to the influx of the 1938–39 *Kinder*. Records, although incomplete because of wartime losses, show that although new organizations emerged to deal with this present influx, those organizations responsible for the 1938–39 effort also remained active for some time after the war. The Central British Fund, for example, assumed financial responsibility for the new arrivals just as they ultimately had for all *Kinder*. To include these postwar children in the Kindertransport saga seems a natural progression. The prominence in this study of the pivotal Orthodox leader in the child refugee movement, Rabbi Solomon Schonfeld, helps correct the lack of knowledge of the role of the Orthodox wing of Jewry in the deliverance of European Jewish children. The release of his papers provides a new insight into the controversial methods of one of the most passionate, but contentious personalities of the refugee movement. Dr Schonfeld's single-minded contribution to the rescue of the *Kinder*, and to the subsequent retrieval of many of them from non-Jewish homes, made him simultaneously an intensely loved and bitterly resented figure. His role in the child refugee programmes deserves more – and a more clear-eyed recognition.

My last chapters look at the lives of former *Kinder* as adults. Some of them were reunited with parents or a parent after the war – not always a joyful event after years of separation and of acculturation by the children to British life. Some of the now adult refugee children remained in England, others emigrated. They followed various paths in coming to terms with the Holocaust, their Jewishness, their new lives and other matters of pervading importance. Relief organizations closed their files but what happened to children still unable to fend for themselves? What were the myriad other painful questions that ensued from the uprooting of thousands of youngsters, and which continued to shape their lives after the war? These last chapters address such questions but, by definition, can wrest only tentative answers from such a complex and open-ended narrative.

No one study can adequately recount the story of the Kinder-transports and those whom they saved. Yet the present work, drawing on sources hitherto little explored, fills a significant gap in the broader understanding of the Holocaust. It is an effort, in the words of child therapist Sarah Moskovitz, 'to wring something life-affirming and productive from massive death and endless evil'.[2] Providing an overview and not an in-depth study, while also addressing the lesser-known aspects of the lives of child refugees, this book is intended to be yet another voice in an effort to keep their story alive.

1

DESCENT INTO DARKNESS[1]

BEFORE Ilse Haas left for England on the Kindertransport her father took her to see her old grandmother in Sachsenhagen near Hanover. One senses Ilse's pride when she spoke of her ancestors living in Sachsenhagen, the family home, since the seventeenth century.[2] She was probably unaware that there had been a Jewish presence in Cologne since AD 321 and in other German cities for almost as long. The Jews were justifiably proud of their contributions to German society, but were apparently oblivious that these had occurred at the cost of much of their religious birthright. The historian John Dippel observes that the majority of German Jews 'subordinated their Jewishness to their Germanness' by various means, especially by marrying into non-Jewish families (by 1930 an estimated one in four German Jews were marrying out of the community),[3] by conversion, or simply by non-observance of their religious heritage. Ingeborg Hecht, for example, remembered that she and her brother knew nothing about the Jewish religion. '[Our] ignorance of Jewish customs extended to the menorah in Father's study, which we simply regarded as a candlestick with seven branches.'[4] Historian Marion Kaplan asserts that, with the children of intermarriage usually raised as Christians and most Jews 'enthusiastically' adopting German culture and social mores, by the 1920s 'some Jewish leaders actually feared the complete fusion of their community into German society by the end of the twentieth century.'[5]

The matter of assimilation was, of course, rather complex and nuanced, but suffice it to say here that, as in Jewish communities elsewhere, there were different kinds and degrees of religious observance among Jewish families in Germany. Observant Jews were largely found among *Ostjuden* (Jews from eastern Europe, especially Poland and Russia), with whom assimilated Jews felt uncomfortable. Assimilated Jews tended to agree with Walther Rathenau, a Jew and German nationalist who became German foreign minister, that this 'alien and isolated race [the *Ostjuden*] ... loud and self-conscious in their dress, hot-blooded and restless in their manner [undermined] their [the assimilated Jews] assiduous efforts to blend quietly into Berlin's business and professional circles to the point of invisibility'.[6]

Certainly, by 1933 the majority of German Jews, especially those in Berlin, had successfully 'blended quietly' into the larger society. Theirs was a proud wartime record for the Fatherland in the First World War, with 100,000 men, or nearly 18 per cent of the entire German-Jewish population, serving in the forces. Of these, 35,000 were decorated and 12,000 lost their lives. Rudi Lowenstein was one among several *Kinder* who remembered that his father, who later perished in the camps, served in the war with pride and was decorated for valour with the iron cross.[7] German Jews had achieved success in industry and business, especially in banking, medicine, journalism, the law, literature and the arts.[8] David Cesarani states that, 'Three-quarters of all Jews in gainful employment were engaged in trade, commerce, the financial sector, and the professions. ... [They achieved] prominence in the arts and sciences. Several of the great publishing houses were Jewish-owned; Jews were over-represented among writers and journalists, in theatre and in the film industry.'[9] The memoirs of the *Kinder* testify to this: Olga's father was 'an important book publisher'; Henry's grandfather a university professor; Hugh's (Horst's) father a musician; Margaret's father a banker.[10] Helen Bentwich, a prominent British Jewish activist, however, said in an interview at the time, 'The reason why Jews got more than their proportion in the medical and legal professions is that till fairly recently, these professions were looked down upon socially and the good Germans went into the army or the diplomatic service.'[11] A more significant reason, perhaps, was that other professions were closed to Jews.[12] Be that as it may, German Jews were generally very well situated in the early 1930s.

In view of their relative prominence, it is important to remember that in 1933 Jews constituted a very small part of the German population – less than 1 per cent, or approximately 525,000 people. What urgency then prompted the Nazis, immediately on gaining power, to promulgate anti-Semitic legislation that forbade the employment of Jews in universities, schools, the legal profession and civil service?

Unquestionably, anti-Semitism was not exclusively a Nazi or even a German phenomenon. As Raul Hilberg writes, 'Anti-Jewish racism had its beginnings in the second half of the seventeenth century, when the "Jewish caricature" first appeared in cartoons.'[13] Yet, by legislation passed in 1869 and 1871, Jews were fully emancipated in Germany, and the German historian Thomas Nipperdey rightly claims that 'in comparison to that of France, Austria, or Russia, German anti-Semitism on the eve of the First World War was certainly not the most extreme.'[14] It appears to have been this very emancipation, however, that triggered new racial tensions in Germany, for it allowed many more Jews to become socially and culturally assimilated and therefore to attain a higher public profile. Reflecting right-wing German sentiment of the time, in 1895 a Herr Ahlwardt insisted in the Reichstag, 'A Jew who is born in Germany, is still no German; he is still a Jew,' and, as a Jew, not a German, he was considered 'widely obtrusive and subversive'.[15] Ironically, from being hated for being different, the Jews were now accused of being too German, too successful at the expense of ethnic Germans. 'We really believed,' remembers a young German woman quoted in Dippel, 'that the Jews were taking jobs away from Germans and therefore we hated them.' To this mind-set, 'race was the distinguishing feature that could not be gainsaid, and it was on these grounds that the Jews were henceforth to be labelled and vilified.'[16] Dippel continues: 'what assimilated ways and secular manner could mask, Jewish racial stereotyping could strip away.'[17] This was the attitude of most German politicians.

Historian Saul Friedlander holds two factors responsible for the failure of assimilation to eliminate anti-Semitism – namely 'the survival of traditional religious anti-Semitism and the related proliferation of conspiracy theories in which Jews always played a role'.[18] Religious anti-Semitism, dating back to the time of Martin Luther and before, was deeply embedded in German culture and religious life. It can reasonably be asserted that it was a greater factor in anti-Semitism than the more modern theories of race. Conspiracy theories, by comparison, were relatively more recent. The most widely promoted of these theories was the Protocol of the Elders of Zion, which purported to expose a worldwide Jewish plot to control the world. It attracted attention not only in Europe but also in England and North America. After the publication of Karl Marx's works, conspiracy theorists inevitably also identified Jews with a revolutionary threat, although the term 'communist' did not come into usage until approximately 1919.[19] In Nazi Germany, even so-called 'liberal' Jews were afraid of being tainted with the communist label. Ingeborg Hecht, 'roped' into joining the German Jewish Comrades' Hiking Association, reacted with boredom when the leaders 'felt duty bound to read us extracts from *Das Kapital*'. She had joined to engage in sports, especially hiking, and enjoyed the fun and the singing. Her parents, however, were 'now doubly afraid ... that our association might be branded Communist as well as Jewish and [be] hounded in consequence'.[20] Many conservative Germans had their fear of a link between Jews and communism confirmed when a few German communist leaders and anarchists were identified as Jews, despite these men neither adhering to the Jewish community nor receiving appreciable support from it.[21]

Adolf Hitler exploited these conspiracy fears and communist anxieties for his own purposes. His obsession, however, focused on a belief that the Jews' ultimate objective was domination of the world and, once this was achieved, its complete destruction. How the Jews were to avoid being destroyed along with the rest of humanity does not seem to have been a consideration. Hitler regarded the destruction of Jews as essential to the salvation of humanity, for beneath the veneer of 'a human look', Jews were subhuman, *Untermenschen*. He promulgated an ideology of racial purity in which Germans, the *Herrenvolk* (master race), Aryans, were contrasted against non-Aryans, Jews, whom Hitler's followers designated *Ungeziefer* (vermin).[22] To be Aryan was to be, among other things, blond and blue eyed. Little Inge, Ingeborg Hecht's half Jewish friend, *was* blond and blue eyed. Her friends teased, 'Hitler and Goebbels would be madly envious of your "master race" looks.'[23]

In *Mein Kampf* Hitler wrote, 'Today I believe that I am acting in accordance with the will of the Almighty Creator: by defending myself against the Jews, I am fighting for the work of the Lord.'[24] Addressing the Hitler Youth in June 1935, Julius Streicher also identified Nazism and its anti-Jewish policies with the will of God when he stated: '[we] became fighters against the Jewish people, against that organized body of world criminals, against whom already Christ had fought.'[25] Many thousands of right-wing Germans endorsed this view that identified anti-Semitism with Christianity and the Jew with international crime, and thus made possible the anti-Jewish legislation of the 1930s. Most Germans, however, were probably unaware of the implications of these laws, and the legislation evoked little interest or enthusiasm among the masses.[26]

Anti-Semitic decrees began in the spring of 1933 with the proclamation of a one-day boycott of all Jewish shops, the forcible retirement of all non-Aryan civil servants except for war veterans and their families, and the prohibition of all kosher (ritually clean according to Jewish law) butchering. Although not legally required to do so, already by 1933, well before the Nuremberg laws were enacted, peer pressure and threats had forced Henry K's grandfather from his prestigious position as a university law professor.[27] Kaplan points out that 'these earlier years shed light on the incremental nature of Nazi persecution.'[28] Insidiously, the pressure escalated. By September 1935 Jewish newspapers could no longer be sold in the street, even though Jewish publications – books, newspapers and magazines – could be sold in shops. The logic behind this appears to be that, being inferior mentally, Jews could not be expected to meet the high standards imposed on the German press, but that it was acceptable to allow shops to retail inferior Jewish literature because they were less public.[29] As repugnant as such racism might be, it nonetheless provided the Jewish community with a channel of communication when other areas were closed and, indeed, it was through the Jewish press that news of the Kindertransport later reached many families.

On 15 September 1935, the Nuremberg laws, the most prohibitive legislation to date, were promulgated. Among other restrictions, these made it a crime against the state to be married to a Jewish spouse and also deprived Jews of German citizenship. Parks, cinemas and swimming pools were closed to Jewish children and adults. To an adult this might not appear to be of serious significance, but to a child it could, and did, result in grievous humiliation. Hana Brady and her little brother George lined up with other children to see the film *Snow White and the Seven Dwarfs*. When they reached the top of the queue, they saw the sign, 'No Jews Allowed'. Weeping and ashamed, they returned home.[30]

A much more serious deprivation, however, was that it became virtually impossible to attend public school or university. David Lewinski was required to leave his school, as was Siggi Wasserman. Rudi Lowenstein's teachers allowed him to stay but his brother suffered greatly from beatings and name calling.[31] Emmi's teacher insisted that Emmi stand in the hallway while the class saluted the flag. 'After all, you are a Jew, not a German,' she said.[32] Heidi Wachenheimer related a particularly distressing experience when the school's principal came to speak to her class. 'He then pointed a finger at me and said, "Get out, you dirty Jew." I could not believe that this formerly kind, gentle person would say this to me. He repeated it, took me by the elbow, and shoved me out of the classroom.'[33] Fortunately, not all school authorities behaved that cruelly. Emile, for example, remembers his school principal 'burst[ing] into tears when forced to forbid Jewish children from taking classes,' while one of Monique's teachers hid her temporarily until a permanent hiding place could be found.[34] The effect of all this negativity was that Jewish children became increasingly isolated. Hana Brady's Aryan best friend promised, 'We'll be together forever, no matter what.' Gradually, however, even she no longer came to play. Her parents had forbidden it.[35] Children appeared to parrot propaganda slogans picked up from the radio and the Nazi paper, *Der Stürmer*, which used such terms as *Judenschwein* (Jewish pig), *Parasiten* (parasites), and *Ungeziefer* (vermin).[36] The situation for both children and parents was becoming untenable.

Not surprisingly, Jewish emigration soared and approximately 33,000 Jews left the Third Reich almost immediately after the first anti-Jewish legislation was enacted, yet many ties kept Jews in Germany. As John Dippel notes, the question was 'why leave? Why abandon friends and family, a comfortable home, a well-paying job, a cherished culture – in short – a rare feeling of truly belonging – for unknown shores, an alien tongue, unemployment, isolation, hardship, and despair?'[37] After all, German Jews had survived anti-Semitism before. Marion Kaplan points out that generally women became aware of their family's increasing vulnerability before the men admitted any danger, possibly because of the women's greater involvement with the community and with schools, shops and servants.[38] There were, of course, many exceptions. David Lewinski's father, for example, applied for David's exit with the Kindertransport against the wishes of both David's mother and grandmother (he was a much-loved only child).[39]

Still, many of the Jewish middle class, as well as the governments of most Western nations, viewed this current rash of extreme anti-Semitism with indifference or as a temporary aberration and felt that life would soon revert to more normal patterns. Many parents of children later enrolled in the Kindertransport shared this optimistic view. Lorraine Allard's father insisted, 'This madman Hitler can't possibly last, and this is all just going to pass over and things will be all right again.'[40] Ursula Rosenfeld's parents believed this to be true as well. Her father, an ex-serviceman, 'had so much faith in the German people that he said, "This will not last. They will see through it. It's a temporary thing."'[41]

Many church officials, both in Germany and elsewhere, also believed that German public opinion would not tolerate the pernicious anti-Semitic legislation. Adolf Keller wrote to Bishop George Bell from Geneva, 'General pressure of public opinion and of the Christian churches will probably lead, as I have reason to believe, to a change of methods in Germany.'[42] Andrew Chandler summarized this attitude succinctly when he wrote:

> Some could not imagine that a people who had given the world the writings of Goethe and Heine, and the music of Beethoven, should for long tolerate such a government. That a modern European society could revive the vices of the medieval era by persecuting Jews seemed extraordinary and unaccountable.[43]

Yet, contrary to expectations, the Nuremberg laws caused no uproar among the German population as a whole. Social historians LeBor and Boyes conclude, 'The simple fact is that even though the mass of German people had ethical choices, they ignored them.'[44]

The Nuremberg decrees, however, 'the most devilish legislation that the history of Europe knows',[45] shocked many hitherto complacent Jews into action. By the end of 1937, 25 per cent of the Jewish population of Germany had already left and many more were anxiously seeking entry visas to any country that might open its doors.[46] As Simon Dubnow rightly concluded: 'assimilation turned out to be in practice psychologically unnatural, ethically damaging, and practically useless.'[47]

The Austrian *Anschluss* (union between Austria and Germany) in 1938 exacerbated this desperate situation when 185,000 Austrian Jews became victims of the Nazi madness. Some 95 per cent of these Jews lived in Vienna.[48] When no new avenues of emigration became available, Gauleiter Bürkel in Vienna declared, 'either the State is found which will take out of Greater Germany the 750,000 Jews and 500,000 non-Aryan Christians [Christians with some Jewish ancestry] or we shall make some concentration camps for these people. Then they will be eliminated in a month.'[49] Austrian Nazis emulated their German mentors with the zeal of the newly converted. Saul Friedlander observed that 'the persecution in Austria, particularly in Vienna, outpaced that in the Reich. Public humiliations were more blatant and sadistic; expropriation better organized; forced emigration more rapid.'[50]

The disfranchisement of German and Austrian Jews should have alerted the Western world to the unimaginable dimensions of Hitler's anti-Semitism. Instead of strong condemnation, however, conferences were convened, the most important of which was the Evian Conference, supported by the Americans. Erich Loewy bitterly denounces this 'window dressing'. He writes:

> Historically, the Evian Conference showed that: (1) the world was hardly unaware of the deplorable conditions in Nazi Germany and the threat hanging over the Jewish population, and (2) beyond pious platitudes, and although it could have done so, the world was not only quite unwilling to interfere but also quite unwilling to help.[51]

Governments at the time discussed emigration schemes ranging from South America to Africa and beyond, and a few Jews found refuge, but there were no open doors to receive the hundreds of thousands.[52]

The situation for European Jewry deteriorated further when the Munich Agreement of September 1938 ceded a portion of Czechoslovakia to Germany and brought yet another Jewish community under Nazi control, with ever greater pressure to emigrate. Where were these people to go? While the German government at this point willingly issued exit visas, albeit with crippling financial prohibitions, almost all the world's doors were closed to Jews. Only Shanghai offered asylum without an entry visa, and here there were job difficulties and severe financial problems. Hugh Schramm's mother left for Shanghai with her youngest son, promising to send for Hugh and his other brother as soon as she had the money to do so. The time never came. She barely survived the terrible conditions then prevailing in China and suffered even more during the Japanese occupation.[53] As Chaim Weizman sadly noted in the *Manchester Guardian* as early as 23 May 1936: 'the world seemed to be divided into two parts – those places where the Jews could not live, and those where they could not enter.'[54]

After *Kristallnacht* (which literally means 'The Night of the Broken Glass') in November 1938, however, a difficult situation became impossible. Mitchell Bard, the Jewish historian, vividly describes this infamous time:

> On November 9 and 10, 1938, rampaging mobs throughout Germany and the newly acquired territories of Austria and the Sudetenland freely attacked Jews in the street, in their homes, and at their places of work and worship. At least 96 Jews were killed [some estimate 236] and hundreds more injured, more than 1,300 synagogues were burned (and possibly as many as 2000), almost 7,500 Jewish businesses were destroyed, and countless cemeteries and schools were vandalized. ... A total of 30,000 Jews were arrested and sent to concentration camps on these days.[55]

Many *Kinder* who later came to England had witnessed these horrors. Siggi Wasserman was seven years old at the time and still clearly remembers the chaos and subsequent fear he felt while he watched the madness from the windows of his family's upstairs apartment.[56] In Vienna Eva Gladdish saw people she knew on their hands and knees scrubbing the pavement under the supervision of uniformed officers. Heidi Wachenheimer, aged 14, remembers her father's arrest. She ran to her aunt's house, where she found her mother. 'Shortly after I arrived there, a human chain of men and boys, shackled together in a row and shoved along by the SS marched past my aunt's house. In this group was my father, uncle and other males I knew. ... I was so traumatized.'[57] Ingeborg Hecht's father was taken off a street car on 11 November and sent to the Orienburg-Sachsenhausen concentration camp. When the directive of 12 December ordered all Jewish detainees over the age of 50 to be released, he returned home shortly before Christmas. 'He turned up with a shaven skull, bent and gaunt, a weary man with heavy eyes. And he was so cold, so very cold.' When he told his family about his experiences in the camp, Ingeborg recalled that 'if he hadn't been our own father, a qualified lawyer, and in his right mind, we would never have believed him.'[58]

The imprisonment of hundreds of men and boys (including many 16 and 17 year-olds who later formed a major component of the first Kindertransport), and the huge fines levied against the community, are well documented. In addition to the human suffering and misery, crippling financial demands were implemented. The Executive Order Pertaining to the Restoration of the Appearance of Streets in Respect of Jewish Business Premises (of 11 December 1938) ordered that all damage sustained by Jewish businesses and homes 'will at once be made good by Jewish householders and trades people' and that the owners of the affected premises would bear the cost of repairs. This directive imposed a crippling financial burden on the community, in addition to the cruel humiliation. Robert M. W. Kempner summarizes 'this unique legalized process' as follows:

> Their [the Jews] jobs were taken away, their possessions were stolen, they were not allowed to inherit or bequeath, they were not allowed to sit on park benches or to keep a canary, they were not allowed in restaurants, movie theatres or at concerts, special racial laws were valid for them, they were deprived of all civil rights, their freedom of movement was taken away, their human rights and their human dignity was trampled into the dust until they were deported to concentration camps and went into the gas chambers.[59]

No delusions remained for the world's nations or for the Jewish community regarding the Nazi intent and, though no one could foresee the Holocaust, Hitler's radicalization became increasingly evident. Sir Nevile Henderson, British ambassador at Berlin, called this organized persecution a reversion 'to the barbarism of the Middle Ages', an 'orgy of violent ill-treatment which even the Middle Ages could scarcely equal'. He recognized that by this 'disgusting exhibition' the Nazis 'turned the whole of the world opinion definitely against themselves'.[60]

The worldwide Jewish community, watching these events in horror, had not remained idle. While the American response continued to be divided, that of the British community was immediate and well organized.[61] Anglo-Jewry boasted a diverse background. The settlement of Jews in medieval England was among the most recent in Europe. While some followed in the wake of William the Conqueror in 1066, that small community was banished in 1290. Jews returned to Britain in the seventeenth century, however, this time largely as a result of German immigration and they were to remain as a permanent presence. After 1914, another wave of predominantly Russo-Jewish immigrants arrived, and this altered the nature of English Jewry.[62] By 1933 most of the approximately 300,000-member community had an eastern European background, although the Germanic connection was also present. Religiously, they were largely Orthodox, but financially they ranged from wealthy and titled to working class and even impoverished. A framework for refugee and indigent assistance had been in place since the establishment of the London Jewish Board of Guardians in 1859, an organization that, among other services, funded schools, orphanages and public housing. The Jews' Temporary Shelter, which was soon again to play an important role in Jewish refugee immigration, was another of its projects.[63]

In 1933 Otto Schiff, a London stockbroker with a keen personal interest in the wider Jewish community was president of the shelter. He was in contact with Rabbi Dr Leo Baeck[64] of Berlin and the two shared their concern about the events following Hitler's rise to power. Both men began preparing for the probability of Jewish emigration from Germany to England: Dr Baeck organized the *Zentral Ausschuss der deutschen Juden für Hilfe und Aufbau* (Central Office of German Jews for Assistance and Culture), which the *Reichsvertretung der deutschen Juden* (Federal Union of Jews in Germany) absorbed a few months later. Otto Schiff brought together various influential members of the British Jewish community to found the Jewish Refugees Committee (JRC) in April 1933. This was to become the largest of all case-working organizations in the refugee movement.[65]

The Central British Fund for German Jewry (CBF) was set up that same year (1933) as a 'Special Committee – to deal with the problems which have arisen, and will arise, in relation to the economic and social welfare of our German coreligionists'.[66] The CBF also attempted to bring together the various elements of the Jewish community for the purposes of relief work and fund raising. Towards this end ten pillars of British Jewry were invited to become founding members of the CBF; they were Lionel and Anthony de Rothschild, Lionel Cohen, Sir Robert Waley Cohen, Sir Osmond d'Avigdor Goldshmid, Simon Marks, Leonard Montefiore, Harry Nathan, Dr Chaim Weizmann, and Chief Rabbi Dr Joseph Hertz.[67] These men represented a wide spectrum of religious and political thought and, though some brought with them antipathies and quarrels that had been long in the making,[68] the plight of their German coreligionists bound them together in a common purpose.

The JRC and CBF moved into the newly-constructed Woburn House in London, from where a vigorous and successful fund-raising campaign was launched. It was the first of many such campaigns, though this was unknown and unanticipated at the time.[69]

Other Jewish organizations set up to save European children on a much smaller scale and organized at different times included, to name but a few, Hechalutz, B'nai B'rith, Youth Aliyah (launched in 1934 and supported financially by the American Zionist women's organization, Hadassah), the Women's Appeal Committee (concerned with the children's welfare after their arrival in the United Kingdom) and the Chief Rabbi's Religious Emergency Council. Most of these groups, plus approximately 70 regional organizations, later worked together under the umbrella of the Refugee Children's Movement (RCM).[70] Elaine Blond of the Children's Movement estimated there were altogether 175 local committees throughout Britain to aid the effort. She noted that 'in some areas we separated Jewish and Christian helpers, but mostly they favoured a joint organization. It was the same at the regional level.'[71]

Anxiety about the fate of European Jews was not entirely restricted to the Jewish community. Margareta Burkill of Cambridge remembers that news of *Kristallnacht* 'went through Great Britain like a sort of electric current; every little town, every village in England said, "We must save the children." It was a fantastic thing.'[72] While *Kristallnacht* may have raised awareness among some members of the British public, that was not evident at the time to many of the refugee committee organizers.

Some non-Jewish groups had, however, already been preparing for such an emergency. The Society of Friends (Quakers), for example, traditionally active among refugees and the downtrodden, was early cognizant of the dangers of Nazism, not only to Jews but also to Christians of Jewish extraction and to political dissenters of all kinds. In 1933 British Quakers organized the German Emergency Committee, later renamed the Friends Committee for Refugees and Aliens, primarily to care for non-Jewish refugees from the Reich, but soon expanding its efforts to assist all who were fleeing Nazi persecution, whether Christian or Jew.[73] Elaine Blond said of the Society of Friends that it was 'the body which did the most to help young refugees. In any appeal for aid, the Quakers were among the first to open their homes and their pocket books.'[74] The Quakers' general secretary, Miss Bertha Bracey, became well known and much loved in Jewish refugee circles for her tireless work on their behalf and was posthumously nominated for inclusion in the book of *The Righteous Gentiles of the Holocaust*.[75]

The Inter-Aid Committee for Children, chaired by Sir Wyndham Deedes and affiliated with the Save the Children Fund (organized in 1919 to assist needy German children after the First World War), by November 1938, had already brought 471 endangered youngsters to Britain and placed them in private homes or schools. In November the committee amalgamated with the newly-formed Movement for the Care of Children from Germany – soon to be called the Refugee Children's Movement (RCM) – under the chairmanship of Lord Gorell and the directorship of Mrs Elaine Laski (Blond) and Mrs Lola Hahn Warburg.[76] Mrs Dorothy Hardisty, its general secretary, was to become a household name in the refugee community, for this organization was to sponsor most of the 10,000 Kindertransport[77] children from Austria, Germany and Czechoslovakia.

As the European situation deteriorated and the refugee position became ever more precarious, helping organizations proliferated: the Church of England Committee for Non-Aryan Christians (organized in 1937), cooperated closely with the Quakers, as did the Catholic Committee for Refugees from Germany (1938) and its sub-committee, Catholic Children's Sub-Committee, and the Riversmead Methodist Committee. In October 1938, the Christian Council for Refugees from Germany and Central Europe, under the leadership of Sir John Hope Simpson, Revd Henry Carter, Revd W. W. Simpson and Canon George Craven, was organized to coordinate the refugee work of the Anglicans, Roman Catholics, Quakers and Free Churches. The council worked closely with the Refugee Children's Movement, especially in its dealings with government. When most of the relief organizations moved into Bloomsbury House in January 1939, the Christian Council was made responsible for the house's administration and day-to-day operations, while continuing to cooperate closely with those groups remaining in Woburn House, the Jewish centre.

These, then, were the major organizations responsible for the approximately 10,000 children who were to arrive in Britain under the Kindertransport movement, most of them reaching the country between December 1938 and September 1939.[78] The rescue was a flicker of light in the descending darkness.

2

EXODUS AND ARRIVAL

ONE of the first tasks the Anglo-Jewish community undertook upon learning of the vicious anti-Jewish boycott in
Germany in 1933 was to designate a representative committee to call on Sir Ernest Holderness of the Home Office to plead
the cause of Jewish refugees from Germany.[1] In their belief that the
situation in Germany was temporary and that no large-scale
immigration was imminent, and to forestall any anti-Semitic tension
that might result from the arrival of European Jews in Britain, the
representatives promised that the Jewish community would bear all
expenses incurred on behalf of these refugees, and that no government
assistance would be required.[2] This commitment was honoured
throughout the 1930s, even as the European situation worsened. There
was to be no publicity related to the project. The minutes of the
Liaison Committee of the High Commission of the League of Nations
for the Refugees Coming from Germany stated, 'there must be no
reporting at all in the press, directly or indirectly. Some harm has been
done … by unauthorized statements.'[3] Such was the sense of
uncertainty related to any influx of Jewish refugees. The Jewish
community's commitment was still in place when a new crisis
developed after *Kristallnacht*. As the *Jewish Chronicle*, 16 December 1938,
noted: 'Lord Rothschild expressed his belief that unless the victims of
Nazi persecution could escape within two years, an immense
proportion of them would be dead.' His was a sadly prophetic voice,

which, at the time, seemed unrealistic and went unheeded by the Western world. Many parents, however, shared Lord Rothschild's fear. After *Kristallnacht* there was a renewed and agonizing outpouring of pleas from European Jewry for refuge for their children. An estimated 60,000 to 70,000 children in Germany and Austria were orphaned or endangered after *Kristallnacht*, and those parents who survived were frantic to find them a place of safety.

The front page 'personal' columns of Jewish newspapers for this period are filled with heart-breaking requests for 'some kind person' to sponsor a son, daughter, grandchild or young dependant. The *Jewish Chronicle* carried the following, among dozens of similar appeals: 'desperate parents beg benevolent people to take care of their boy' (14 July 1939); 'a mother begs good-hearted people to get a permit for two charming girls, 11 and 12 years of age. Father in Dachau' (16 December 1938); 'please help me bring out of Berlin two children, 10 years, very best family, very urgent' (23 December 1938). Even national papers such as the *Manchester Guardian* opened its pages to these appeals.[4] The response, however, could not begin to alleviate the need and Helen Bentwich (Mrs Norman Bentwich) and Dennis Cohen of the Jewish Refugees Committee were therefore asked to formulate a plan whereby 'the largest possible numbers' of children could be moved out of the Greater Reich 'with the greatest possible haste'.[5] In an incredibly short three days the two drafted a plan that became the basis of a proposal the Council for German Jewry submitted to Prime Minister Neville Chamberlain on 15 November 1938.[6]

The refugee situation in Great Britain at this time was complex. Labour unions and professional organizations just recovering from the Great Depression feared that an influx of refugees might jeopardize British jobs. If children were allowed, surely their parents would eventually follow? Only a year earlier, 3,800 Spanish refugee children from Bilbao had been allowed entry 'on condition that they were maintained from private funds',[7] and now to agitate for the admission of thousands more children was a politically volatile act. Sir Neville Chamberlain therefore expressed only 'benevolent interest' in the scheme for rescue. A more positive meeting was convened on 21

November with the home secretary, Sir Samuel Hoare, a Quaker who was warmly sympathetic to the proposals.[8] Indeed, later that same day, a Mr Logan, speaking in the House of Commons, castigated those who worried about the financial implications this scheme might have for the British taxpayer and concluded:

> Today an opportunity is offered to the British nation to take its proper stand ... to protect a minority that deserves well of all the nations of the world. ... Tomorrow may be a hard day for us, but I feel that, by doing the things that are morally right, we shall achieve something which is worthy of the name of the British nation.[9]

On 23 November the government agreed to the plan the Inter-Aid Committee for Children from Germany proposed, whereby an unspecified number of unaccompanied children from the Greater Reich, under the age of 18, would immediately be granted admission to Britain 'for educational purposes' and for a period of two years, provided they would not become a liability to the British taxpayer.[10] 'These children were admitted with a view to their being maintained and educated [in Britain] and being emigrated at a later date when they were old enough, if conditions in Germany were still such that they could not be returned to their parents,' reads the entry in Hansard, the British Parliamentary record.[11] The *Jewish Chronicle*, 25 November 1938, quotes Lord Samuel and Lord Selborne, joint chairmen of the British Committee for the Care of Children from Germany as declaring that 'at least 50,000 children must be brought out of Germany at once'. This recognition of the need proved to be utterly unrealistic in fulfilment, but this, of course, could not then be known.

Yet, even while recognizing the need, the opinions expressed in the British House of Commons were not unanimous: were 'part-Jews' more desirable than 'whole Jews?' asked one member. Mr Lloyd, speaking for the cabinet, answered without hesitation that no such distinctions would be made. Another member argued that admitting Jewish refugees, even children, would only be 'an incitement to foreign rulers to get rid of people who, in their opinion, are either racially or politically undesirable'. Miss Wilkinson responded that 'there is a very great deal of public feeling in this country that would welcome the unfortunate people for the honour of our country,' and so the debate raged both for and against allowing the German refugee children asylum.[12]

By 1 December, however, the discussions in the House of Commons had shifted from uncertainty about the desirability of admittance to dismay at the slowness of granting visas to unaccompanied children. The Home Office responded by simplifying the entrance procedure. It authorized the Inter-Aid Committee to issue individual two-part identity cards; the committee would retain one portion as a travel document for the child and forward the other to the Home Office.

Strangely enough, in all these discussions, the Jewish MPs remained silent. Elaine Blond, active in the Refugee Children's Movement, and a daughter of Michael Marks of Marks & Spencer, commented how:

> many prominent Jews were genuinely frightened of stirring up public hostility by seeming to press too hard for special treatment. This was certainly true of Jewish MPs who, in the long debate on refugees in ... 1938, actually took a vow of silence. Their muddled reasoning led them to believe that saying nothing would help their credentials as model citizens.[13]

Despite the Jewish politicians' silence, the government paved the way for the entrance of unaccompanied children, and refugee organizations immediately implemented plans to evacuate children from Germany, Austria and Czechoslovakia. Regional committees were set up in Manchester, Birmingham, Bristol, Cambridge and Battersea (south London) to enlist foster parents and to organize hostels and other accommodation. By September 1939 there were 12 regional committees and 65 area committees, and by the end of the war the area committees had increased to 175.[14]

The children were to be brought out by various means, but mainly by train. Only children up to and including the age of 17, and a minimum number of adults for supervision, were allowed on these transports, which the German rail authorities quickly dubbed *Kindertransporte* (children's transports), a term quickly adopted in England as well. According to the Inter-Aid Committee agreement with the government, the children were to be in Britain, supported by the Jewish community, for educational purposes for up to two years, by which time they were expected to have re-emigrated. Optimistically, a letter to the chairman of the Germany Emergency Committee, dated 2 May 1939, notes, 'as regards the length of stay in England, I am informed that the greater proportion of refugees will be emigrated in the course of a year.'[15]

There were to be both guaranteed and non-guaranteed children. The guarantee involved an assurance that the guarantor, whom the child's parents usually arranged, would be fully responsible for the maintenance and education of the child up to the age of 18. Legal adoption was not an option at this time.[16] Margareta Burkill of the Cambridge Refugee Committee remembers that there was 'a tremendous difference between the guaranteed child and the unguaranteed child', since the guaranteed youngster would go into a home where 'people were expecting the child lovingly and would do their utmost to put it at ease', whereas the unguaranteed child was placed in a camp until a sponsor could be found.[17] By May 1939 a new and 'more lenient' policy regarding guarantees had been put into place. On 26 May the *Jewish Chronicle* reported:

> the children are to be divided into three categories: (1) those for whom guarantors are willing to pay £50 [the newly imposed deposit to assist in the child's ultimate re-emigration] – whose arrival is then expedited; (2) those specifically nominated by a committee or an individual who cannot pay the deposit. The case history is then sent to the Movement in Germany and if a report is received that the child is in danger, they will be brought over; (3) those whose names were sent by the agents of the Movement as being in danger or in desperate need.

Guarantors were often relatives or friends. Some were found when parents placed advertisements in British newspapers, such as the *Manchester Guardian* or *Jewish Chronicle*.[18] Occasionally, as in the following letter, the child would ask assistance personally, usually from someone known to the family. This letter, addressed to 'Miss Amy', a refugee servant, was forwarded to the Worthing Refugee Committee. It was sent from Vienna and dated 15 February 1939.

> Dear Miss Amy!
> My brother Kurt and Ma wrote me, that I shall bestow on you, about a permit to come to England. I am thirteen years old and I am alone at my parents at home, who are banished, and therefore I must seek a home for me. My parents can't take me along with, and so I pleased you to help me spend my childhood in England. I should like to come into a Jewish house and I will endeavour me to make you always honour and joy. My dear parents would be very thankfully you would be so kind to help me …
>
> [signed] Paul.[19]

Paul found a sponsor, but not every child was that fortunate, especially those with physical handicaps who always required a guarantor. Yet, even here, the Movement for the Care of Children from Germany managed to find places in British institutions for many disadvantaged youngsters, as those, for example, from the Jewish School for Deaf and Dumb Children in Berlin-Weissensee who arrived in July 1939, and the Jewish Blind Society children who were placed in institutes for the blind throughout Britain.[20]

Non-guaranteed children were to be placed in camps until homes 'suitable' to their religious and cultural background could be found.[21] The final decision in choosing unguaranteed children for each transport was left in the hands of the European committees – the *Kinderauswanderung* (Child Emigration) department of the *Reichsvertretung der Juden in Deutschland* (Federal Representation of Jews in Germany) in Germany, working with the (Christian) *Paulus-Bund* (Paul's Association) and the Friends Service Committee; the *Jüdische Kultusgemeinde* (Jewish Religious Community) in Vienna again in cooperation with the Quakers.

The situation in Prague differed somewhat in that several groups as well as individuals were active in the rescue operation.[22] The British Committee for Refugees from Czechoslovakia (BCRC), headed by Doreen Warriner with the invaluable aid of Bill Barazetti, worked mostly with adults,[23] until Nicholas Winton, a banker, arrived on the scene. Winton, who has been called 'England's Schindler',[24] declared himself head of the BCRC children's section, a section that existed only by his own initiative and that began his largely independent and quite extraordinary efforts that resulted in saving 669 Czech children. He not only gathered and selected the children but also found placements for them in Britain. Trevor Chadwick, a schoolmaster who assumed responsibility in Czechoslovakia when Winton returned to England, later assisted him.[25] Chadwick was a person of both ingenuity and daring, as was Winton. On one occasion when some of the children being sent to England were found not to have the proper documents, Chadwick simply provided counterfeit papers and the children were allowed to proceed.[26] The Archbishop of Canterbury and the Chief Rabbi were both honorary presidents of the BCRC.

There were also, among other Quakers, individuals such as Jean Hoare, Jean Bannister and Tessa Rowntree, who worked independently, while the 'official' Quaker organization was everywhere involved.[27] The MP Eleanor Rathbone visited the area and subsequently became an ardent supporter of the refugee cause in parliament, while convent-educated Josephine Pike brought 'a little happiness and laughter and some order and stability into the children's drab and insecure lives'.[28]

Nicholas Winton reported that many of the orphaned refugee Czech children had been living in 'damp, overcrowded and unsanitary camps', for three months already, and that those outside the camps were in 'even worse plight. … In some instances mothers are forced on the street in a desperate effort to get money with which to feed their children. … It is getting worse.'[29]

The first of the 'Winton' children left for Britain on 14 March 1939, the last on 2 August 1939.[30] The Czech Trust Fund, set up by the British government[31] and by personal guarantors whom Winton, the Quakers and others recruited, provided for these Czech children on their arrival in Britain.

Three transports of Polish, mostly Orthodox, Jewish children arrived in England in February and August 1939.[32] Previously, 300 Orthodox Viennese children had arrived and, since it was vacation time, Rabbi Schonfeld was able to open his schools for them for temporary housing. The classrooms were emptied of all furniture and the Jewish Boys' Brigade asked to lend beds and bedding.[33] A furniture manufacturer also eventually loaned 150 beds to the secondary schools.[34] Finding foster homes for so many children caused much anxiety. Finally, most of them were assigned to hostels, which seemed to alleviate their fear that it might be impossible to be strictly observant in their new environment.

As parents anxious for their children to find refuge besieged the organizations, those responsible for selecting them in Europe had an emotionally draining task. One *Jewish Chronicle* correspondent reported that mothers followed him on the streets, begging him to take their children away. 'The parents were unanimous in their desire that the children should be saved first.'[35]

The procedure for obtaining a place on the Kindertransport involved sending an application and photograph to the German provincial social worker who then forwarded them to Berlin. The application included 'a signed statement from the parent ... agreeing to entrust the child to the care of the [Movement for the Care of Children from Germany] Committee and to any step the Committee may take in the interest of the child'.[36] The last question on the form asked them to state their religion from the following options – 'Jew Orthodox, Jew Liberal, Jew but not practising, Protestant, Catholic, Quaker, Freethinker?'[37] Parents were also required to sign a document agreeing to have their child placed in any available home, even with a non-Jewish family if no Jewish accommodation was obtainable. It stated: '*Ich erkläre mich damit einverstanden, dass das Kind ... gegebenenfalls –*

wenn keine jüdische Unterkunft gefunden werden kann – auch in einer nichtjüdischen Familie untergebracht werden darf.[38]

When a child was chosen, his or her documents, including a health certificate, were sent to the Refugee Children's Movement in London, then to the Home Office for an entry permit and Passport Control Office stamp. The document issued read: 'This document of identity is issued with the approval of His Majesty's Government in the United Kingdom to young persons to be admitted to the United Kingdom for educational purposes under the care of the Inter-Aid Committee for children. THIS DOCUMENT REQUIRES NO VISA.' Permits were then returned via airmail to Germany and submitted to the German police. 'Inexplicably, some were always withheld by the German police,' writes Esther Baumel, although most were returned to the refugee organizations, which distributed them to the Kindertransport leaders.[39]

Orphans were given priority at all centres and some desperate parents abandoned their young children at the doors of orphanages to give them an added chance of life. Children with a parent already in a camp or in danger of incarceration, and teenaged boys released from camps or threatened with detention were also classified as 'urgent' and were among the first to leave.

News of the Kindertransport spread rapidly in Europe in various ways – 'the Rabbi's wife told my mother'; 'my mother's doctor informed her'; 'my cousin was going' – as well as through Jewish newspapers and organizations. Some Jewish communities recruited boys from local youth organizations to call on people with children in their homes to inform them of the opportunity, while the Quakers formed a mobile unit to 'disseminate technical information' and interview candidates.[40] The designated committees worked tirelessly, often around the clock and on occasion at very short notice – sometimes less than 24 hours but usually from two to fourteen days – to document and assemble the children who were to leave. In a little over four weeks, some 1950 children were transported from Germany and Austria to Great Britain.[41]

Psychologically, many of the older children were ready to go. They had witnessed the humiliation of their parents, the imprisonment of fathers and older brothers, or had even been in camps and were then let out on the understanding that they would leave Germany within a short period of time, usually between two weeks and two months. Such was the experience of Rudi Lowenstein, who was picked up during *Kristallnacht* and then released. At the age of 16, with nowhere to go, he heard about the Kindertransport and was immediately accepted.[42] Walter, an Austrian Jewish Christian who was severely beaten on *Kristallnacht*, also found a place on the transport to England.[43] Many Jews had been forced from their homes; many from wealthy families, now penniless *Untermenschen*, came to welcome a meal from a soup kitchen; children were stoned on their way to and from school. In some instances, even elderly Jews were made to scrub sidewalks and toilets with toothbrushes under the taunting vigilance of both guards and bystanders. The humiliations they suffered were incredibly degrading and the older children certainly understood the imperative to leave.

While to a certain extent parents and older children were prepared for departure and separation, younger children generally were not. Certainly, they had endured their share of anxiety. Children from Christian homes would be devastated if they were expelled from the Hitler Youth with its uniforms and parades.[44] Despite the stone-throwing on their way to and from school, the humiliation by teachers in the classroom and more, they still felt a sense of security with their parents. Now these over-burdened parents must struggle to prepare their children for separation. Some attempted this by teaching them English. David Lewinski, an only child as well as the only grandchild of a wealthy Jewish family with one Aryan grandmother who remained certain her family would never be touched, remembers that his father registered him for the Kindertransport despite the objections of other family members, even his mother. Although David was only nine years old, his father bought English textbooks and began learning English with him, assuring the boy that he and David's mother would join him in England soon. He encouraged David to enjoy the trip and think of it as a holiday. Siggi Wasserman, at seven, enthusiastically entered the train taking him to England. It was all a 'big adventure'.[45] This was also the experience of Edith Bowen and her sister.[46] Ten-year-old Hana and her twin brother Hans were told they were going to England to learn English and they, too, regarded the trip as 'a great adventure'.[47]

Other parents delayed even telling their children about the impending separation. One youngster wrote: 'it was only on the way to the station that our parents informed us that they would have to stay behind "to clear a few things up". My brother and I were to travel to England alone. He was seven and I was eight years old.'[48] Children who believed that their parents would be joining them soon could not understand why there was so much weeping when the train pulled out. As one child remembered, 'everyone was crying and I did not know why. I was seven years old.' Another was very fearful. 'My mother cannot hold her tears back and I plead with her to constrain herself as she could draw the attention of the Gestapo men who are there observing the passengers.'[49]

If they had any money, some parents went on shopping sprees and bought their children the best clothes they could afford. As a result, these particular youngsters arrived in British foster homes considerably better dressed than local children, but in fashions the European parents thought of as 'English'. 'Tweeds were much in demand', Barry Turner writes, 'for boys who were togged up to look like young versions of Sherlock Holmes'.[50] Plus fours (knickerbockers cut very full and bagging below the knees) were very popular, as evidenced in surviving photographs, as were breeches and knee-length boots.

Yet, it seems that the majority of parents 'deliberately made life as ordinary as possible in a vain attempt to ease the inevitable trauma, or simply as a way of holding off reality'.[51] For the parents themselves, the decision to send their children away to a foreign country to be brought up by strangers and then to see them actually board the train not knowing if they would ever see them again, was an act of incomprehensible desperation and selfless courage. Sonja Pach remembers, 'Papa, with tears streaming down his face, [putting] both his hands on my head. He wanted to part from me with the traditional Jewish blessing of the Priests.' Eric Lucas had a similar experience. Before leaving, 'first my father and then my mother had laid their hands gently on my bowed head to bless me.'[52] It was a moment never to be forgotten and, for many, a blessing never to be received again. Such harrowing farewells were to be repeated later by parents whose children stayed behind and who, as the situation worsened, sought desperately for hiding places for them.[53]

While some families were eager to see their children sent off to safety in England, there were others who had decided to send a child away but, especially if the child was only two or three years old, would break down at the last moment and withdraw him or her from the train. In fact, Lory Cahn's father pulled her from the train through a window by her wrists after the train had already begun to move.[54] Dorothy also remembered that some parents 'snatched' their children back.[55] But by far the majority of parents had come to terms with the necessity of separation to ensure the child's survival. Some parents became so frantic if they failed to receive a permit for a place on the Kindertransport that they took drastic action. Emmy Mogilensky described how one mother pushed a laundry basket into the carriage as the train door was about to close. When Emmy finally mustered up enough courage to peer into the basket, she found it contained twin baby girls. Another child remembers her mother taking her three-and-a-half-year-old twin brother and sister to the railway station when a transport was about to leave and, amid the confusion, pushing them into the crowd of youngsters and walking away. 'They too came to England.'[56] Such substitutions would have been impossible at stations where guards refused to allow parents onto the platform, or where officials counted heads meticulously. Yet, with hundreds of small children and few adults, as was the case on most transports, there must always be some confusion, whether at the station, on the platform, or while boarding the train. And it was on this that these desperate parents depended.

The scenes of farewell were often chaotic. One child remembers that 'at the station we were ushered into an enormous waiting room which was packed with children and parents weeping, crying and shouting.'[57] In a few places parents were not even allowed to enter the station. Bertha Leverton recalls that when she and her brother left, the families were forced to say their goodbyes in an anteroom. Her younger sister watched with her parents as 'the children filed down the stairs with their rucksacks and little suitcases, and off they went to the station.'[58] Joe Schlesinger remembers how 'we sat on a wooden bench next to the tar-coated urinal [in a washroom] while my younger brother, Ernie, slept beside us. We were waiting for a train and had taken shelter in the toilet because, as Jews, we weren't allowed into the waiting room.'[59] In other places parents stood silently in small groups, not wanting to draw attention to themselves or their children. After the children had boarded, the trains often moved so slowly that many parents took taxis and followed the children from station to station for one last look.[60]

As traumatic as this parting was for the parents, some children, though not all, also suffered greatly. One woman remembers crying bitterly and saying, 'please, Mummy, please don't send me away.' She was 11 years old at the time. Edith Forrester was only seven when plans were made for her departure. 'My mother tried to explain,' she recalled, 'but I could not grasp the awfulness of the situation.' When she boarded the train she could 'not get near a window to see my beloved mother. ... I cried "Mutti! Mutti!" and somebody lifted me up and I was able to catch a last glimpse of her face. ... To my dying day I shall never forget the expression on her face.' Other *Kinder* have similar memories.[61] This separation from their parents was to remain one of the greatest traumas the children could remember in later years.

What awaited them in England was a subject of some discussion among the older children. Many felt it was an adventure and actively anticipated their arrival. Bertha Leverton:

> thought of England as a land of lords and ladies because of the king and queen, and the two little princesses appealed to us very much. A year or two before, we saw pictures in newspapers of the coronation with their ermine clothes and their crowns on their heads. And we really thought in England that's how people got dressed – perhaps not every day, but sometimes on Sundays. So that was our expectation of England.[62]

Two main routes were chosen for the Kindertransports: the vast majority went by train, almost invariably by night, departing from major centres such as Berlin, Vienna and Frankfurt, while a smaller number left by ship from Hamburg's port at Bremerhaven to Southampton. Margaret Heller (now Goldberger) was on an American ocean liner that stopped at Southampton to discharge a few children.[63] A smaller number still were flown out of Czechoslovakia. A few transports went to Sweden and at least one to the United States. Palestine was, of course, the preferred destination for those whom Youth Aliyah sponsored, but those sent there directly from Europe were not involved with the Kindertransport.

The European committees reserved the seats, sometimes whole coaches (usually third class) or even entire trains, for the required number of children on the trains designated to carry Kindertransport children. If possible, the parents paid the fares, but if the child was an orphan or destitute then the committee did.[64] Each child had been tagged with a card around his or her neck, on which was either a name or usually only a number. Each was allowed a small case on the train and usually one larger one in the baggage car. Anything of value was strictly forbidden, although some children were allowed to bring their musical instruments. The small case generally contained a change of socks and underwear, and a favourite book or toy. Bertha Leverton now laughs at what she packed. Along with photographs of her family, some clothes and a book, she selected a cup and saucer and a single setting of silverware.[65] The strangest sight however, was probably the two-year-old with a chamber pot strapped onto his back![66] The case also contained a lunch carefully packed by a parent, but often with nothing to drink. With such crowded conditions the organizers were afraid that toilet facilities on the trains would be woefully inadequate if children were allowed liquids – practical, perhaps, but hardly comforting.

Adults from the sponsoring refugee associations, sometimes from Britain but usually from Europe, accompanied every train. These individuals, 'ranging from former youth leaders to unemployed Jewish professionals', to Quaker relief workers, generally remained with the youngsters while they transferred to the ferry and until they reached the designated British port, usually Harwich.[67] The European chaperone was then required to return to the continent. Should one of them decide to seek asylum in England as a refugee, he or she knew that it would jeopardize the transportation of children still waiting for a place. It seems that among the many hundreds of trips the chaperones made only one person defected, yet many were later sent to the camps and to their deaths.[68] Norbert Wollheim was only 25 years old when he became involved with the Kindertransport and began escorting children to Britain. His English relatives urged him to remain, but he refused. 'It's impossible because that would stop all the work for these children. How can I take that responsibility? They couldn't understand. It wasn't easy to return, but after the first time, it became almost routine.'[69] Wollheim survived the camps, but his wife and three-year-old son perished.

On very rare occasions a parent would act as chaperone. Ruth Michaelis's mother took her and her brother 'all the way to their first foster family … in Kent, and then she went back to Germany'. David Lewinski's mother accompanied him to the Dutch border.[70]

In addition to an adult, if an adult was in fact available, older girls in the coach were made responsible for younger children, or where there were siblings, the older looked after the younger. Shulamit Amir was only 12 years old when she was made totally responsible for two toddlers who were not her siblings, both under two years of age, on a journey lasting three days. She recalls, 'I used the overhead luggage racks to bed them down, while we older children sat up all night and tried to keep warm.'[71]

The arrangement of using older children worked only insofar as the older child was responsible enough to provide the care that was needed. It was, after all, children looking after children. Sometimes, indeed, the whole car was in turmoil, with everyone 'wailing, screaming and crying', in a coach that was 'absolutely packed' with 'kids in corridors, standing, sitting, lying'.[72] Edith Bowen remarked that on her train there were about 150 children ranging in age from six months to 14 years, all in the charge of 'English Quaker ladies'.[73] And so it was that some were comforted while others, also only children, were the comforters.

In some cases the windows and doors of a Kindertransport were sealed once the children were on board; in others, the children travelled in ordinary passenger cars. These scheduled 'civilian' trains made their regular stops, and many of the children wrote postcards to their parents at every station.[74] Sometimes SS guards were assigned to a particular train, and the children were very afraid of them. One child, by contrast, remembers that 'the [German] railway officials were not merely courteous; they were even helpful.'[75]

The trains halted at the German–Dutch border and the few mothers who had accompanied their children now left to return to their uncertain future. Then came the German border guards' search. Siggi Wasserman was only seven, but he clearly remembers the fear and apprehension that the children felt at this point.[76] Sometimes the soldiers' search was perfunctory, even kindly or occasionally generous, as in the case of the guard who noticed the laundry basket on the floor of Emmy's train. Emmy recalled the young German demanding that the basket be opened. When no one moved, he himself lifted the lid. 'The guard stares. He looks at his list and you know [the twins] are not there. ... He closes the lid, turns and walks out without another word.'[77] At other times a particular carriage might be uncoupled and the children made to undress while every piece of clothing and luggage was examined.[78] Norbert Wollheim, an escort on the first transport, remembers that when the train reached the border at Bentheim, the SS and not the German border guards entered the children's coaches. 'They behaved like animals,' he wrote later. 'They did not attack the children but they tore into the luggage. ... It was awful.'[79] One train from Vienna was held up for four hours by German passport and customs officials, during which time the children had to sit in absolute silence.[80] The stress this must have occasioned in the younger children especially is hard to imagine. Occasionally, German border guards demanded the ten marks each child was allowed to take out of the country, and confiscated any valuables such as watches and jewellery. Some parents had anticipated this and so Maria Siegal found bank notes among the lettuce of her sandwiches, while another child wore shoes for many months until a shoemaker realized that its hollow heels contained her mother's rings.[81]

The children's reactions to crossing the border into the Netherlands differed greatly. Edith Bowen had expected 'a great feeling of relief at being safe at last, but it did not happen'. Colin Anson, by contrast, remembers that moment as the greatest emotional release he has ever experienced, so intense in fact that he thought he would faint.[82] Other children burst spontaneously into song: 'It sounded like Beethoven's 9th Symphony in its jubilation,' wrote an accompanying adult. Still others, released from fear, 'opened the windows, shouting abuse and spitting at [the Nazi guards]. It was terrible that we children should have learned such hatred.'[83]

Arrangements had been made with the Dutch government for these youngsters to cross through the Netherlands on their way to Britain provided they had the required identity cards.[84] Once across the border, Dutch volunteers greeted the children and offered them cookies, snacks, lemonade, hot chocolate and sometimes games or dolls. A few of the older boys, some with their heads shaved from internment and very apprehensive, managed to get hold of stronger stuff. 'We lads from Cologne had a couple of bottles of egg flip,' admits Ernest Jacob. 'I can't tell you how drunk we were.'[85]

A few children, either because their papers were not in order or because they had been so destined, remained in the Netherlands or were sent from there to Belgium or Sweden. Most *Kinder*, however, continued to the Hook of Holland to board a ferry bound for an English port, usually Harwich or sometimes London. Many were terribly seasick during the crossing and that, added to their tiredness and the trauma of leaving their parents and being in the company of total strangers, brought especially the younger children to the edge of panic. One nine-year-old travelling with her eight-year-old sister later remembered, 'We were very much alone. I can't remember any grown-up coming to see if we were all right. ... I felt very anxious and responsible [for my sister].' Another remembers hearing her older sisters quietly crying for most of the night She was four and her sisters were five and seven years old.[86]

The youngest and those who were shy suffered most, as did those older children who felt such a huge weight of responsibility for their younger siblings, a responsibility their parents often imposed before their departure. Herbert, Jochi and Hanna Najmann remembered their brother John:

> He more than abundantly kept his promise to our parents to take care of us, his three younger siblings. ... In fact, John was both father and mother to us. ... We never really felt parentless: we had John, this charismatic, joyous person who was looking after us and making sure we never lost contact as a family.

How very fortunate these children were, but how great was the older boy's responsibility.[87] Yet older boys often enjoyed every minute of the journey. One fellow described exploring the ship from top to bottom:

> Everything was new to me, it was fascinating. ... I spent the night in one of the saloons, which had been improvised into a dormitory. Not much sleeping was done. There were about 40 or 50 boys, all between 15 or 16 years old in that room. We were all a little over-excited. ... We did not need to look over our shoulders or lower our voices and the realization that we could say what we liked with impunity engendered an atmosphere of enormous gaiety.[88]

The first Kindertransport children arrived at Harwich at 5.30 a.m. on Friday 2 December 1938. The ship, the *De Praag*, carried eight teachers accompanying 206 children, most of them survivors of a Berlin orphanage burnt by storm troopers, also children from one-parent families, older boys threatened with internment if they did not leave the country and children whose parents were already in concentration camps. Ten days later a second transport arrived from Vienna with another 630 children, the youngest only two-and-a-half years old. 'Thereafter there were at least two children's transports a week, until the movement reached its peak in June and July 1939, with transports arriving daily and all but overwhelming the organizers.'[89]

Not all children came by train and boat. The Quakers in Prague, for example, and the Movement for the Care of Children from Germany, initially decided that it would be unwise to transfer children across Germany by train, so they therefore hired small aircraft. The Barbican Mission did the same.[90] Only 20 children per flight was the norm. These children did not spend time in the reception camps but went directly to sponsors, obviously a much less traumatic journey. The flights from Prague ended with the arrival of the German army on 15 March 1939 and thereafter Czech refugee children also entered the United Kingdom by train and/or ship.

Although the majority of the children came from Germany, Austria or Czechoslovakia, there were also those with Polish roots. In October 1938 the Gestapo rounded up Jews in Germany with Polish passports, together with their German-born children. They were deported to Zbanszyn, on the Polish border, where they were 'hounded by the Nazis across the German frontier', refused entry by Polish guards, returned to German territory, then forced back into Poland again. When the Germans set dogs on these refugees the Poles relented, allowed them into no-man's land, and placed them in rat-infested barns and pig sties. Later admitted into Poland, the Polish Jewish Committee sought sponsors for these children and 185 of them found refuge in Britain.[91]

On arrival in England, medical officers examined all the children and customs officials validated their documents. One boy refused to open his case for customs and when he was finally persuaded to do so it was found to contain 'some earth taken from the boy's home'.[92] Children with guarantors could board a train directly for Liverpool station in London or for Victoria station if they had arrived in Southampton by ship. Elaine Blond commented that 'for the first hour after our arrival [at the station] it was the adults more than the children who were likely to misbehave,' for they might snatch a child without informing the organizers or show their terrible disappointment on seeing the youngster whom they were to foster.[93]

The procedure upon arrival at the station was to be as follows: the guarantors were to remain behind a barrier until their names were called, when they were to come to a table, sign appropriate documents and claim their child.

At the end there were always a few guarantors without children (quite possibly taken off the train at the Dutch border; the armed guards liked to give a lasting impression of their authority) and a few children without guarantors. These last joined the bus party waiting to go to one of the RCM hostels.

But not everyone joined the last bus party. John Fieldsend, aged seven, was met by his guarantors as arranged, but when they were ready to leave they realized there was still one child left on the platform. It was John's older brother. The family took him home with them without hesitation until other arrangements could be made.[94]

The first frantic priority for those whom guarantors did not meet immediately was, of course, temporary shelter. When it was suggested that two summer holiday camps, now empty and located conveniently near Harwich, could be rented cheaply, the committee thought its problem had been solved. Younger children were placed in a children's home in Broadstairs, Kent, while all the others would be housed at a resort area called Dovercourt or at the Pakefield holiday camp in Lowestoft. Anna Essinger, a German teacher who had emigrated with her entire school in 1933, and was now headmistress at Bunce Court, a well-known residential school in Kent, was asked to administer the camps.[95] Preparations were not yet complete when the first children arrived. Transferred from the docks by double-decker bus, 60 at a time, the *Kinder* were first given a hot drink, which one boy described as 'a peculiar liquid which looked like coffee, tasted like poison and was said to be tea'.[96] Tea, in Germany at that time was an adult's drink, served without milk and seldom allowed to children.

The accommodations at the camps might have been adequate in

summer or even perhaps during a mild winter, but the winter of 1938–39 was one of the coldest on record. The *Kinder* were so cold that some stayed in bed as long as possible, wearing coats, sweaters and even gloves. One morning 'the children gathered in the dining room to find snow fluttering through the rafters and piling up over the breakfast plates.' Water pipes froze solidly and the children could neither wash nor use the lavatories. 'Even the urine in the pots froze,' claimed one lad.[97] Enough was enough and while Dovercourt was deemed adequate, the 550 children at Lowestoft were evacuated either to a Salvation Army hostel for sailors in Norwich or to St Felix School in Southwold. Yet 'another batch' was sent to the Samuel Lewis Convalescent Home at Walton.[98]

Despite such mishaps, a prodigious effort was put into keeping the children at the receiving camps healthy, happy and occupied. The movement had insured the children 'against 72 serious illnesses and mishaps', so medical attention was not a problem.[99] Volunteers were recruited to play games, teach the children English and provide entertainment. A 'form of schooling' was introduced almost immediately, 'not only to keep the children occupied, but also to tell them something about England and English ways'. At Dovercourt and Lowestoft there were even programmes to teach the youngsters English manners and customs.[100] The *Jewish Chronicle* carried advertisements requesting teachers who knew German to come and teach at Harwich. The community assisted in practical ways: one non-Jewish person drove 40 miles to 'bring a hundred-weight of sweets; a local dentist, also non-Jewish', offered his services free of charge. Marks & Spencer provided surplus shoes and clothing, a butcher supplied beef sausages for the Sabbath meal. 'An anonymous friend sent a dozen cases of fruit every week for several months. ... Nine Jewish barbers gave up their free time and came down on Sundays to do haircutting.'[101]

The refugee societies hired a German rabbi to look after spiritual needs and to comfort the lonely and the frightened. Dr E. Grumpter was put in charge of religious education at Dovercourt and Rabbi M. Katz at Selsey Camp. They organized Friday evening and Sabbath morning services, and 'usually' conducted services every morning.

Those children who were in camp during the Purim holiday received fruit and sweets. Several bar mitzvahs were celebrated, and a small Jewish library started at Dovercourt. Provision was also made for those of a non-Orthodox background, with visits from Rabbi Brasch of the Liberal Synagogue.[102] Unfortunately, tensions quickly developed between the Orthodox and non-Orthodox boys and the chief rabbi, Dr Hertz, made plans to visit Dovercourt to see what could be done. Dr Grumpter wrote to Dr Hertz: 'I should be very glad if you could mention in your address to the boys that some of the so-called liberal boys should show more tolerance and understanding for the religious boys, and be more Jewish themselves.'[103]

On the other hand, the *Jewish Chronicle* reported that in the camps 'a great number of children who knew nothing at all about Orthodoxy had been attracted by the services and of their own accord were taking a great interest in a form of life which they would never have found in their own homes.'[104] The services reached others as well. In his report of 16 April 1939, Dr Grumpter writes:

> The boys immensely enjoyed the Seder Nights [the eve of the first day of Passover], and even more, they were deeply touched. … Many of them told me … how much they have missed the Seder Nights which are observed in their homes … though they come from more or less liberal homes.[105]

Despite all the efforts by the Jewish community and refugee organizations, however, the camps were not home, nor were they meant to be. Ideally, the children would stay only for a day or two and then leave for foster homes so that new arrivals could be accommodated. When it proved difficult to find homes, especially for older boys, more hostels were opened so that the entry of 'new' children would not be impeded. Dovercourt served as a reception centre until March 1939, when it returned to its intended use as a holiday camp.[106] For the majority of Kindertransport refugees, the camps remained in their memory as their first impression of England, for better or for worse.

Some children, including many who were non-guaranteed, went directly to the Midlands, by-passing the camps altogether. Siggi Wasserman went by train to Manchester, where a childless Jewish couple were waiting for him. When they insisted, after one year, that their intention had always been to adopt him, and when Siggi's parents, at that time still in communication, refused, the couple returned him to the receiving camp. He was only eight years old.[107] Manchester had a large and active Jewish community that was, on the whole, well prepared to receive these *Kinder*. Eli Fox, an insurance agent, had already travelled to Germany in 1937 to 'bring out as many boys as possible', and had purchased a large house in which to house them until they could be placed in local Jewish homes.[108] This advance guard, as it were, had prepared the community, which now opened its doors wide to receive the Kindertransport children. On 23 December 1938, Mr H. Pels, secretary of the CRREC, wrote to the South Manchester Hebrew congregation, 'Two hundred and fifty children from Orthodox Vienna families are arriving today and we should be glad to hear at your earliest that you are prepared to take over a number of these children, boys and girls of seven to sixteen years.'[109] Manchester obliged. In April 1939, older children received a warm letter of greeting, of which part read:

> We are glad to welcome you to Manchester. We hope you will be happy here and that you will soon be able to fit yourself into the life of the Community. We strongly urge you to join either one of the special classes in English arranged by the After Care Committee.

Some classes such as 'textile fabrics', for example, were taught in German, for those interested in the clothing trade. The refugees also were welcome to attend any of the lectures the university provided for them.[110] The community arranged sports, boating, swimming and walking tours for the newcomers and did everything in its power to make them feel wanted and at home.

These Manchester and district refugee children were thus much better prepared to face the strange new world into which they had been thrust than many who spent long weeks in reception camps. Certainly, this was a strange new world and, just as certainly, they were indeed the 'strangers within [England's] gates'.[111]

3

STRANGERS IN YOUR MIDST

AFTER shelter, the refugee committees' main task was to place the children in foster homes as quickly as possible. Couples who had sponsored a child but not a specific one were invited to the camps and, during the lunch hour on a Saturday or Sunday, would walk between the long rows of tables and choose the child they wished to take home with them. The children were terribly apprehensive, not understanding English well enough to grasp this selection method. When one little girl heard her name called out, she cried, '*Ich bin verkauft*' (I've been sold). It is hardly surprising that the older children began to refer to the selection period as 'the market'.[1] Even the Orthodox CRREC selected this method for placing its children. Rabbi Dr Schonfeld wrote to prospective foster parents: 'we shall arrange a meeting when you may choose the child whom you would like to take into your home.'[2] And again, 'we beg to inform you that you can call at the girls' hostel … as soon as you are ready. If you will bring this letter with you, you will be shown the children, and select a suitable child.'[3] Insensitive as this method of selection may have been, it is small wonder that the soon-to-be foster parents wished to have at least some discretion when it came to deciding who would be sharing their homes and their lives with them for an unknown length of time. It was probably the best that could be done under these very difficult circumstances. As Nicholas Winton commented many years later, 'choosing a child was terribly commercial but it was the quickest way'.[4]

41

There were also those who came out of curiosity and not necessarily to choose a child. The *Jewish Chronicle*, 16 December 1938, printed a request from the refugee committees asking people not to visit the camps without written permission and certainly not to remove any children!

The child who was never chosen suffered beyond words – the too plump or too thin, the not so beautiful, the child with acne – these often remained in the camps for several weeks, long after most of their companions had left. Many were older children, adolescents, and most of them were boys. It appeared that foster parents first of all chose young children and then, when these were no longer available, for whatever reason, older girls, often, it must be assumed for the work they could perform in the household. The Refugee Children's Movement, therefore, decided to place the older boys in hostels, usually large homes supervised by paid English or refugee staff, located throughout the country. Harris House in Southport for boys, and Tunbridge Wells for girls as well as some younger boys, were two of many such hostels. The majority of Orthodox children were sent to the Cardiff Refugee Hostel, Avigdor House or Northfield. Eight refugee boys between the ages of 16 and 20 found a home in a Liverpool *yeshiva*. It was an unhappy experience. On visiting the *yeshiva* 'M.A.R.' wrote that the house was in the slums, 'in a very bad state and a danger of disease exists'.[5]

The historian Jacob Newman, in his study of the Kindertransport refugees, states that 'most children were happiest in a hostel'.[6] Elaine Blond, who was both active in the movement and Jewish, also felt that hostels provided the happiest experience for older children, better than private homes because there was more independence and the young people never had to face the decision of whether or not to call another couple 'Mother' or 'Father'. In any event, most of the older children, even those in happy foster homes, referred to their adoptive parents as 'uncle' or 'auntie' and seldom by the more intimate familial appellation.

In addition to the older children the Refugee Children's Movement sponsored, organizations like Youth Aliyah and the Council for German Jewry, among others, brought hundreds of teenagers into

Great Britain, specifically as agricultural trainees in preparation for re-emigration to Palestine.[7] They also were generally placed in hostels or on farms. Wittingham House near Edinburgh, the former residence of Lord Balfour, was one of the homes placed at the disposal of Youth Aliyah, although it was stated specifically that children of every class, every standard of education and every degree of orthodoxy would be accepted. When the question of age arose in connection with these young people – who was and who was not a 'child' and therefore eligible for sponsorship – the decision was reached that 'a refugee should be deemed to be a child until he, or she, reaches the age of 21 years, it being pointed out that they remain wards of the Court up to that age.'[8]

An effort was made to keep siblings together, whether the children were placed in private homes or in hostels, but this was not always possible. Enforced separation caused tremendous additional trauma, especially to a younger child who relied on the presence of an older brother or sister to ease the pain of separation from parents. Older children frequently felt such keen responsibility for the younger siblings their parents had entrusted to their care that it is difficult to know whose anguish was the greater. Twins were frequently chosen together. One poignant photograph depicts three-year-old twins, Susi and Lotte, Lotte with her arm around her shy sister as though for protection, saying in the broken English learnt from their mother, 'Mein Susi, meine Schwester, mein lovely sister.'[9] ('My Susi, my sister, my lovely sister.') They were placed together in a Baptist minister's home.

As it was not always possible to place siblings together, it also became increasingly difficult to billet children with foster parents of their own religious persuasion, though this had been the original intention. Many German and Austrian children were not Orthodox, but the majority of those with a Polish background were and the refugee agencies now found that there were not enough Orthodox homes available for this influx of religious children. In the end, as the number of *Kinder* far exceeded those anticipated, it was found that there were not even enough Jewish homes. In a letter to the *Jewish*

Chronicle, the Marchioness Reading, Elaine Laski and other refugee leaders expressed their 'grave anxiety' that 'there are practically no offers of hospitality from homes left in our records.' They conclude, 'we cannot plead too strongly for more offers of Orthodox homes,' warning that it is 'almost impossible to bring over Orthodox children because of the acute shortage of hospitality for them'.[10]

As Amy Gottlieb comments: 'while there was generous financial support from the Jewish community for the rescue of the children, the same spirit of beneficence was not manifest when foster families were needed.'[11] Rabbi H. Poppers echoed this unhappy state of affairs in several letters to the chief rabbi and other Jewish officials, letters in which Poppers laments 'the difficult task of finding Jewish families able and suitable' to take in refugee foster children. He then defends the placement of youngsters in non-Jewish homes on the grounds that 'the Jewish public did not come forward with offers of vacancies when the children first came to this country.'[12]

While there was a dearth of Jewish homes, hundreds of Gentiles offered hospitality and so, to the observant community's consternation, Jewish children began to be billeted in non-Jewish homes. This was abhorrent to Orthodox Jews and Rabbi Schonfeld wrote angrily to Viscount Samuel. 'This meeting of Rabbis of London, having heard with dismay that Jewish refugee children … have been placed in non-Jewish homes, registers its strong protest.'[13]

The RCM, however, had no other options, short of aborting the rescue operations. Indeed, in January 1939 the Council for German Jewry noted that, 'for some weeks the work of bringing fresh children over has been suspended, except those for whom individual guarantees have been obtained.'[14] Norman Bentwich wrote in a similar vein to Dr Josef Loewenherz of the *Kultusgemeinde* in Vienna:

The Movement for the Transport of Children, again, cannot bring over more unguaranteed children until those already here have been placed. I regret that it is of no use to continue to ask for more help than we are giving, because it is not in our power to grant it.[15]

Elaine Blond of the RCM succinctly described the difficult solution to this impasse, namely placing the children in Gentile homes. 'What we did was to accept as many children as we could get in – orthodox, liberal, and non-believing – on the assumption that all other problems were secondary.'[16] This policy continued throughout the Kinder-transport immigration.

Not all Jewish children initially assigned to a Christian billet accepted it without protest. Paula Hill's brother, 'deeply religious and fearing for my Jewish soul', insisted that his sister stay among Jews. When a 'beautiful, childless, fur-coated, elegant lady with tears in her eyes' pleaded that she would provide kosher food and even a Jewish education for the little blonde, blue-eyed girl, the brother stood his ground and refused to allow a Christian to foster Paula, though legally he had no right to do so. Paula refers to him as 'my remarkable older brother, forced into the adult world long before his time and to whom childhood was denied'. Many staunchly religious children were placed in hostels, though Paula and her brother eventually found billeting with Jewish families.[17]

Initially, working-class families were considered too unstable financially to be guarantors, but as the number of children arriving far exceeded all expectations, so long as they passed the inspection any families willing to open their homes, even single women, were recruited. People from all walks of life accepted children – fish-mongers and clergymen, rabbis and boardinghouse keepers, rich and working class.[18] The British public's generosity was overwhelming. The Bernard Schlesingers, for example, though admittedly well to do (Dr Schlesinger had a Harley Street practice), shared their comfortable lives by setting up a hostel for twelve children and taking a thirteenth into their own home.[19] Jim and Fanny Lewis, a working-class family, initially agreed to foster one boy, but when his brother had not been chosen by the time they were leaving the station, they took him home also. When a third brother arrived three weeks later, he too was received with love. 'These relatively simple people did not allow their traditional doubts about Jews or their current hate of Germans to deter them from taking into their modest home us foreign-speaking and strangely dressed youngsters,' remembers one of their foster sons.[20]

Prospective foster parents made their application either to the local refugee committee or directly to a refugee organization such as the Refugee Children's Movement or the Chief Rabbi's Religious Emergency Council. The CRREC and B'nai B'rith application forms included the following questions. 'Occupation of head of household? Is yours a Jewish home? Do you wish the child/children to be orthodox, non-orthodox or fairly orthodox? Does anyone [in your home] speak German? Can you take [the child/children] permanently? If not, for how long could you receive them? Do you wish for a boy(s) or girl(s)? About what age? What education will the child be given?'[21] Religious, personal and bank references were also required.

The RCM questionnaire was similar but more extensive. Among the questions it asked were the required age, sex, religion and social position of the child.

> Religion of the Befriender. If Jewish, is he orthodox? Can Child be maintained until it is eighteen? Does Befriender realize parents or relations may claim child at any time? What is the husband's or breadwinner's work? Is he or she in regular employment? Can two references be given – Bankers and personal? Is German spoken by anyone? Is a maid kept? What will be the sleeping arrangements for the child? What plans for education and/or training have been made? When can the child be taken?[22]

To become a foster parent was obviously an enormous responsibility and yet, amazingly, thousands of Britons responded without hesitation.

Once the questionnaire had been completed, a member of the local committee would make a home visit to determine the suitability of the family to receive a child. The home inspection covered 'cleanliness, space, furnishing, facilities for regular baths, separate beds, playing space'.[23] The prospective foster mother's attitude was noted 'to judge whether the hostess will understand the child's need of love and security; whether he/she will be made a welcome member of the family; whether he/she will get training, moral, social and intellectual'.[24] Not all inspectors' reports were complimentary. One family had asked to foster a 15-year-old girl, but the inspector noted that, 'in my opinion she will give up the daily woman [daily household help] once the child is in her house.'[25]

Once approved, the guardian was required to sign a document promising 'unconditionally [to] guarantee to hold myself responsible for [the child's] maintenance and upkeep until such a time as he/she is reunited with his/her parents or other recognized guardians; or until he/she reaches the age of 18'.[26] Since not all families felt able to commit to such a long-term undertaking for a child they had never seen and did not know, some agencies instituted short-term trial periods ranging from six months to two or three years, though the three-year minimum period was preferred.[27]

Children without guarantors were 'boarded out' to families, schools or institutions. The refugee committees provided for holidays and clothing, in addition to a weekly rate, which varied from one area to another but averaged about 17/6d (85½ pence), much like that paid for British orphans in similar situations. Sometimes, however, depending on the child's age and the location of his or her placement, the cost was as high as 27/6d (£2.37½ pence) per week, and even this did not cover the entire cost of maintenance.[28]

Aware of the tremendous financial requirements of this refugee project, at the request of the Christian Council for Refugees, Lord Baldwin, the former British prime minister, appealed for assistance on a radio broadcast. He described himself in this broadcast as

> an ordinary Englishman who is shocked and distressed by the plight of those despised and rejected people and their innocent children. They may not be our fellow subjects but they are our fellow men. … [I am left] with the uneasy feeling that somehow our Christianity is not worth much if we cannot in some way help in alleviating the mass of suffering.[29]

The Lord Baldwin Fund raised £522,000 in short order, of which £30,000 was immediately allocated to the Refugee Children's Movement as an emergency measure. In total, £237,000 was made available to the movement for its rescue operations. Some of the Lord Baldwin monies were also set aside to cover the £50 deposit the movement required of guarantors as of April 1939 to assist in the anticipated re-emigration of children over the age of 12. This, of course, never materialized, but the RCM could not know that, and re-emigration was initially one of the stipulations for receiving the children. The *Jewish Chronicle* of 13 October 1939 stated that, 'on account of the Fund 8,000 children are now being cared for'.

To ensure as far as possible the acceptance of these thousands of children in the community, and to avoid overt anti-Semitism, it was thought advisable not to billet too many in the same neighbourhood or community. 'We are anxious to spread our children as far over the British Isles as possible,' wrote Helen Bentwich in the *Jewish Chronicle*. 'We do not want too great numbers of them in one place.'[30] The German Jewish Aid Committee shared this concern and went one step further in its advice to the refugees by publishing a small pamphlet entitled *While you are in England*. Among other suggestions, it encouraged them to learn English as a priority, cautioned against speaking German 'in a loud voice' on the street or on public transport and, it emphasized, 'do not criticize. … Do not speak of how much better this or that is done in Germany.' The chief rabbi, Dr Hertz, addressing a letter to 'My dear child,' expressed concern about the same issues: behave quietly and politely, wait 'for your turn in getting into buses, trams or trains', remember 'that English people always admire quietness and gentleness' and 'always remember to show and express your thanks for what is done.'[31]

Sometimes even parents added instructions to those already bedevilling the child. Marietta's mother, for example, reminded her daughter to 'be good, grateful for everything. … Don't forget to thank [your foster parents] for taking you in.'[32] Lorraine Allard's parents, in virtually every letter she received from them, prompted her to 'strive to please your foster parents by good behaviour which is a way of showing them your gratitude,' or again from her father, 'I cannot insist enough on asking you to show these wonderful people your constant appreciation and gratefulness.'[33] Small wonder that some of the young people developed an 'emotional resentment' against this constant reminder always to be grateful, to be thankful, to be polite, to show 'first class behaviour'.[34] Vera Loewy said it so well: 'I loathed ... having to be grateful all the time. Being in this situation seemed so demeaning.'[35]

Yet, both the pamphlet and the chief rabbi's letter had their basis in fact, for some refugees caused concern by their public behaviour. Max Rittenberg, who drafted the pamphlet, complained to Otto Schiff, 'I am bound to say from my own personal experience that the refugees are pestitential [sic] in the matter of derogatory remarks about various things in this country.'[36] Of course Rittenberg was not referring to *Kinder* exclusively or probably not at all. When one considers, however, that many of these children came from upper middle-class urban families with servants – as Elaine Blond comments, 'the children were used to a standard of living higher, on average, than that enjoyed by their foster homes' – and might now be billeted in rural homes with outdoor privies and no electricity, and be asked to help with chores such as milking cows, or were sent to working-class homes in London's East End – the injunction not to criticize but always to be thankful, must have been almost impossible to follow.[37] The fact that such a mediocre home might be that of a relative was scant consolation. Mitzi Raynor writes that her uncle always wrote that he was poor, 'but I did not expect such bad living conditions.'[38]

Some children, of course, were billeted in homes that were much more affluent than their own. For example, the celebrated pianist Dame Myra Hess fostered children, as did Lord Attenborough's family, the Sainsburys and the de Rothschild, who took in more than 26 children. Lord Sainsbury's family cared for 25 children and paid for their education, while Harry Jacobs of Times Furnishing set aside a whole wing of his mansion to house *Kinder* and provided all the required staff, including a cook and a nurse.[39]

Many of Britain's best schools, among them Cambridge and

Oxford colleges, Winchester, St Paul's Cathedral and Westminister Abbey schools, offered residential scholarships, some preferring blocks of boys from similar schools in Germany. ORT also sponsored boys from the ORT school in Berlin,[40] thus sparing the children the trauma of being 'chosen'.

Some families offered homes to children because their own families had grown up and were no longer living at home; others hoped that a child of a similar age would be a companion for their own son or daughter; yet others requested orphans with a view to permanent adoption.[41] There were as many reasons for accepting a refugee child as there were families opening their homes.

For many youngsters, however, problems were not necessarily solved, even when a family had chosen them. One girl remembers that within an hour of her arrival, after a hot drink, 'I did the ironing for the whole family.'[42] Some of the girls were obviously chosen to act as household help or as a nanny to care for younger children. Older boys, on the other hand, were suspicious of sponsors who were farmers or owners of family-run businesses where they might be expected to supply cheap labour.

It was especially difficult for adolescents who were placed in the work force on arrival and who were, as a result, relegated to blue-collar jobs, thereby losing the middle-class status most had enjoyed in Austria and Germany in prewar days. Dorit Whiteman cites the case of Franz, who remarked that as a mechanic's helper in England's 'class-ridden' society, he was very aware of 'being a social inferior'.[43] Being made to feel inferior had overtones for the *Kinder* who remembered only too well the feelings they had experienced after the Nazi takeover, when they were no longer allowed to attend school or university, to ride on certain buses or walk on certain streets – they were made to feel inferior, of no worth. Yet, in Germany the intention went far beyond social stigma; the objective was to humiliate the Jews to the extent of dehumanizing them. This was not so in England and therefore most *Kinder* who experienced the loss of their middle-class status regarded it as a small price to pay for their freedom. 'Better this than Germany,' was their attitude.[44] The majority of them, by hard work and education, escaped the initial stigmas of social inferiority and bettered their condition. However, for those who did experience the negative impact of English society as it was in the 1940s, it created one more hurdle to overcome and made adjustment just that much more difficult.

Some children, though not made to feel inferior in class terms, felt unwanted from the very beginning of their relationship with their foster parents, even when these might be relatives. Some were treated 'condescendingly' as 'poor relations', or as a liability to Jews wishing to remain out of the limelight. Sonja Pach knew she could have fitted in with her uncle's family 'if they had wanted me, but I soon realized that they really had been made to take me in'. Marion Marston was evacuated with her school to Reading when she received a letter from her wealthy Jewish guarantors informing her that they would no longer be responsible for her. They 'were forwarding my belongings. I was shattered and didn't know what to do.'[45] Another child, Lieselotte, rebelled against being made to feel she was accepting charity. It was so sad when a child was 'housed and fed but never loved'.[46] Esther Baumel goes so far as to say that, 'as in Emma Lazurus's famous poem, the Jewish children were treated by many British Jews as "the wretched refuse of your teeming shores. ..." [They] gave reluctantly of their money and never of themselves.'[47]

Occasionally, children were accepted by foster parents but not by the children already in the home. When the parents' own children proved to be jealous of the newcomer or disliked him or her, this tension exacerbated the child's loneliness and need for his or her own parents, and often resulted in feelings of acute depression. Ruth remembers that 'the loneliness was worse than any fear of air raids. Suicide entered my mind.'[48] The RCM actually listed one suicide in 1941.[49] Reports of bed-wetting, nightmares and running away were not uncommon.[50] Such situations created many difficulties for even the most helpful and kind foster parents. As Dorit Whiteman points out, 'depressed children do not necessarily cry. Some develop eating and sleeping disturbances, some turn rebellious and some become withdrawn. It can take a great deal of sympathetic understanding to help a depressed child.'[51] Unfortunately, not all foster parents were sympathetic and understanding.

Some families were simply unsuited to being foster parents, sometimes because they were too young (a recently married couple in their early twenties who applied were refused) or because they were too old. Paula Hill was placed 'with a Jewish couple of advancing years who were neither prepared nor equipped for the traumatized child who entered their lives'.[52]

A few individuals abused the child, either verbally, physically or sexually. Friederka, for example, was raped not only by her foster father but also by his 19-year-old son, while Margaret was chased and assaulted whenever she was alone with her foster father.[53] It took Henry K well into his adult years before he could speak about the sexual abuse he suffered as a six-year-old over a long period of time while in the care of a 'children's home'.[54] Sometimes the abuser was a neighbour, family friend or, as in one case, a neighbourhood shopkeeper who always wanted refugee boys 'to run errands for him'.[55] It took much counselling and many years before adults who had been abused as children could cope with their horrific experiences at the hands of those who had been in positions of trust and authority.

Yet, fortunately, it would appear that these cases of abuse were the exceptions. Most foster parents took their role very seriously and many far exceeded their obligations. An English vicar and his wife gave their charge a 'wonderful wedding'. Helga Samuel says that her 'truly wonderful' Jewish family treated her 'like their own. I lacked for nothing in either material things, comfort, love, understanding, protection, kindness.'[56] Steffie Segerman also remembers being greeted with love by the entire family and made to feel like one of them. Vera Gissing was taken to a receiving home in Bloomsbury and, when the door opened:

There stood this little old lady, barely taller than myself. … Suddenly, her face broke into the most wonderful smile, and she ran to me and hugged me, and spoke to me words I did not understand then, but they were, 'You shall be loved.' And those were the most important words any child in a foreign land, away from her family, could hear. And loved I was.

John Fieldsend is effusive about his foster parents' kindness, while Paul Kohn remembers with deep gratitude the efforts of the Revd B. Morton and his wife 'to learn the intricacies of orthodox Jewish observance'. The list goes on.[57] Indeed, the majority of *Kinder* remark on the kindness, understanding and love their foster parents and often even their school mates extended.[58] Mordecai Ron, for example, recounts, 'I met kindness, understanding and compassion and to this day I admire the way the people conducted themselves during the bitter days of total war.'[59]

Part of this admired conduct was Britain's initial acceptance of the Kindertransport children, while a major component of the *Kinders*' own adjustment was the quality of the homes in which they were placed. As Dorit Whiteman shows, many 'factors … determined the degree of the children's adjustment. The best results were obtained when characteristics of the external situation, such as type of placement, and the personality and expectations of the guardian, coordinated well with the value system of the child.'[60]

Orthodox children faced additional problems, for there were relatively few homes available in which the guardian's expectations coincided well with the child's value system. Occasionally, even a young child would become very upset about the lax religious observances in his or her foster home. Rabbi Schonfeld cites the example of one little lad of about seven who had been returned to Avigdor House (an Orthodox centre). 'He had cried all day long and had seemed very unhappy. When the child was questioned it was found that the family ate without caps, did not "bench" [pray after meals], and were, to his mind, very unorthodox in every respect.'[61]

Some Anglo-Jewish families felt ashamed of the way these European children dressed and did not wish to be seen on the street or even in synagogue with them. Certainly on arrival, many of the children were easily identifiable as foreigners. Kurt Fuchel remembers walking into the home of his foster parents, the Cohens, as 'a little boy dressed in his Austrian finery: short pants, jacket, long wool stockings held up by a suspender belt, and high-rising boots'.[62] In Fuchel's case, the offending clothes were burnt and the host family thereby spared the embarrassment of public incredulity, but many families could not afford another set of garments and the child would be forced to attend school in his or her conspicuous garb. There were also cases of a refugee child being better clothed than the other children or even the mother in the foster home, and being forced to relinquish a treasured item, such as new boots or even an entire wardrobe.[63] This, fortunately, was a rare occurrence.

Their clothing was not the only source of pervasive strangeness the *Kinder* encountered. Failing to understand what was spoken was a cause of great confusion and because of this many children learnt English with amazing rapidity. Kurt Fuchel wrote to his parents after six weeks in England, 'I no longer speak German.'[64] While most youngsters took considerably longer than a mere six weeks to learn English, to speak without an accent proved an unattainable goal for a few, much to their consternation.[65]

Not only were clothing and language sources of strangeness, but codes of acceptable conduct differed in England from those on the continent. A well brought up German adolescent, for example, behaved differently from his or her English counterpart. 'It was a while before Gunther realized that the way he greeted people must seem odd. There was no need to make a slight bow while clicking one's heels, as he had been taught in Germany.'[66] When Walter Fulop reported for work 'dressed in continental fashion' he also clicked his heels and offered his hand to be shaken.[67] In his case, his employer quickly found him a second-hand suit and instructed him in English greeting customs. Lenore Davies's experience was different but no less embarrassing. The first morning in her foster home, she remembers, 'like a well-brought up little girl I took my bed to pieces, stripped the sheet, placed the pillows on the window sill, upended the mattress – and suddenly my hostess stood in the door, threw up her hands in horror and said, "Shocking, what will the neighbours say!"' Like almost every refugee child Davies therefore had to make adjustments. 'That was the first of many innocent misunderstandings to come; my table manners were different, not wrong; my phraseology was poor, not impolite; my English general knowledge was limited, not stupid.'[68]

This strangeness, in addition to their German or Austrian background, opened the child to that bane of the school playground, peer-group teasing. Unfortunately, this was not always limited to public places. The son in Margaret Furst's foster home teased her so incessantly that she was always in tears.[69]

Some of the teasing had its roots in the child's foreign name and foster parents frequently changed the youngster's name, often quite arbitrarily. So 'Horst' became 'Hugh', 'Arvid' became 'David' and the little twins, 'Lotte' and 'Susi' became 'Eunice Mary' and 'Grace Elizabeth'. A number of children assumed the surname of their foster parents.[70]

The classroom could be a place of absolute disaster or of kindly and sympathetic integration: much depended on the teacher or local school authority's attitude. When some local authorities raised objections over the cost of educating the new arrivals, the Home Office ruled that 'a refugee should have treatment comparable to that of an average English child in receipt of free education.'[71]

Not all refugee organizations, however, officially upheld the goal of assimilation into English culture. A 1942 Church of England committee report noted that the refugee children 'should be encouraged to value their heritage of German language, literature, and culture, instead of trying to dissociate themselves from everything connected with their national background', but this was only after the war had already made all these aspects of Germanism highly suspect.[72] Yet, even those who should have known better occasionally disregarded this injunction to value the children's heritage. Gertrude Burns remembers that her headmistress, though kindly and friendly, 'made me read to her every night from the *Financial Post* to improve my accent [and] made me sit next to one of the staff at every mealtime, to be trained in making polite conversation during meals'.[73] The teacher seemed to be trying to assimilate her into English culture in as short a time as possible, which she probably felt to be for the child's own benefit.

That not all refugee organizations agreed on the question of assimilation compounded the children's difficulty of acceptance. In 1942 the RCM declared:

One of the most vital tasks of the Movement is to enable its children to be assimilated into the life of the country and to take their place as normal and useful citizens. Many of these children have unfortunately developed a kind of 'refugee mentality' which causes them to regard themselves as objects of curiosity and pity, and as a race apart.[74]

Whether Vera Gissing would have been seen as such a child is a moot question. She had been placed with a Methodist family and was well cared for, but nevertheless was desperately homesick, 'not just for my parents, but for everything Czech ... for the food, the education, the company of other Czechs'. She was therefore fortunate to be offered a place in a recently-opened Czech school, the Czechoslovak State School, first in Shropshire and later in Wales, where she spent the next three years. Here also she got to know Joe Schlesinger, who was to become one of Canada's foremost broadcasters and journalists and who became her close friend. 'They were the happiest years I had in England,' she remembered, 'I was very glad that I was with people who understood.'[75] Joe Schlesinger shared this appreciation. 'These years remain in my memory among the happiest, most carefree times of my youth,' he wrote in his autobiography many years later.[76] Both young people were also, by virtue of being billeted with fellow countrymen, never required to assimilate in quite the same way as children placed in British homes and schools, for they were able to retain their language and culture, and build friendships with other Czech children. Despite her desire to be with people from her own background, Vera Gissing continued to regard her foster parents, the Rainfords, as her 'dear little English Mummy and Daddy' and she visited them regularly.[77]

At the beginning, a few children had great difficulty adjusting to the British diet. Vera Schaufeld wrote to her parents and 'complained that

I didn't get enough to eat, which I don't think is factual ... I just think that the kind of food they had wasn't satisfying, so that's why my parents sent these [food] parcels and must have been very worried.'[78] So much strangeness for so many homesick children!

The RCM encouraged the children to write home frequently to maintain some semblance of still 'belonging' and to assuage some of their loneliness and separation anxiety. The organization even provided postage when it was necessary. After the outbreak of war, some of the children, like David Lewinski, were able to remain in contact through family members in neutral countries, especially if they lived in America. When the United States entered the conflict, however, even this avenue was closed.[79] After 1942, when many parents were already in camps, postcards were received via the Red Cross. The last of these cards arrived 1942–43, after which there was silence and the older children began to suspect that their worst fears were being realized.[80] In August 1942, the *Jewish Chronicle* headlined, 'Death in the Gas Chamber' and in December of that year, 'Two Million Jews Slaughtered: Most Terrible Massacre of All Time'. There was no longer any doubt, though the individual child remained hopeful.

Since Youth Aliyah trainees were not generally placed in private homes, the treatment they received was different from that of the Refugee Children's Movement. Youth Aliyah, which feared assimilation as much as the Orthodox community did, set up *hachschara* centres – Zionist job and agricultural training facilities – where the children lived, attended classes and worked on agricultural projects in preparation for re-emigration to Palestine (Israel). Even here, though, not all was necessarily smooth sailing. In March 1940, for example, some adult refugees, together with about 20 children from the Youth Aliyah centre at Bydown, were moved to Braunton to work on a large farm specializing in growing bulbs, flowers and vegetables. The children were in the fields eight to ten hours a day, with only two half-hour breaks. Fred Dunstan, one of the leaders, later wrote that 'this would not have mattered so much if the children had been older, but the farm did not want to employ 17-year-olds and older ones, as they would have to pay them higher wages.'[81] Needless to say, this particular scheme was soon abandoned and the children were returned to the Bydown centre. Barry Turner points out that this experience was not unique to Braunton, but 'by and large, it was the same story at many of the smaller training centres,' including the Hale nurseries near Bournemouth.[82]

Youth Aliyah seems to have enjoyed a more favourable financial situation than many of the sponsoring organizations in that in July 1939 Eddie Cantor, the Jewish American comedian and actor, raised £100,000 in support of its centres. The American Hadassah organizations also supported it well, perhaps because of its commitment to send 'their' children to Palestine.[83]

There were, of course, hostels other than those the Youth Aliyah supported, and of these many, but not all, were Orthodox.[84] The children placed in these enjoyed the same sense of comradeship as the Youth Aliyah trainees. Several of the homes took in younger children as well as adolescents.[85] Sessi Jakobovits and the girls in her Leeds hostel were supplied with 'games and mountains of wool and knitting needles. The Older girls taught the younger ones to knit.'[86] The daily schedule at Barnham House, which the RCM ran, was as follows:

> Nursery of 18 boys, ages 9 and under. Most of these have short lessons in the morning. They are taken for walks, play games and are generally supervised by competent workers from the time they get up to the time they go to bed.
>
> Boys 10 to 16 years of age have school all the morning from 9.30 to 12.15. The basis of the teaching is English and they are grouped in accordance with their knowledge of English.
>
> Boys of 16 years of age and upwards do field work all day. This is done under the supervision of a trained agriculturist. ...
>
> Boys of 14 to 16 years do field work in the afternoons only.
>
> With the exception of the cooking, the whole of the domestic work of the building is undertaken by children supervised by staff. The laundry, except for sheets and towels, is done by the boys under the supervision of a washer-woman.

There is a tailor's shop, carpenter's shop, and a bootmaker's shop, all run by the boys under supervision.[87]

Whether in hostels or private homes, the children had barely settled when the war began. Now they faced an even greater trauma, as heightened concern for their families was added to their own uncertain future. The chief rabbi encouraged them not to fear but to 'remember the G-d above Who neither sleeps nor slumbers. Into His hands do I commend my spirit, when I sleep and when I wake.'[88] The *Kinder*, especially the older ones, had need of all the comfort, prayers and support the community could offer, for there were even more difficult days ahead.

4

EVACUATION AND INTERNMENT

B RITISH authorities had long feared that an outbreak of war would mean the bombing of London, and therefore a plan to evacuate all school-aged children and those not yet in school, as well as several other categories of people at risk, had been in place since the late 1930s.[1] The evacuation, initially intended only for London, soon also included foreign-born children in all security-sensitive coastal areas. Called 'Protected Areas' these included 'almost all of Scotland, the East and South coasts, Devonshire, Cornwall, a large area north of the Bristol Channel, Pembrokeshire,' and a large area around Liverpool. In these areas 'no alien may remain without permission, which is granted only in rare cases'.[2]

School headmasters and headmistresses had already been notified in early January 1939 that evacuation would occur in the case of war and on the last day of August 1939, the order was received on the BBC via the code words, 'Pied Piper tomorrow'. The following day, 1 September, 2,000–3,000 refugee children, among tens of thousands of other school children, were marched, as previously practised, to trains and buses for evacuation to the countryside. Even teachers and parents were not told of the children's final destinations, possibly for fear of enemy sabotage.[3]

Evacuation was a familiar exercise for the Kindertransport

children. Joe Schlesinger remembered that he felt as though 'Czechoslovakia was happening all over again … just as I was getting used to my new home, I was shipped off again.'[4] The headmistress of the Jewish secondary schools reported that the refugee children, whose ages ranged from five to 17, 'were still in the first confusion of the bewildering change of circumstances, unsettled and homeless'. Orders had to be repeated in German because so many of the youngsters did not understand any English.[5] Moreover, many of the recently arrived refugees came dressed in 'very scanty clothing and we now have to provide the necessities for the winter months'.[6] The children were tagged again with their names and again carried a lunch. This lunch, however, had not been prepared by the children's parents but was issued by the evacuation authorities. Each child was given a bag containing a tin of corned beef, two tins of evaporated milk, two packets of biscuits and a large chocolate bar, so that when they arrived at their various reception centres there would not be a run on food stocks from the local shops.[7] They were also equipped with gas masks. Orthodox children questioned whether a gas mask could be carried on the Sabbath, and the rabbinical answer was yes, if there was 'a real and present danger', or if it was 'considered a necessary adjunct to one's clothing'.[8]

Parents or guardians were asked to contribute what they could afford towards the cost of maintaining the child. The cost was computed at an average of nine shillings a week, but the government decided to fix six shillings a week as standard for each child, and those who could show that such a sum was an 'unreasonable burden' could pay a reduced sum, according to their circumstances.[9] Thus, the government bore a large part of the financial burden of the evacuation, but the children and their parents paid an enormous emotional price.

Some refugee children were evacuated with their foster parents but most were sent into the country with their schools. Such *Kinder* suffered less than those placed individually in remote areas without the companionship of friends. Isolated children not only experienced greater loneliness, but they were also frequently the object of suspicion among locals, even branded as spies for innocuous behaviour such as sketching the village green or describing their homes in Vienna. The child's inability to understand the local dialect added to the villagers' suspicion and to the child's fear and distress.[10] Margaret Heller (Goldberger) comments that many adult villagers simply regarded them as German refugees and that their attitude reflected a total ignorance of what the Jewish children had experienced in Germany.[11]

Whole villages were requisitioned for the evacuees and reception centres were hastily organized in church halls, schools and other public buildings. When children were left without a billet at the end of a day, placement officers would go from door to door, accompanied by the hapless and tired youngsters, and not infrequently forced an unwilling householder to accept an evacuee. Judith Baumel reported that 'by the end of the day many children had broken down both emotionally and physically.'[12]

This was not an auspicious beginning for any child. To compound the trauma for the Orthodox, there was very little recognition of the absurdity of placing an Orthodox evacuee in a Catholic convent or Anglican vicar's home.[13] In this emergency, however, such things happened. To exacerbate the chaos, British Jews were largely urban and many villages to which children were now evacuated had never before encountered a Jewish person. On the lists of placements in the district of Stetfold, for example, no Jewish names appear as hosts, although it is possible, of course, that some had anglicized their names. Be that as it may, in some remote villages the *Kinder* were regarded as curiosities, pariahs or wholly undesirable foreigners.

Some 14 hostels, as well as Rabbi Dr Schonfeld's Orthodox Jewish secondary schools in which 350 refugee *Kinder* were enrolled, were evacuated *en masse*, the latter to three villages in Bedfordshire. Most children not in hostels or evacuated with their schools were placed individually, sometimes far from other evacuees. This scattering of Jewish children worried the leadership. How was religious life to be maintained unless children were evacuated together in schools or at least in groups that could be placed in the same village or district? What about the older children, the teenagers? 'We are very worried about the Jewish evacuated children. They are let loose in entirely strange townlets and villages, and unless some meeting places and controlling influences are established ... we are faced with the probability of losing the loyalty of an entire Jewish generation,' wrote a Mr Hausenball on 1 November 1939.[14] Or, as an editorial in the *Jewish Chronicle* asked, 'do you want thousands of Jewish children to run wild in various parts of the country and to grow up ignorant heathens, bringing reproach and hatred to the name of Jew?'[15] The fear of anti-Semitism is only thinly veiled in these expressions of concern for their children, yet it was a very real fear for British Jewry.

Chief Rabbi Hertz took the initiative in stemming the Jewish children's anticipated apostasy by organizing the Chief Rabbi's Canteen Committee, which began work in October 1939. Kosher canteens were placed in each centre with a sizeable Jewish evacuee population. Sometimes the canteen found a home in a caravan, trailer, school room or even church hall.[16] The canteens proved to be an instant success. They served kosher meals and games, books and musical evenings, as well as other entertainments, were provided. 'Our children sleep with local residents', wrote the principal of one Jewish school, 'but spend the whole day with our school'.[17] This contact proved to be that very necessary link to the child's Jewish roots about which the leadership was so concerned.

Not all Jewish children, however, were within reach of a canteen. To those in isolated areas, the chief rabbi sent a message of instruction and encouragement. He enjoined them not to eat meat in a non-Jewish home, although all fish except eels and shellfish were permitted. 'Never make a fuss,' he admonished, 'your foster mother may never have known a Jew before; when you face any danger, say, "God is with me; I am not going to be afraid."'[18]

Fear of local repercussions caused resident Jews in some areas to oppose a large-scale celebration of Jewish festivals, such as the Passover, and even a few 'responsible Jewish teachers' hesitated to organize this observance. However, the decision was made to use the kosher canteens wherever possible and in this way the eight days of Passover were celebrated in 24 canteens, reaching almost 2,000 children.[19] Later, it was discovered that canteens were not the only places where the Passover was observed. In Holt, Wiltshire, the Anglican church hall and a Wesleyan hall were placed at the disposal of the evacuees 'for all religious purposes', while in Fordham all activities in the local village hall were cancelled for nine days to allow for the celebration.[20]

In assessing the impact of the Passover celebration on the local community, the conclusions proved to be very positive. Local dignitaries and clergy had visited; villagers donated scarce fresh vegetables, while some foster mothers assisted with washing up the dishes and other chores. Although the Fordham committee reported that there were 'ill-feelings in the district', another group concluded, 'it [evacuation] is a precious opportunity for eradicating any superstitious beliefs about Jews, [and] for allaying prejudice.'[21]

This diaspora of Jewish children into predominantly Christian villages, however, created problems as well as 'precious opportunities'. The number of children in non-Jewish homes had now soared dramatically. Elaine Blond notes that approximately one-third of the Refugee Children's Movement charges were placed in Christian homes before evacuation, but 'many more' after September 1939. Chief Rabbi Hertz's figures substantiate this estimate, showing 3,457 children in non-Jewish homes and only 1,844 in Jewish billets. In Scotland the imbalance was even greater, with only 27 children in Jewish homes and 146 in non-Jewish billets.[22]

The arrival of Jewish children in a community could cause unforeseen difficulties and these were not all related simply to finding homes for the young evacuees. There were some among them who required social welfare assistance, namely services that were much better developed in London than in rural areas. Also, included among the children of the Jewish schools were recent refugees who were found to 'need a great deal of medical and dental attention'.[23] Jewish dietary laws loomed large in the thinking of Jewish leaders and of the refugee organizations. Jewish religious observance was at stake.

Here was a rural vicar, [Blond wrote], who went out of his way to make two Jewish refugees feel at home by recruiting them to his church choir; ... a farmer's wife who persuaded her husband to kill the fatted pig so that the family and their Jewish guests could enjoy a slap-up roast. Acknowledging our sins of omission, in 1941 we made a direct appeal to Jewish organizations to support religious education.[24]

By May 1940, the Orthodox community had already formed an organization, the Joint Emergency Committee for the Religious Education of Jewish Children from London, which combined representatives from the Jewish Religious Education Board, Union of Hebrew Religion Classes, Talmud Torah Trust and the Central Committee for Jewish Education in a common cause, primarily to provide teachers, prayer books and other literature for the evacuees.[25]

To help the movement maintain contact with all the refugee children, wherever they were placed, the 12 regional committees, initially established to look after the children on arrival,[26] expanded their activities to include the following subcommittees and departments – general, guarantee, German, hospitality camps and hostels, transport, finance, and after-care departments.[27] Their responsibilities included visiting the children and keeping abreast of address changes and any problems that might arise, as well as monitoring the religious instruction they received. To facilitate the instruction, which was to be 'according to the faith of his or her parents', the various branches of Judaism cooperated to extend the earlier Orthodox initiative and formed the Joint Emergency Committee for Jewish Religious Teaching, under the aegis of the Refugee Children's Movement. A correspondence course for more isolated children was prepared and, in addition, a rabbi was to instruct such children at designated times. Occasionally, religious instruction resulted in an unusual twist in the young child's mind, as when the seventh commandment, 'Thou shalt not commit adultery' became 'Thou shalt not kick a duckery.'[28]

While the plan for joint instruction appeared feasible on paper, in actuality serious problems were soon evident, problems chiefly related to the acrimony existing within the Jewish community itself. As Blond remembers it, 'a plethora of orthodox and liberal [groups] promptly took up cudgels against each other. [The Orthodox made the RCM] sound like undercover agents for the Archbishop of Canterbury.'[29] This acrimony was to last throughout the evacuation period and beyond.

Yet, for many of the observant children, even those billeted in Christian homes, evacuation proved to be a positive experience, as Rabbi Schonfeld's Jewish secondary schools pupils, for example, discovered in the Bedfordhire villages to which they were sent. The youngsters found the Biggleswade Rural District Council 'especially helpful' in arranging for homes, while a Mr Ashby of the Free Church 'bought a chapel, specially redecorated and allocated it for our free use',[30] to mention but two of many positive actions on the part of the host communities. Many of the older children adjusted to all the disruptions of evacuation with the same courage that marked their arrival in Britain just months earlier. Kurt Weinberg, for example, sent to Cornwall, remembers joining the Boy Scouts, becoming a patrol leader and eventually organizing salvage collections for the whole of west Cornwall.[31]

As on their arrival from the continent, most children were much happier when not alone among strangers. The billeting authorities therefore sought to place siblings together, now as on their arrival in Britain. When this was not possible, children would practise the most ingenious subterfuge to avoid being separated, as the story of Gina and her brother illustrates:

> Mrs Bell, a case worker, went to a home to take only Gina and not the boy. While she was at Gina's billet, the boy came along with his luggage, with a message that the billeting officer had instructed his hostess to send him with [*sic*. The message was a fabrication] ... I am told that it would be most difficult to separate the two children.[32]

Evacuation also affected operations at Bloomsbury House where great anxiety was felt for the safety of their records since these contained the only legal documents that most refugee children possessed. Therefore, a house, the Grange, was rented in Hindhead, Surrey, and the files relocated, together with 15 staff members and the after-care department of the RCM.[33]

The after effects of evacuation remained with the children well into adult life. It exacerbated the refugees' sense of insecurity and created in some, as in Ruth Inglis, 'a lasting passion to stay in one place'.[34] Some reported recurring nightmares and an inability to make decisions, among many other symptoms, which supported the theories of psychiatrists such as Anna Freud (daughter of the world-famous doctor, Sigmund Freud), who were 'implacably opposed' to evacuation, contending that bombs were less distressing to the child than separation from parents,[35] even foster parents.

Other authorities, however, argued that the move from the city to the country 'probably benefited the evacuees' because they were generally better fed and experienced a healthier lifestyle. In reviewing the larger picture, Ruth Inglis concludes that 'the legacy of the ... evacuees totally benefited the welfare of British children born after them,' chiefly because children were no longer regarded as chattels.[36]

The older *Kinder* did not remain in the evacuation communities for long. In October 1939, some weeks after the outbreak of war, tribunals were set up throughout Britain. These courts generally consisted of a King's Counsel or county court judge, with a police secretary in attendance. The tribunal's purpose was to sift through the alien population resident in Britain to determine who among them might be a threat to the security of the state. Czech refugees, whose sympathies were assumed from the outset to be anti-German, were not required to appear before the tribunals.[37] For those born in Germany or Austria, however, the mere process of appearing before the tribunal was traumatic, for it reminded them of their Nazi experiences.[38]

In May 1940 the government began to intern 'enemy aliens' aged 16 years of age and older, grouping them into three categories, namely 'A' – deemed suspect and interned immediately; 'B' – to remain at liberty under restrictions; and 'C' – not considered a security risk. Most *Kinder* fell into category 'B', which meant that although they remained free, even their bicycles, cameras and radios were impounded. By 12 May, however, some 'B' category refugees, including many of the older *Kinder*, were being interned, often without explanation to either the child or the foster parent. Obviously, this caused considerable confusion and anxiety. By the end of that month all Germans and Austrians between the ages of 16 and 70, both male and female, classified in category 'B' were ordered interned, together with some in category 'C'. Some common sense fortunately prevailed and Connery Chappell records that 'the automatic internment of "C" category women and girls was halted … after approximately a week.'[39] A few of the older girls were fortunate in that they were spared such trauma altogether. Margit Diamond, placed in Trinity Hall school for girls, remembers that the headmistress, a Miss Lobb, 'had to make special arrangements for me to be there lest, in the event of a German invasion by sea, I should aid the enemy!'[40]

The children billeted in the Stoatley Rough School had a similar experience. Those over 16 were required to appear before a tribunal in Guilford, but so many British citizens vouched for them that they were all placed in 'C' category. In April, however, this decision was rescinded and four boys and two girls were interned. The school history reports that 'these children were interned because they had only just turned 16 and had not appeared before a tribunal to establish their loyalty. … Dr Lion [the principal] spent the next two months trying to get them released.' Eventually, in July 1940, four were released and returned to school. Unfortunately, two were transferred to Canada (they had already been transferred when the Home Office granted them release). One boy, sent to Australia, committed suicide when he heard about his mother's death in a concentration camp.[41] Several of the boys whom the CRREC had brought to England were interned together in 'Camp Two' at Tatura in Australia. They wrote to Rabbi Schonfeld that they were managing to stay together and had successfully petitioned to receive kosher foods.[42]

A future Nobel Prize laureate, Walter Kohn, was among these interned students. Thinking the internment was a mistake and that Walter would shortly be released, his school sent his books to the camp but, unlike the students from Trinity Hall and Stoatley Rough, however, there was no rescinding of his incarceration.[43]

Refugee organizations as well as individuals made courageous attempts to defuse the situation. A memorandum was circulated that contended that:

> Refugees as a class are neither enemy aliens nor POWs. They were invited and welcomed here as victims of Nazi oppression and offered asylum. ... The Paton Commission which unites [the welfare of refugees and POWs] is a serious error in Organization. ... So far as the State is concerned, it is wrong that the War Office should be charged ... with the task of dealing with refugees.[44]

Nonetheless, the internment of men and boys continued for some months.

The internment proved to be understandably traumatic for many of the young refugees, despite kind officials often doing their best to mitigate the fear and anxiety involved in the process. One of the internees remembered:

> I was interned as an enemy alien in 1940, a thing which was a great shock to me as, naturally, there was nothing 'enemy' about my feelings for this country, and it was a pretty awful moment when I, a girl of 17, was fetched by two policemen and shipped off to an 'unknown' destination.[45]

The 'unknown destination' proved to be either an internment or a transit camp. The internment camps, most but not all of which were located on the Isle of Man, were so hurriedly put together and so inadequately staffed that often even basic amenities were unavailable. The transit camps in England to which the men and boys were sent, initially as gathering points, were particularly wretched. Among these, Warth Mill near Bury, Lancashire, was arguably the worst, with rotting floors, buckets for toilets and rat infestation. Some camps were set up at racetracks and the internees billeted in stables and tents. Fortunately, the boys did not remain in the transit camps for any length of time, but were moved by train and ship to the Isle of Man as soon as the accommodation there could be made ready.[46] Seafront hotels and homes on the island had been requisitioned for use by the military, with the town of Douglas serving as the centre for the camps.

The first prisoners, 823 of them, mostly Jewish refugees and including Kindertransport children, arrived on 27 May 1940. An attempt was made to continue the education of those who had been taken out of school and after a few months, once they had settled in, the internees organized their own orchestras, plays, athletic competitions and other activities. Rabbis and Christian ministers came to conduct services. It is interesting to note that the interned Christian women and girls did not want the ministrations of a German pastor, so strong was their anti-German feeling, and therefore Sister Annie Whisler, who had worked for many years as a deaconess in Upper Silesia and spoke fluent German, was appointed to hold services.[47] A youth institute was opened.

Despite attempts to maintain normality, however, the refugees found the mere fact of internment frightening and humiliating. A very angry 'Statement of the Representatives of 688 Internees Transferred from Central Camp, Douglas, to Onchan Camp, IOM', asserted that several houses were without electricity or gas, that there were broken windows and furniture and that the rations were very poor. The most troublesome factor, however, was the Onchan camp commander's harsh discipline and general behaviour, which included racist remarks, ordering embarrassing body searches in full view of local civilians, and making the men stand in a cold wind for two hours. This was deemed 'dangerously close to those [tactics] adopted by the Commandants of German Concentration Camps'.[48] The fact that anti-Nazi Jews were billeted with Nazi sympizers and even prisoners of war exacerbated an already tense situation. The latter's attempts to intimidate the former resulted in near riots and physical violence. Ya'acov Friedler, interned at Port Erin, clearly remembers the tensions between the refugees and Nazi sympathizers. The Nazis would raise their arms in the German salute and smirk when they encountered a Jewish youth. Often these encounters led to fist fights and other physical violence.[49] When this became known, refugee committees sent strongly worded letters 'by prominent men' to *The Times* (of London) and other daily papers insisting that Nazis and anti-Nazis be accommodated separately.[50]

The situation worsened when the government decided forcibly to deport large numbers of internees to Canada and Australia. Rudi Lowenstein remembers the fear and anxiety of facing U-boat infested waters, the desolation of the first Canadian camps and the poor treatment meted out to the evacuees, who were regarded as prisoners of war.[51] Walter Kohn was among those *Kinder* sent to Canada. He recalled that his imprisonment lasted almost two years, but that, during this time, he attended classes organized by a Professor Heckscher, which prepared him for the matriculation examination at McGill University in Montreal, one of Canada's most prestigious universities. He was more fortunate than most internees.[52]

The indefensible maltreatment and brutality inflicted on the *Kinder* and other internees sent to Australia on the *Dunera* was exceptionally bad and caused a major public outcry when it became known. 'Kicks, blows from rifle butts and savage beatings by the troops were a daily occurrence,' while valuables including rings and watches were stolen, valuable papers destroyed and property vandalized.[53] One refugee committed suicide rather than continue after his visa to Argentina was torn up and thrown overboard.[54]

British and Canadian soldiers also mistreated, searched and robbed the internees aboard the *Ettrick*, which arrived in Canada in July 1940, though fortunately this proved to have been an isolated incident.[55] It soon became evident, however, that these internees were not what Canada had expected. Indeed, Charles Ritchie, at the Canadian high commission in London recorded in his diary:

I now hear that the ferocious internees whom the British Government begged us on bended knee to take to Canada … are mostly entirely inoffensive, anti-Nazi refugees who have been shovelled out to Canada at a moment's notice where they may have a disagreeable time, as our authorities have no files about them and will not know whom or what to believe.[56]

The *Dunera* passengers and other internees in Australia were released in 1941 and offered either work in Australia or repatriation to Britain. By 1947, some 1,451 *Dunera* internees had returned to Britain, 165 had emigrated to other countries, 13 had died and 913 had decided to remain in Australia.[57] Among the latter was a young count, Christopher Wallenstein, who began his medical training at this time[58] and later emigrated to Canada as a fully qualified physician.

As a result of the recommendations of HM Commissioner of Prisons A. Paterson, who was sent to Canada to investigate conditions in Canadian camps, some internees were allowed to return to Britain and, by June 1941, 891 had done so.[59] It was not until 11 November 1942, however, that the Canadian government circulated a letter announcing that the refugees were now 'regarded as friendly aliens enjoying temporary liberty in Canada'.[60]

Needless to say, the Jewish community, refugee organizations and prominent citizens, including the Archbishop of Canterbury, raised strenuous objections to the refugees' internment, even before the scandals of the deportations became known, but to no avail. The well-known Quaker activist Bertha Bracey was the first representative of a welfare organization to arrive in person on the scene when she visited the Isle of Man, yet even her representations were ignored.[61]

In Britain, however, the absurdity of imprisoning anti-Nazi refugees became apparent earlier than in either Australia or Canada. Bishop George Bell recommended that the Church of England in Canada and Australia make its members aware of the plight of refugees deported as prisoners of war, but in those countries his suggestion seemed to fall on mostly deaf ears.[62] By late 1940 the British Home

Office had already released the first internees under a White Paper and, by 1941, most of the genuine refugees had been freed, though curfew restrictions remained in place for all 'friendly aliens' until 1944 and longer inside the protected areas. At the end of the war 1,198 internees remained on the Isle of Man, none of whom appear to have been Kindertransport refugees.[63] Statistics show that 1,000 *Kinder* had been interned and, of these, 201 were deported to Australia or Canada.[64]

Some of the older *Kinder* released from internment now entered the workforce, though they were too young to have acquired any job skills. Many enlisted in the British armed forces. British naturalization was not an option at this time, so these young German and Austrian nationals enlisted initially in the Pioneer Corps, called by some the 'Jewish Brigade', which was designated as a behind-the-lines unit.[65] It was not the perfect solution. The boys complained privately that 'the labour service offered in the Corps gave very little scope for intelligent and well-educated boys.'[66] As the war progressed and their loyalty was no longer questioned, many transferred to the regular service, with a surprising number choosing to become commandoes. Even more *Kinder*, because of their linguistic skills, were seconded to the intelligence service. Colin Anson managed to combine all three categories, serving with the Pioneer Corps, then volunteering as a commando and finally acting as an interpreter with the Field Intelligence Agency.[67] Altogether, 754 boys and 157 girls enlisted in the British forces. Of these, 30 were killed in action.[68]

Upon enlistment the government urged the recruits to anglicize their names, both as a step towards assimilation and for protection in case of capture by the Germans. The latter seems a rather specious argument, since it would not have taken long for the true identity of a prisoner to be revealed. Nevertheless, for various reasons, many of the young recruits did anglicize their names at this time.

Children who were too young for internment or military service meanwhile continued their education, despite the local authorities' initial trepidation at the costs involved, an uncertainty that parliament firmly repudiated.[69] The RCM reported that more than 6,000 refugee children attended school in the years 1939–44. Those passing the entrance tests and in a position to pay the prescribed fee were allowed to continue to secondary school. Since the school-leaving age in Great Britain at this time was 14, many of the refugees in poorer homes were unable to continue their education but were required to enter training schools or apprentice positions, often in Jewish establishments. The garment and fur industries, hotel management, manufacturing, the jewellery trade, tailoring, and upholstering were all considered suitable occupations. Many girls entered schools of nursing, became secretaries or dieticians or even took up chicken farming.[70] An estimated 2,000 *Kinder* over the age of 16 were in training or apprenticeships during the 1940s.

Some youngsters were fortunate enough to have been placed in schools or relatively wealthy homes that allowed them secondary and even post-secondary education, though the number attending universities was initially very small.[71] Individuals like Gerta Burkill of Cambridge, the German-born wife of a college don, worked tirelessly on behalf of higher education for refugee children by ferreting out scholarships and grants for which the children could apply. One of 'Burkill's' boys earned a scholarship to both Oxford and Cambridge, which was an almost unheard of feat at that time.[72] Fees for higher education were sometimes paid by the British business connections of a student's parents or even by the parents themselves. The Quakers, for example, would sometimes pay a child's school fees in pounds sterling, if the parents had funds in Germany with which they could reimburse them.[73] The precarious situation after *Kristallnacht*, however, when the Kindertransport children arrived, made such transfers virtually impossible. Yet, most refugee children accorded great importance to education and the number enrolled in evening classes and on correspondence courses was disproportionately high compared with the general population.

While foster parents or even refugee organizations acted *in loco parentis* for their wards in education, as in other matters, there were situations, such as illness or a minor's determination to marry, in which a legal guardian was urgently required. Before the Guardianship Act of

1944 the parents of children in the care of the Refugee Children's Movement were still legally considered to be alive and in control of their child's life. By 1943 it was apparent that this might no longer be the case, and the government moved to appoint a legal guardian. The Union of Orthodox Hebrew Congregations presented a strong case to appoint the chief rabbi, Dr Hertz, at least as a joint guardian,[74] but there was too much dissent in the larger Jewish community. Finally, after the bill 'to provide for the guardianship of infants who have come to the United Kingdom in consequence of war or persecution' was passed into law, Lord Gorell of the RCM, a Christian, was appointed 'guardian' of the children in England and 'tutor' of those in Scotland.[75] This bill carried the proviso that due attention must be paid to the wishes of the ward's parent or nearest relative with regard to religious matters. It is of interest, therefore, that a Christian became the legal guardian of Jewish children and a Protestant the guardian of Roman Catholic children. Lord Gorell wrote:

> It was a wonderful thing that my guardianship was so generously and unsuspiciously [sic] accepted not only by the Chief Rabbi ... but also by Cardinal Griffin, who indeed even asked me to extend it, so as to include some other Roman Catholic children who had not been brought over by the Movement.[76]

In his autobiography, Lord Gorell summarized his unique responsibilities:

> I thus became the first Christian, I think, ever to be legal guardian to Jewish children and certainly the first Protestant to be in that position to Roman Catholic children. ... It is simple, unusual – and also, as it happens truthful – to be able to say that I have had more children, legally, than any man since Solomon.[77]

It was not all smooth sailing. Dr Schonfeld's records relate that 'an attempt is being made, in a test case, to establish the legal guardianship of Lord Gorell over Jewish children. The Chief Rabbi has offered to act as guardian for the child in question, either alone or jointly.'[78] Since there seems to be no further reference to the case, one therefore assumes that a legal problem had been solved. Many other difficulties, however, vied for the attention of the harassed refugee committees.

5

CRISES, CRIES AND
LAMENTATIONS

T HE appointment of a guardian accorded the refugee organizations much more authority in situations such as removing
children from abusive homes. The Orthodox community
wanted to extend this mandate to removing all Jewish children from
Gentile homes. Such a move, however, was both impractical – there
were too few Jewish homes available – and unwise in that the children
were by now fairly well settled, even taking evacuation into account,
and another upheaval could do untold damage. As the Manchester
Jewish Refugees Committee concluded:

> Removal might mean the destruction of three years of hard
> work and sacrifice on the part of the foster parents in effecting
> adjustments in the refugee's behaviour patterns. ... Now, a new
> foster parent, however worthy, would be faced by tremendous
> difficulties, including antagonism of the young person of being
> uprooted from the home in which he had found refuge and
> love.[1]

Observant Jews had from the very beginning objected to billeting
Jewish children in non-Jewish homes and had no intention of easing
the pressure at this point. 'We shall not hesitate in stopping this

apostasis [sic] of children,' insisted Rabbi Dr Schonfeld, but exactly what measures he could take in the face of there being too few Jewish homes was unclear.² Even the *Jewish Chronicle*, which was usually sympathetic to Dr Schonfeld, commented:

> Have the Jews of this country ... nothing to reproach them-selves for this sad business? Again and again have appeals been made for homes in which these children could be reared in the traditions of their creed. If these appeals are to be ignored, at least part of the blame for what will follow will lie on the heads of those who could help, but who refuse.³

Fear of conversion to Christianity loomed large, however, and with the placement during evacuation of thousands of Jewish children in Gentile homes, the matter assumed crisis proportions in the Orthodox community's eyes. In June 1940 the Chief Rabbi's Religious Emergency Council circulated a pamphlet entitled *Save Jewish Children for Judaism*. In it the writer appealed to all branches of the Jewish faith to unite to:

> salvage them [the children] from the waters of baptized and unbaptized apostasy. ... In many cases there is, in addition to *treifus* [eating non-Kosher food], a deliberate alienation from Judaism. They are drifting towards *Shemad* [apostasy]. ... If we remain inactive, there is no future for Judaism in this country ... everyone must join in a great sacred effort to salvage them from the waters of baptized and unbaptized apostasy.⁴

The *Jewish Chronicle* of 13 May 1941 printed a letter written by F. Weil, which stated in part that two refugee children brought up 'strictly observant' but living in a non-Jewish home for two years:

> have lost all interest in things Jewish ... [are] rapidly veering to the point where they might be completely lost to the Jewish faith. ... How many [parents] if they had known how their

children were now being brought up here in England, would not have preferred them to share with their parents their martyrs' existence?[5]

Conversion was seen as an even greater catastrophe after the war when the full horror of the Holocaust became known. In 1946 Gerhart Riegner, general secretary of the World Jewish Congress, pointed out that, 'after the wholesale murder of European Jews together with their children, all these children who have been spared are of vital importance to the Jewish community and its reconstruction.'[6]

One organization that the Orthodox community singled out as especially predatory to the Jews was the Barbican Mission, which brought out a small number of children from Czechoslovakia even before the major effort that Nicholas Winton spearheaded had begun. Revd B. Walner, the mission's representative in Prague, selected these first children, while the Revd Davidson, director of the mission in Britain organized the second Barbican transport.[7]

The mission was accused of allocating space on its transports only after the child's parents had signed a document permitting baptism and conversion.[8] Even Lord Gorell, a Christian, condemned the practice.[9] The Barbican Mission, unrepentant in its response, insisted that:

> The great majority of our children were only Jewish on one side and knew nothing of Judaism ... no child had been taken by us without their parents' full consent and understanding of the conditions in which we proposed to bring them up ... that is, that our first objective would be to teach them the Christian faith.

The response continued. 'Their parents, by mutual consent, seemed to have left the question of religion entirely out of their calculations; the children had received no teaching whatsoever, and neither Church nor Synagogue held any place in their lives.' The parents were given 'written assurance that children under 16 would not be baptized without the parents' consent'.[10] Indeed, some of the children were baptized in Prague prior to leaving for England, obviously with the consent of their parents or guardians.[11]

Various refugee agencies visited and questioned the children placed first in the mission's homes at Chislehurst in Kent and again after their evacuation to Devonshire. Although the youngsters were seen to be healthy and happy, several were removed. The majority of the more than 100 refugees, however, remained with the mission, which also saw to their secular training and education. The joint committee reluctantly concluded that 'the [Barbican] Mission appeared to have legal right to the guardianship of these children whilst in this country.'[12]

As a result of this outcry against the Barbican Mission, however, the Archbishop of Canterbury, Dr Temple, sent guidelines to all Church of England clergy, urging them not to proselytize. After Lord Gorell's appointment as guardian, Dr Temple 'agreed that it would be most improper for any Clergyman to baptize any Ward without first ascertaining the wishes of the Guardian.'[13] The Christian Council informed its clergy and ministers that 'the Guardianship Act is now in operation and children should not be baptized without reference to the Legal Guardian.'[14] Despite such instruction, however, the archbishop's correspondence reveals that in some cases the guidelines were ignored and children were baptized either upon their own request or that of their foster parents.[15] In March 1942, Bishop Bell noted that there had been conversions at the Christian hostel at Riversmead:

> The Children's Advisory Committee had carefully considered certain cases of Jewish children who had been baptized ... each case must be carefully considered on its own merits ... every effort should be made for refugee children to receive religious instruction in accordance with the faith of their parents, and that in the event of a transfer of any child from one religion to another the most careful consideration be given to all relevant factors in the case.[16]

In response to a request to remove a child from his foster home, as late as 1 November 1945 Kenneth Macmorran gave his legal opinion in a letter to Archbishop Geoffrey Fisher:

> It could well be that Lord Gorell could take the child away from a religious institution or from adoptive or foster parents who were bringing up a child of Jewish parentage in the Christian religion. But I cannot see what remedy is open to him if an incumbent of the parish ... baptizes such a child at the request of its adoptive or foster parent. ... It is suggested that such an incumbent ... is under a duty to obtain Lord Gorell's consent before baptism. ... In my view such a suggestion cannot be upheld under English law.[17]

And so the battle raged. Strangely enough, because Baptists only baptize adults and not infants or children, the observant community feared evangelical Baptists less than the liturgical churches.[18]

There is no doubt that conversions and baptisms occurred and that certain geographic areas evinced more proselytizing than others. Cecil Roth, for example, wrote to the chief rabbi about the many conversions in Oxford, especially among older girls who were joining the Anglicans, Lutherans and even Roman Catholics, 'particularly at Blackfriars', a Catholic college. He concluded that 'the number of refugee youths – especially women – now professing Christianity in Oxford is deplorably high.'[19] Conversions among young women who joined the armed forces or who married Englishmen were also more common. It seemed to give them a sense of security to be assimilated into the dominant culture and religion.[20] Conversions also occurred in homes that took care not to proselytize but that, through their love and care for the child and their own consistent religious life, attracted the child to Christianity. The loving, non-coercive family with which he was billeted so impressed John Fieldsend, for example, that when he reached the requisite age, he informed the rabbi responsible for his religious instruction that instead of celebrating his bar mitzvah, he, John, wanted baptism.[21] When the court of the chief rabbi contacted the Bishop of London in 1947 about an older child's request for baptism, the bishop wrote to Canterbury, 'I doubt whether in the last resort … we have the right to refuse baptism to anyone who sincerely desires it and has the necessary disposition.'[22]

It is impossible to ascertain how many conversions occurred and under what circumstances. Chief Rabbi Hertz asked Rabbi Poppers from the Joint Commission for Religious Education to investigate the situation, and he responded that conversions occurred under the following circumstances:

- when the child was residing with parents in England;
- after a '*Konfessionslos*' education in Europe;
- after attending church in Germany; or
- after a previous education indifferent to anything Jewish.

He concluded that 'the number of genuine Baptism Cases appears to be small.'[23]

Elaine Blond agreed. She stated that 'there were numerous cases where young people lost interest in formal religion (a sequel of war which touched every faith), several cases of intermarriage, and a few cases where Jews converted to Christianity.'[24] The Board of Deputies put on record:

> The conversions to which so much public attention has been drawn in the Jewish press within recent years, were almost entirely conversions of refugees, many of whom had already gone in that direction in Germany itself – though there were some cases of children who, but for the circumstances which brought them to this country and placed [them] in a non-Jewish environment, might have grown up in the Jewish faith.[25]

In a letter to the *Jewish Chronicle* of 23 May 1941, however, a Mr F. Weil asserted that 'there are literally hundreds of children … in non-Jewish surroundings, becoming estranged from all things Jewish. I am told that a considerable number have been baptized and go regularly to church.'[26] In 1948 the same publication placed the total number of baptisms 'as far as can be gauged [at] 129. Of those, 23 [children] were living with parents in this country; in 13 others, parents were alive but not in this country,' in 15 cases the mother was non-Jewish, in four the father was a Gentile, while 14 were baptized before legal guardianship came into effect (1944). Of the remaining 60, 20 were baptized with their parents' consent. 'Of the 400 children from concentration camps, none were in non-Jewish homes and none had been converted.'[27] Whether there were few or many conversions, or whatever the circumstances of their conversion, every child mattered to the Jewish community. Even a few conversions were too many.

To be fair, however, not all the blame for conversion was placed on the shoulders of the Christian foster parent or proselytizing by the Christian Church, or even on the individual child. As Mr Weil wrote in the *Jewish Chronicle*, in his letter of 23 May 1941, 'The blame cannot be laid on the child. ... The blame lies with our Jewish community, with our public bodies and their leaders.'[28] Mr H. Poppers, writing to the chief rabbi, also acknowledged that many of the problems could be traced to the Jewish community, 'by reason of the fact that the Jewish public did not come forward with offers of vacancies when the children first came to this country'.[29]

There were also conversions within the spectrum of Jewish religious observance. Some non-observant children placed in observant homes became observant while others, placed in unhappy Gentile homes, blamed their unhappiness on Christianity, or the lack thereof, and turned to Orthodoxy. A few Orthodox children, on the other hand, were only too relieved to be billeted in a home that was less demanding in religious observation than their own home had been, but whether this can be called a 'conversion' to less rigid Judaism is a moot point.

Occasionally, there was an unexpected turn to a conversion. Olga Drucker, for example, born into a home in which no Jewish holidays were celebrated and who had never been inside a synagogue in Germany, 'liked going to church and prayer meetings and hearing missionaries and singing hymns'. However, when she later married an American Jew, she began exploring her heritage and, in June 1991, at the age of 63, she celebrated her bat mitzvah.[30] The importance of spiritual comfort obviously could not be denied, whatever form it happened to take. One might even be tempted to agree with Thea Feliks Eden, who concluded, 'I think of religion as causing trouble, as opposed to faith which I think gives people something.'[31]

Closely allied to the fear of conversion, was the effort, especially on the part of the Orthodox community, to remove children from non-Jewish homes. The reason for the many hundreds of Jewish refugee children in non-Jewish homes was, of course, that, while there were too few vacancies in Jewish homes, the non-Jewish community opened its doors wide. Although most of these children were placed in private homes, the Board of Deputies' files hold scores of offers similar to the following. 'Through the Sports and Social Club of my factory, I can arrange to rent a house, and I will furnish same, as a sort of Kindergarten, and engage the necessary nurses to look after, say six or eight children.'[32] The fear for such children, but especially for those in private homes, being weaned away from Judaism was very real, and was expressed succinctly in a memorandum to the chief rabbi:

> The danger of conversion of the children in private homes cannot be over emphasized. Those offering hospitality are generally sincere church-going Christians, who are impelled by humanitarian motives for which no praise is too high, to help relieve the sufferings of the Jewish people. The child will, therefore, see Christianity under its best and most favourable conditions, and the influence of the home in which he is will be such as to conduce [*sic*] towards a desire to become like them.[33]

To the Orthodox mind, therefore, the obvious solution was to remove the child from its Gentile foster parents by whatever means. Since too few Jewish homes were available, hostels or Jewish schools were prepared to receive these youngsters. Sometimes the child was simply approached when away from his or her foster home and persuaded to leave for Jewish accommodation. The minutes of a joint committee contain a 'long discussion' related to a boy over 16 'who was removed without knowledge of his custodians to a *Yeshiva* [seminary] in Gateshead'.[34] But not all children wished to be moved. Joseph, aged 12, wept at the thought of being taken away from his foster parents, saying, 'I've lost a home and want not to lose another. I am frightened. I had Nazi bayonets behind me. I can't bear it – I can't bear it.'[35]

If a child had been with the same foster family for four or five years and the relationship was loving and the home atmosphere happy, the trauma of removal was increased. After Lord Gorell's appointment as guardian, the removal of children from non-Jewish homes became a major issue. Lord Gorell, in contrast to some refugee agencies, went on record as opposing placement of children in hostels or schools. 'In the vast majority of cases a home must always be preferred to a hostel,' he said, and 'the uprooting of a child from its home might do irreparable damage after a period of five years of a happy, settled life.' Furthermore, he pointed out 'the great difficulty in obtaining a Jewish home which is a counterpart of the home in which the child may have lived.'[36] The upshot was that refugee committees, apart from the Orthodox ones, did not seek to remove Jewish children from non-Jewish homes except at the direct request of an unhappy child or relative.

For administrators in the refugee organizations, the conversion and removal crises, if that term may be used, caused less immediate stress than the financial and organizational woes besetting them. A memo from the Central Committee for Refugees, dated 28 April 1941, for example, states that 64 guarantors 'have failed',[37] while the CBF reported that the guarantors for three children were killed in an air raid.[38] Records are replete with criticisms related to the disorganization at Woburn House, Bloomsbury House and German-Jewish relief work in general. The Board of Deputies' records reveal many letters of complaint, including the following that M. Domb sent to Neville Laski in December 1938:

> the increasing number of complaints … appear[s] to show that the chaos at Woburn House is increasing rather than decreasing, and what is even worse, the amount of work being

thrown upon the shoulders of the people there is leading them to be extremely rude to those people seeking information ... files appear to be in such a deplorable state that no trace can be found of previous correspondence or entries or anything of that description.[39]

This litany of woes was echoed in complaints about Bloomsbury House, where the 'terribly over-worked' staff, doing their utmost under 'barely tolerable conditions' were accused of such ungracious behaviour that 'Christian sympathizers were chilled and repelled by the way ... their offers of help had been met.'[40] Phrases such as 'gross mismanagement', 'lack of organization', 'the administration is very bad indeed and simply a disgrace', abound in the letters of complaint.[41]

Lord Reading and Otto Schiff, leaders in the refugee movement, felt swamped in their efforts to rectify the situation, while Lord Hailey tendered his resignation as chair of the coordinating committee for refugees because of 'his extreme dissatisfaction, not to say disgust, with the devious and unbusiness-like manner in which problems have been handled'.[42]

Even the self-sufficient CRREC was drawn into the fray. The headmistress of the Orthodox schools now evacuated to Bedfordshire wrote that 'our canteen workers are all either in bed or have left or are on the verge of a nervous breakdown.' 'The house is overcrowded and our nerves are shattered.' 'It is not fair. ... It is disgraceful.'[43] Rabbi Schonfeld seemed to agree, for already in 1939, in a letter to I. Kestenbaum of the B'nai B'rith, he remarked that 'neither the Chief Rabbi's Council nor the B'nai B'rith has at the moment, in my opinion, an organization fit to deal with all the aspects of the orthodox children's problems.'[44]

While acknowledging the problems, Otto Schiff nevertheless came to the relief organizations' defence. He pointed out that almost the entire staff of the forty or more organizations involved with the *Kinder* consisted of volunteers, both refugees and non-refugees. This could and did create language and therefore communication problems. Moreover, the volunteers were also trying to coordinate all aspects of the transports with all the various groups, which might have totally different agendas one from the other. Add to this overwork – the 66 workers at Woburn House received 'no fewer than 1,500 letters a day ... all requiring individual and sometimes very complicated attention ... [also] between 600 to 1,000 "callers" a day' – it was no wonder the staff was 'overwhelmed by an onrush which was not of their creation'.[45] In July 1939 the *Jewish Chronicle* reported that Bloomsbury House now received about 20,000 letters a week, but that the volume had reached up to 40,000 in November 1938.[46]

Obviously, despite the refugee organizations' good intentions, reorganization was desperately needed if lives were to be saved. M. Domb suggested to Neville Laski that the chief officer of the refugee organization should be 'a non-Jew, because I think that such a person would not then be open to the personal pressure which is at present apparent upon the part of interested parties'.[47] Berthold S. Kisch, however, a Jew and treasurer of the Movement for the Care of Children from Germany, was appointed to head the restructuring and, shortly thereafter, he tabled the following recommendation. This was that professional staff should largely replace volunteers unless the volunteers could provide full-time service; the professional staff would 'systematize efforts to secure additional offers and guarantees ... decide the allocation of children to individual homes and hostels ... [and] maintain a routine of inspection'.[48]

Kisch's recommendations were accepted and the movement was incorporated as a company in April 1939. Sir Charles Stead, a non-Jew, was appointed executive director. Otto Schiff wrote to Neville Laski on 24 May 1939:

Two of Messrs Marks & Spencers's organization are at present going systematically through the whole German Jewish Aid Committee with a view to reporting and making recommendations. I do not doubt for one moment that they will find many things which can be improved and I candidly think that expert advice ... of this type is worth a great deal more than the volumes of criticism which have no constructive remedies.[49]

There were very few complaints after this restructuring. At the outbreak of war when Sir Charles Stead entered the military, the movement's secretary, Dorothy Hardisty, succeeded him.

Rabbi Schonfeld had his own agenda for cutting expenses, which differed substantially from that of Berthold Kisch and the Refugee Children's Movement. Schonfeld offered the CRREC a room in his private home as an office, free of charge, so that all donations received could be spent directly on refugees. Further, except for the secretary, he directed that volunteers or refugees maintained by the council should do all the work for the council.[50] Being so much smaller than the RCM, the CRREC could obviously be differently structured and still function efficiently. Yet, as a note in the Schonfeld papers admitted, 'we are literally struggling ... and are terribly hard up. As soon as money is coming in from payments a fight arises between Miss Sassoon [his secretary] and myself over the way it is going to be spent because there are so many bills.'[51]

All these organizational and administrative woes could have been overcome quite easily with adequate financial resources, but where were these monies to come from? The Quakers' German Emergency Committee and several other organizations, 90 per cent of which were Jewish or had a large Jewish component, had been carrying the burden of refugees since 1933, with each group raising its own funds. Some money was coming in from overseas – the Chief Rabbi's Religious Emergency Council, for example, had offices in Montreal and Toronto – but wartime exigencies brought the voluntary organizations to the brink of bankruptcy. While admitting that his records were in disarray because of inadequate staffing, in December 1939 Rabbi Schonfeld recorded an income of £1,000 and expenditures of £7,550.[52] His records also reveal numerous cheques bouncing, staff unpaid for months on end and even threats of legal action.[53]

As the chief rabbi lamented, 'the need of our refugees ... is greater by far than the will to help,'[54] but he was not altogether correct. There *was* a will to help and various proposals were examined to raise even more money than the CBF's fund-raising efforts had garnered. The Board of Deputies, for example, anxious to bring in 100,000 refugees (not only children) suggested a 20 per cent levy on the income of all British Jews over and above current giving, regardless of family size or commitments.[55] Schonfeld thought that the community should pay so much per synagogue member. The truth of the matter was that the Jewish community, both Orthodox and non-Orthodox, had been wrung dry. Certainly, some could have given more generously and it is always true that some simply will not give at all, but others gave sacrificially and simply could give no more. By the middle of 1940 the community had raised an estimated £6 million sterling, up to £8 million if gifts in kind were included. Truly, many took literally the adage, 'charity delivers from death'.

Despite such massive giving, with the greatly increased flood of refugees after *Kristallnacht* the demands on relief agencies spiralled beyond all expectations. For the months of January to July 1939 alone the Central Council for Jewish Refugees, the umbrella Jewish fund-raising agency,[56] spent £250,000 on refugee relief while 'in all of the six previous years the JRC had spent [only] £233,000'.[57] Such a sudden and dramatic increase in expenditure exhausted the council's resources. Lord Reading, Simon Marks and Otto Schiff were asked to scrutinize the council's desperate financial situation. After due consideration, they recommended approaching American Jewry for a 'substantial contribution'. The response proved to be incredibly disappointing, largely because the 'Americans were convinced that the Anglo-Jewish community's generosity was evidence of unlimited wealth and they were not prepared to bail it out.'[58]

The breaking point was reached in the spring of 1939 when the council declared its position so desperate 'that for the first time since its inception approaches to the government for possible loans to the JRC were considered'.[59] The Christian Council for Refugees, whose plight was less precarious, offered a loan of £25,000, guaranteed by Anthony de Rothschild and Sir Simon Marks, which was to be repaid by 31 January 1940.[60] But this amount was woefully insufficient to meet the ever-escalating need.

There seemed to be no alternative but to approach the government for assistance, yet Sir Robert Waley Cohen believed that the Anglo-

Jewish community should not come as supplicants 'but as claimants for recognition that the burdens they have borne for six years by their own personal sacrifices are now shown to belong to the whole civilized world'.[61] He was right, of course, and other prominent Jewish leaders shared his view. Professor Brodetsky of the Board of Deputies, for example, wrote in the *Jewish Chronicle*, 'It is about time that it was made clear that the problem of the Jewish [refugees] was not a Jewish problem ... because the defence of the Jewish community was only the beginning of the defence of all humanity against barbarism.'[62] The situation became so desperate that the government was informed that the relief organizations would 'have to close down on Monday next, or at the latest a week later,' a move that would, in effect, throw the refugees onto the local ratepayers.[63]

After several meetings with the Home Office in which Bertha Bracey of the Quakers and Henry Carter of the Christian Council joined Anthony de Rothschild, Otto Schiff and Lionel Cohen, the Treasury, through the Home Office, offered the refugee organizations a loan. Anthony de Rothschild immediately responded that 'it would be impossible and in fact immoral for them to accept a loan ... they had no reason to believe that they would ever be able to repay.'[64] Sir Alexander Maxwell then made an offer, backdated to September 1939, whereby the government would equal the sum the voluntary agencies expended. This would enable the agencies to continue operating until the end of February.

In the government, Sir Osbert Peake, who had been active in negotiations with the refugee committees, warned of the 'appalling consequences which must follow if their Organization collapsed and if some 13,300 Jewish refugees were left to be maintained out of public funds', and of the anti-Semitism that would be sure to follow.[65] The end result was a government offer to grant an initial £100,000 to the agencies, then to pay half the cost of the refugees' care and maintenance, provided the total grant did not exceed £27,000 a month. The Jewish agencies would receive approximately 85 per cent of the grant and the Christian Council the remainder. This offer was accepted with gratitude.

An executive committee of the Central Office for Refugees, which Henry Carter and Anthony de Rothschild co-chaired, was formed to administer the funds. Otto Schiff was appointed chair of its provincial department to serve as 'the principal channel of communication between Government departments and the refugee organizations', as well as between these and the 12 regional councils, which in turn had 450 committees throughout the British Isles, 'most of which were concerned with the welfare of children'.[66]

Although guarantors totally maintained thousands of children at no cost whatsoever to the British taxpayer, this action by the government now facilitated payments to be made for non-guaranteed children who were 'boarded out'. The government proposed a rate of 15 shillings a week, which was found to be insufficient, and eventually an agreement was reached whereby each child was allotted 18 shillings a week plus one shilling a week for clothing. This amount did not cover the full cost of maintaining a child, but the sponsoring refugee agencies paid the remainder.[67]

However, the monetary problems continued, with the minutes of the Church of England Committee for Non-Aryan Christians, for example, noting that its current account was overdrawn by nearly £760.[68] Although a financial 'melt-down' of the refugee agencies had been averted in 1940, continued fund-raising was imperative if the programmes were to continue. It was to this and to other problems that the refugee committees now addressed their efforts.

And 'other problems' there were in abundance. In 1942 the CBF reported four deaths from disease and nine from accidents.[69] The report for December of the next year noted that 'we are up against problems of psychological difficulty [sic] and breakdowns, and in some cases, suicide.'[70] No elaboration followed. Of lesser importance but still critical for any child were the reports of unsuitable foster parents and ongoing efforts to remove children from non-Jewish homes; there were guarantors who defaulted and 'problem' children. Turner suggests that the reports that Bloomsbury House received of problem children show that in 'at least 50 per cent of the cases, education or the lack of it, were a contributing factor'.[71] 'Sheer frustration with low-paying, undemanding work', added to anxiety, triggered many of these problems. When the Education Act of 1945 broadened access to secondary schools and higher education, much of the energy that had gone into vandalism, running away or other forms of defiance, was channelled into more constructive activity. Boredom was also a factor in some cases of so-called vandalism. Sometimes the older refugee boys, for example, were simply interested in how things worked. This was the case when the water heater in a hostel 'had been pulled away from the wall, the spout of the machine unscrewed and the interior fallen out of position'.[72] 'Proper supervision' was the answer in this particular case.

Very few *Kinder* ran into trouble with the law. During the second year of the war juvenile delinquency in England rose by 52 per cent, according to Basil Henriques, but among the Jewish refugees there was a drop in the numbers involved in altercations with the police.[73] This makes Turner's estimate that 'possibly as many as one in ten found themselves up against the police or other bastions of social authority'[74] highly suspect, unless he includes boys hauled before headmasters for minor school infractions or before hostel supervisors for such things as taking a water heater apart. Elaine Blond puts the figure at a more realistic ten cases that were actually brought to court.[75] Approximately 50 boys were deported to Germany between 1945 and 1947 for unspecified reasons, and 36 were confined to mental hospitals. 'By the end of the war, Bloomsbury House maintained a small department of welfare workers whose job it was to care for the chronically ill,' which included those with tuberculosis and those in psychiatric care.[76] By and large, local committees dealt with minor problems, while the central offices of the refugee organizations addressed the more serious cases, especially where long-term medical assistance might be required.

One of the more serious administrative issues facing the voluntary associations centred on one of its own members, the Czech Refugee Trust Fund. In contrast to its sister organizations, the Czech Fund was created by a grant of £4 million from the British government to care for refugees from that country, and children also were recipients of this largesse. In March 1940 the CBF circulated a report entitled

'Refugees from Czechoslovakia', which stated that the work done by this organization 'is open to grave criticisms', criticisms that included 'a marked tolerance' for 'increasing political dissatisfaction' expressed by members of certain communist groups, and 'blindness to actual cases of anti-British propaganda', 'lack of reference to local refugee committees' and 'gross dilatoriness and procrastination in dealing with essential correspondence'. The memo concludes with the following remarks. 'We wish to emphasize the very serious danger confronting the whole body of refugees of which the disaffected section of the Czech refugees form only a minority. Public opinion is already highly sensitive to what it suspects to be ingratitude and disaffection among refugees.' The report noted that in Leeds, the communist refugees in a hostel made 'themselves so unpleasant that they would have to be separated [from other refugees]. English people in the neighbourhood who used to visit frequently now refuse to do so.'[77] It is not indicated how many Kindertransport children, if any, were involved or what actions were taken.

Suffice it to say that while the various crises were being dealt with and the financial burdens were alleviated for the moment, human nature being what it is, problems of all kinds continued to trouble the refugee agencies and were to do so until well after the war had ended.

95

6

THE ORTHODOX EXPERIENCE

AN ongoing difficulty for the Jewish refugee committees was that long-standing tensions had created dissension within the Jewish community. As the *Jewish Chronicle* noted in December 1938, shortly after the Kindertransports began to arrive in Britain:

> Already one hears of a struggle between Zionists and non-Zionists, between Orthodox and non-Orthodox, between the charity-contributors and social workers, between all the different factions of Anglo-Jewry. ... It is surely necessary to place the future well-being and happiness of these refugee children before all private prejudices or vested interests.

Only a few months later the *Chronicle* became yet more critical. 'Only in Jewry are [such] raucous tones on internal dissension heard. "Long live domestic strife!" is the Community's motto! "Let us eat, drink and quarrel, for tomorrow we die!" A queer motto for any community of rational men. God help us!'[1] Much of the paper's cynicism was based on incidents similar to the altercation in a meeting of the Board of Deputies when the president was forced to rebuke a 'distinguished Orthodox deputy who denied that Liberal Jews were Jews at all'.[2]

At the centre of much of this controversy, although certainly not solely responsible for it as the *Chronicle* pointed out, was the Orthodox wing of Judaism and at the centre of the Orthodox community was

Rabbi Dr Solomon Schonfeld. Rabbi Schonfeld insisted that it was he, rather than others, who had the 'future well-being and happiness' of the refugee children at heart and that his actions proved it. In 1938 Dr Schonfeld was only 26 years old. He had been ordained as rabbi of the Adas Yisroel congregation in London in 1933 when he took over the work that his father had started. That same year he became presiding rabbi of the Union of Orthodox Hebrew Congregations and principal of the Jewish Secondary Schools Movement.[3] He is described as an achiever: 'Where others petitioned and prayed, he demanded, and what is more, he got.'[4] His critics, on the other hand regarded him as 'impossible ... aggressive ... arrogant ... a bigot ... a trouble-maker ... [and] irresponsible'.[5] Yet, even his opponents admired his charm, ability and dedication. Rabbi Schonfeld also had 'almost explosive' energy, imagination and religious zeal, all of which he now turned to the rescue of Jews, especially of Jewish children from the Greater Reich.

A telephone call from Julius Steinfeld, an Orthodox leader in Vienna, began Dr Schonfeld's mission on behalf of European Jews. After hearing about hundreds of Austrian children left homeless and alone, he contacted a friend in the Home Office and, by personally guaranteeing their care, managed to obtain the necessary documents for 300 children. He set up dormitories for 260 children in two schools of which he was principal. Historian David Kranzler maintains that Dr Schonfeld took the other 40 of the 300 children into his own home, while he slept in the attic,[6] but this seems to be open to debate because in 1938 Dr Schonfeld was still sharing a not overly large house with his mother, brother and sister. While it is possible to squeeze 40 children into one house, it was clearly not a situation that was to be tolerated for any length of time.[7] In any case, there is no record of these children living in the Schonfeld residence, so perforce their stay must have been a very short one indeed.

Rabbi Schonfeld soon realized that, despite his enthusiasm and energy, he was unable to work as effectively alone as with an organization. Consequently, he approached Chief Rabbi Dr Joseph Hertz, whose son-in-law he later became and who was also personally

Orthodox in observance.[8] Together, in July 1938, they formed the Chief Rabbi's Religious Emergency Council (CRREC).[9] Later that year the CRREC discussed the 'question of close co-operation with the B'nai B'rith Committee for Children … and the Chief Rabbi urged that we would not be doing our duty if we did not co-operate with all people who were working on the same lines.'[10] The B'nai B'rith had already been active in bringing children to Britain, and cooperation seemed a viable endeavour. Harry Goodman, secretary of the World Agudas Yisroel Movement, shared the CRREC's views and so, with the Anglo-Orthodox community now solidly behind him, Rabbi Schonfeld's efforts, especially on behalf of Orthodox children, intensified. However, his methods – 'he had no time for committees or budgets or precedents or permission or red tape'[11] – brought him into sharp conflict with other refugee organizations. Elaine Blond claimed that Rabbi Schonfeld 'gave us more trouble and occupied more precious time with petty fogging complaints than all our other critics put together'.[12] He in turn accused the other organizations of discriminating against religious Jewish children,[13] and wrote the following to his brother Moses in the United States:

> With regard to our relation with the Board of Deputies and the Joint Emergency Council, the matter is rather delicate. … Sir Robert Waley Cohen, a Vice-President of the Board, is at cross-purposes with the Chief Rabbi. For the same reason, the Executive of the Board of Deputies would like to hamper our activities.[14]

One of the harshest criticisms of Dr Schonfeld's relief work, which notable leaders such as Norman Bentwich shared, accused the rabbi of putting children at risk by refusing to allow a Kindertransport to leave Germany on a Saturday, the Sabbath on which no Orthodox Jew may travel any distance. The CRREC did not, however, come to the decision lightly, and when informed that the train would wait, the relief of the Orthodox community in Germany was palpable. Neither Schonfeld nor the German leader, Rabbi Dr Leo Baeck, felt that the crisis was serious enough to warrant breaking the Sabbath.[15] If they had, the '*pikuach nefesh*' (the preservation of life) would have been invoked as it was in other cases, especially in the rescue of hidden children in postwar years. According to the Talmud, if an action involves saving life, the transgression of Torah law, or any other law, is not only permitted but commanded.[16]

The uneasy relationship between refugee children of differing religious observances was exacerbated almost immediately on arrival at the receiving camps in England. The Orthodox boys wrote a very angry letter to the chief rabbi complaining about the lack of provision for keeping *kashrut* (the Jewish dietary laws). They also vented their indignation at the treatment they received at the hands of other Jewish children in the camp who, they said, threw snowballs at them, shouted abuse and were altogether offensive. These Orthodox children regretted ever having come to England, for nobody cared about them. Two of their number had already left Orthodoxy and, as they put it, '*der Rest steht auf einem Fuss*' (the rest are standing on one foot).[17] This situation infuriated Rabbi Schonfeld who, as the chief rabbi's representative, immediately investigated and just as immediately acted. The situation in the camps changed with admirable alacrity, yet not before some of the children had already been living on bread and water for two weeks because they suspected that the kitchen was not strictly kosher (ritually clean). Siggi Wasserman, at eight, was one of the youngsters who survived only on bread until he became ill. He remembers how very much he appreciated the rabbi's actions.[18]

Fortunately for future relations between the Orthodox refugee organizations and those with a Christian component, Rabbi Dr Grumpter was quite explicit in his defence of the camp authorities. As he wrote to Dr Schonfeld, 'I should like to state definitely, it was not due to lack of good will on the part of the Christian manager but to an impression gained somehow, that there was no need to bother too much about it [*kashrut*].'[19]

These young adolescents showed admirable faith in adhering to their religious beliefs despite such obstacles. One of the children remembers with gratitude the 14 and 15 year-olds who took the initiative to 'save our traditions. ... They organized a prayer meeting and general duties. [On Friday night] we grouped ourselves in one corner and sang *Zemirot*, the traditional Sabbath [table] melodies as we had been taught at home.'[20]

The problems for the Orthodox *Kinder* partly arose because notions of Orthodoxy were different in Germany and England. As Rabbi Dr Grumpter wrote to the chief rabbi from the receiving camp at Dovercourt:

> Many problems have their roots in the different conceptions connected with the word 'orthodox' in England and in Germany. The Camp Authorities are continually requested not to send 'too' Orthodox boys to a hostel. Jewish boys who lay *Tefillin* [phylacteries] every day, refuse to turn the light on Sabbath (or sometimes those who expect that food is not cooked on Sabbath) are, as a rule, considered 'too' Orthodox.[21]

Dr Grumpter further complained that the Bradford committee, for example, 'refused to take orthodox boys only, although the Hostel will be run strictly kosher [ritually clean according to Jewish law]. They are afraid, the boys in their strictness, will give them too much trouble.'[22] Yet, even the British Orthodox community was seldom completely unified in its practices although it maintained rather proudly that the percentage of Jews keeping *kashrut* was higher in England than on the continent.[23] Still, differences between English and German usages of the same terms proved to be a source of continual confusion and was to cause the refugees more problems as they sought to adapt to life in the Anglo-Jewish community.

The evacuation exacerbated the kosher kitchen problem a thousandfold. With the arrival of the Jewish schools in Shefford, a village in Bedfordshire, for example, so unaware were the women of the village of Jewish dietary laws that they carefully prepared a festive meal of various meats with all the trimmings. The children, of course, spurned the food, which left everyone, including the refugees, angry and embarrassed. Fortunately, human kindness and common sense prevailed in Shefford. The community went out of its way to accommodate its uninvited guests and in time – the children stayed for six years – they became comfortable with each other. In 1943 Rabbi Schonfeld received a letter signed by several of the *Kinder*, telling him that 'Shefford has become a real Jewish home for us'.[24] Accommodation obviously was possible when goodwill was present on both sides.

The Orthodox community did its utmost for all its displaced children, including the refugees, during the enforced evacuation, but it was especially concerned about the 200–300 youngsters billeted in isolated locations.[25] To prevent undue hardship for children who refused to eat non-kosher food but who had no access to kosher canteens, the chief rabbi reminded them in a circular letter that the law provides that where there is danger to life, *kashrut* may be disregarded.[26] This assurance evoked a great collective sigh of relief, from Orthodox children and foster parents alike.

Orthodox children did not always wait for others to make the crooked way smooth for them. In several documented instances, those arriving at evacuation centres took matters into their own hands. An account describing the entrance of Orthodox children into a village in Bedfordshire during evacuation is very moving. Two boys headed the procession carrying *Sefer Torahs* (a leather or parchment scroll of the Pentateuch). Billeted in the parish church hall and arriving on a Friday, the older boys set up tables and chairs, the girls set aside one set of dishes as 'milk' and another as 'meat', then proceeded to spread white paper on the tables in lieu of cloths. Rabbi Schonfeld arrived from London with four large army mess tins and some food. The children's meal that night consisted of one sausage and a piece of bread, but they celebrated the Sabbath as they had been taught. The teacher observing this wrote:

The Shabbos [Sabbath] Queen had arrived for the first time in history into this small village in Bedfordshire and she was welcomed by hundreds of young voices singing in the dimly lit

[St Michael's] Church Hall, '*Lekhu Dodi*' ['Come, My beloved'], and '*Lekhu N'ranenah*' ['Come, let us sing before the Lord'].[27]

Some time later the *Jewish Chronicle* reported, 'The evacuated Jewish youth at Bedford [*sic*], who have conducted Sabbath services from the early days of their dispersal, have now decided to form themselves into a Youth Synagogue. ... Services are held Friday evenings and on Sabbath mornings at ten o'clock.'[28] These youngsters deliberately chose to live their faith, to walk the Jewish walk, even in exceptional times.

The teacher who observed these Orthodox youths' actions with such admiration had her own difficulties. She wrote to Dr Schonfeld requesting payment of £6 owed her because she was facing:

The problem of hard-up-ness peculiarly 'evacuational' ... namely the necessity of buying 14 Xmas [*sic*] presents for the household with whom I am billeted! I am sure none of us foresaw, among the hundreds of nightmare possibilities ... that evacuation might bring, the one of becoming a forced partner to the Xmas customs of our hosts. Please don't think this a joke – it's only too true and a worrying problem for me.[29]

This peculiar problem might well have faced the children as well as the teacher.

The various evacuation crises notwithstanding, the Orthodox community took especially seriously the placing of any Jewish child in a non-Jewish home and attempted to thwart such billeting by subterfuge if necessary, even if it meant antagonizing a sister Jewish agency. A letter to the CRREC regarding responsibility for several children urged that action be taken 'before they make contact with Mrs Bentwich's organization [Movement for the Care of Children from Germany].'[30] The Cambridge refugee committee also complained about official Orthodox behaviour, accusing these people of being 'extremely difficult to cope with ... and all sorts of things'.[31]

While the CRREC acted unilaterally in what it considered a Jewish child's best interests, with scant attention to other refugee organizations, it was the Barbican Mission that caused the greatest concern. Rabbi Schonfeld regarded the mission's relief efforts as a ploy for conversion and appointed Rabbi Dr L. Rabinowitz to undertake 'the hard but holy task of preventing these children from being baptized'.[32] He was to work in consultation with Dayan H. Swift. The Barbican Mission, in turn, reported that its children, particularly the boys, 'were waylaid on a number of occasions on their way to and from school. ... Some were intercepted on their way to us and never reached our care. One boy was taken from the train. ... [They] stooped to the most unprincipled pressurizing.'[33] Margareta Burkill of the Cambridge refugee committee also complained that the 'orthodox Jews kidnapped children who were in Christian homes' and that 'two children were kidnapped by wealthy orthodox people and it nearly got to a case [for] the high courts'.[34] From the Orthodox viewpoint, these tactics in fact worked, for the CRREC reported that not only had Dr Rabinowitz 'been successful in preventing some intended baptisms,' but that Rabbi Swift in the Cambridge area had achieved similar success.[35]

What prompted the Orthodox community in general and Dr Schonfeld in particular to 'stoop to the most unprincipled pressurizing' of these children? It may be that the answer lies, at least partially, in their application of *pikuach nefesh*. If one can accept the opinion of the historian David Kranzler, which seems debatable, 'they [the Orthodox leaders] never relinquished their primary weapons of bribery, ransom, or the use of illegal methods as a means of assuring the survival of the Jewish people.'[36] Should this indeed have been the case, then it is small wonder that there was friction between Orthodox and non-Orthodox refugee agencies.

Whatever reservations one may have about David Kranzler's position, it was the chief rabbi, albeit inadvertently, who really exacerbated the situation. In a letter to *The Times* he accused non-Jewish foster parents of 'sectarian snatching of souls from a rival faith' and of 'spiritual kidnapping'.[37] Rallying to the defence of non-Jewish billets, the non-Orthodox community described Dr Hertz's accusation

'as disingenuous as it is ungracious'.[38] After several weeks of acrimonious correspondence in the public press, Lord Gorell of the RCM
then wrote that he believed that the chief rabbi was referring to hidden
European children who were only now being discovered in homes
throughout Europe, and 'not to those who have lived in Great Britain
for the past six years'.[39] This seemed to defuse the conflict, but the
Orthodox community had thereby endeared itself neither to the rest of
Anglo-Jewry nor to the British public.

The harm the Orthodox position wreaked on Christian–Jewish
relations is further evinced in the exchange of letters between Dayan
Swift and Lord Gorell, related to the proposed conversion to
Catholicism of a 15-year-old girl. Lord Gorell concluded his response
to Dayan Swift's acrimonious letter of resignation from the RCM
because of Lord Gorell's stand in the matter by writing, 'I do not
remember you ever saying a word in acknowledgement of the
unstinted care and loving kindness which, for years on end, Christian
foster parents have, in hundreds of cases, lavished upon Jewish refugee
children. Always you have shown suspicion and even rancour.'[40] It was
a difficult and frustrating time for all concerned.

The Orthodox community was not a homogenous body. In the
midst of postwar bickering, even the *Jewish Chronicle* felt compelled to
feature several articles under the title, 'What is Orthodoxy?'[41]
However, strenuous efforts to achieve unity, at least in its refugee
rescue operations, were initiated as early as December 1938 when the
chief rabbi urged the Orthodox congregations to 'co-operate in every
way', while Rabbi Schonfeld pleaded, 'can we not … substitute the
present chaos by a well thought-out plan of orthodox co-operation?'[42]
Probably as a result of this urging, the Joint Orthodox Jewish Refugee
Committee was formed, incorporating the Agudas Yisroel
Organization, the CRREC, the Federation of Czechoslovakian Jews
and the Union of Orthodox Hebrew Congregations.[43] When the B'nai
B'rith, originally a non-sectarian Jewish social organization, decided to
remain outside the committee, Rabbi Schonfeld urged its collaboration
for greater efficiency within the Orthodox camp.

It must be said, however, that Dr Schonfeld was all too often the cause of discontent and friction even within the Orthodox refugee agencies. He antagonized the Mizrachi Federation of Great Britain, the Jewish Committee for Relief Abroad, and also Sir Robert Waley Cohen in the latter's many capacities.[44] The rift with Waley Cohen became a legal matter, and Schonfeld wrote to his brother Moses, 'I, personally, am having a legal arbitration with Waley Cohen over his defamatory implications in the United Synagogue's letter to the Home Office. The relations between us ... are practically non-existent ... and therefore we have no compunction in giving them as much trouble as we can.'[45]

And trouble he did give. A. G. Brotman, for example, complained to Ivan Greenberg that Rabbi Schonfeld had arranged a meeting between Jewish members of both Houses of Parliament without consulting the Board of Deputies, which was legally responsible for such liaisons. Dr Brotman added that 'this is not the first effort by Dr Schonfeld to do political work without the knowledge of the community,' and he worried that the rabbi would 'destroy the status of Anglo-Jewry by introducing division, irresponsibility and carelessness into Jewish work'.[46] In despair, Dr Brodetsky of the Board of Deputies also wrote to Greenberg, 'Jewish life is so difficult, and the sense of discipline so weak in Jewry, that it is an almost superhuman task to secure co-operation between different bodies.'[47]

Even after the war was over, the South African Board of Deputies accused Dr Schonfeld of, among other things, 'pestering' them for funds. The CBF, to whom this correspondence was addressed, replied that it was sure that the South Africans realized 'the difficulty of anybody controlling Rabbi Schonfeld'.[48] It seems from other correspondence, however, that there were long-standing tensions between the CRREC and the South African Jewish community. For example, an apparently unpublished article with the title, 'Why South African Jewry Should Assist the CRREC', contains the following remark. 'Posterity will know how to judge the smug announcements of the South African Jewish War Appeal while starvation, poverty and disease are rampant in Europe.'[49]

Finally, Dr Schonfeld also broke with Zionist organizations, though the CRREC had supported many projects in Israel. He had come to believe that refugee children under Zionist auspices were given inadequate religious training and were, in fact, deluded into opting for a non-religious upbringing.[50] He also complained to his brother that 'the Zionists are sworn enemies of any successful organization in this country [the UK], which is not entirely managed by them and whose funds are not completely used for their purposes.'[51]

While an organization's religious policy and practices were relatively simple to identify, it was another matter to determine which British Jewish homes were Orthodox, Liberal or Reform. The Movement for the Care of Children from Germany attached an addendum to the questionnaire that the Joint Committee for Religious Education of Jewish Refugee Children distributed in Germany that asked parents the following question. 'If suitable facilities are available, do you desire your child to be brought up in Konservative, [sic] Reform or Liberal Judaism?'[52] Yet, even this information had different connotations in Germany and Great Britain. 'There is a big difference between what you call Liberal Judaism in England and Liberal Judaism in Germany,' wrote Rabbi Dr Nussbaum in the Jewish Chronicle. 'In Germany, the Community which has gone in for extreme reforms is known as Reform, while the Liberal Judaism of Germany corresponds closely to the practice of the United Synagogue in London.'[53] This same problem of semantics had plagued the Orthodox community from the first days of the Kindertransport. The joint committee, therefore, of which the CRREC was a member, determined 'perhaps it would be helpful if it were asked whether kashrut was observed and how the Sabbath was kept in their homes.'[54]

These criteria were ultimately unsatisfactory to the CRREC. Its solution was rather to place as many Orthodox children as possible in hostels, which Habonim personnel largely supervised, and in religious educational facilities such as those provided for yeshiva (seminary) students,[55] but even these measures were only partially successful. Vivian Simmons, for example, complained to the chief rabbi that 30 students that the CRREC had brought over were 'living in great discredit to the Jewish community ... an appalling state of affairs'.[56]

But Rabbi Schonfeld was doing his best under very difficult conditions. After the war he looked as far afield as Ireland to place his second wave of refugee children. Again, however, he acted unilaterally: he (Schonfeld) 'quietly' brought approximately 100 children into Eire despite the local committee being 'very much against refugee children coming to Ireland'.[57]

Throughout his involvement with refugees, Dr Schonfeld remained adamant that Jewish children, especially Orthodox ones, many of whom had Polish rather than German or Austrian roots, should, under any and all circumstances, be billeted only in Jewish homes or hostels. Yet, as early as January 1939, the flow of Orthodox children exceeded the availability of spaces for them. As a result, the arrival of unguaranteed Orthodox children was, in fact, halted for a time in June 1939.[58] In a letter to I. Kestenbaum of the B'nai B'rith, a correspondent identified only as 'EM', addresses the matter of cooperation with the CRREC and the influx of Orthodox children. He notes that the:

B'nai B'rith Committee has large waiting lists of children whom they have not placed and apparently cannot place for some time and further, they are drowned with hundreds of individually guaranteed cases. The Chief Rabbi's Council has the Viennese children on their hands. In the meantime the orthodox children arriving in Camp are simply left to their own fate for an indefinite time. Moreover, those placed in orthodox homes are not looked after by an orthodox authority, nobody feeling responsible for them.[59]

At this point, overwhelmed by the waves of Orthodox children and the dearth of accommodation and supervision for them, it almost appears that Schonfeld tended towards sharing the philosophy of David Ben-Gurion who, in December 1938, when the Kindertransports were just getting underway, stated: 'were I to know that the rescue of all German Jewish children could be achieved by their transfer to England and of only half that number by transfer to Palestine, I would opt for the latter.'[60] Rabbi Schonfeld's objective was not, of course, to 'transfer' the children to Palestine but he did feel strongly that to save a child's physical life only to lose its Jewish soul and identity had little purpose. As Nicholas Winton questioned: 'what is better, a converted Jew or a dead Jew?'[61] The Orthodox community's horror of conversion is reflected in the response of the Polish mother of a hidden child when she told a Catholic nun, 'I would rather see [my daughter] die as a Jew than to grow up as a Catholic.'[62]

Such an attitude, whether voiced or not, proved to be a major point of contention between most Orthodox and non-Orthodox refugee organizations. The Orthodox maintained that no children should be brought over who could not be placed in Jewish homes, while other groups argued that the priority was to save lives and then work on their religious education. Elaine Blond wrote that 'offers of orthodox homes dried up as early as April 1939. … What we did was to accept as many children as we could get in – orthodox, liberal or non-believing – on the assumption that all other problems were secondary.'[63] Nicholas Winton endorsed such a view, saying, 'I was after saving lives, not souls.'[64] This was not Rabbi Schonfeld's philosophy and his actions raised the ire even of other influential Orthodox leaders such as Norman Bentwich and Sir Robert Waley Cohen. Cohen wrote to Schonfeld, 'I do not think that the whole [Orthodox] Community is so dead to spiritual forces that they are willing to let them [the children] die rather than join forces with those whose views of ceremonials and observances differ from their own.'[65] Dr Schonfeld finally concurred and thereafter he brought in non-Orthodox children, children without religious training of any kind, and even baptized children, saying that 'we do not believe a sprinkling of water makes any difference.'[66]

True to his convictions, however, he sought earnestly to convert such youngsters to the teaching of the Torah, for, he insisted, the Orthodox 'worked through Torah, the [Liberals] without and often against Torah.'[67] Dr Schonfeld held a high, almost poetical, view of the Torah. He wrote:

Given the will, the essentials of *Halacha* [or *Halakah*, Jewish laws, supplementing written laws or custom] – the Jewish walk – are both feasible and happy. *Tefillin* is a daily betrothal. *Kashrut* is aristocracy. *Berochoth* are heartfelt 'thank yous'. *Tefilla* is a song of nearness to the Almighty, Sabbath a weekly reunion, Solemn Days are oases in our desert life. Festivals are landmarks in our drab existence. Each *mitzvah* if practised and experienced is a spring of inexhaustible beauty.[68]

Given such an exalted view of Orthodox observance, it is small wonder that he wished this for all refugee children and viewed anything other as lesser in quality.

Dr Schonfeld's life was not without its problems. In May 1946, for example, he was accused of mishandling food supplies destined for Europe. His accuser wrote to the rabbi: 'The matter will be regarded as a private one so as to leave you the final outlet of a personal apology to me.' It was the wrong approach! Dr Schonfeld replied that the fault-finder was 'allaying your evidently disturbed conscience. I hope that by next Erev Yom Kippur you will be sane enough to realize your wrong.'[69] The matter was apparently dropped. The larger community obviously respected and believed in the rabbi's impeccable honesty. As some sought to diminish Dr Schonfeld's reputation, there was apparently at least one attempt to harm him physically. Ruben Katz, a Polish refugee, noted that an attempt was made on the rabbi's life in Poland after the war. There are no details and no further references to the matter.[70]

When Dr J. H. Hertz died in 1946 and a new chief rabbi, Dr Israel Brodie, was chosen,[71] the question of continuing the CRREC became an issue. Dr Brodie 'made it clear that he would not be prepared to associate the name of the Chief Rabbi with a fund'.[72] Instead, he designated the CBF as 'the only body in England and Ireland dealing with refugees from Nazi Oppression'.[73] The CBF, with some reluctance, consented to assume this responsibility, together with any of the CRREC's outstanding debts.[74] The CRREC executive committee minutes of 5 February 1950 record the resolution 'to dissolve the Council as of 15 February 1950' with Dr Schonfeld appointed liquidator.[75] The *Jewish Chronicle*, generally a supporter of Rabbi Schonfeld, hailed this 'winding down' of the CRREC and predicted that it would 'mark a beginning in the process of co-ordination and co-operation that is so sadly wanting in the charitable no less than the Jewish political sphere'.[76]

Rabbi Schonfeld requested that he be allowed to continue using the CRREC name and letterhead, but permission was denied. He was also denied any further influence on the children he had brought to Britain. Leonard Montefiore stated unequivocally: 'I don't want Schonfeld connected with the CBF directly or indirectly.'[77] Despite this opposition, it seems that Dr Schonfeld's involvement lasted for several more years, for in 1954 he wrote to Anthony de Rothschild on CRREC letterhead, asking the CBF to take responsibility for the last of the renovations done to Clonyn Castle in Ireland (a hostel for refugee children). 'You will find that, in the long run, the taking over of that Council [CRREC] has not been a heavy burden to the Central British Fund,' he added.[78]

Just how many children Rabbi Schonfeld and the CRREC brought out of Europe is difficult to determine, for statistics available in the CRREC records overlap those of the Refugee Children's Movement. Orthodox estimates, which include postwar children, place the number of 'Schonfeld *Kinder*' at 'more than 3,700 children, adolescents and adults'.[79] Chief Rabbi Hertz lists fewer than 2,000 but this does not include Schonfeld's initial 300 or the postwar children.[80] An anonymous writer in Bertha Leverton's book claims the number to be 750 children in the 1938–39 movement alone.[81] Whatever the actual figure, the lives of many hundreds of children were saved because of the indomitable Rabbi Dr Schonfeld.

When the chief rabbi's council was dissolved in 1950 and responsibility transferred to the CBF, there were still 98 *Kinder* from the 1938–39 group, and 161 young people brought over in 1945–47, for whom the council 'have a contingent liability'.[82] Rabbi Schonfeld insisted that the CBF ensure the children's 'recent standards of religious surroundings and instruction' and that no child be transferred to another billet before a rabbi nominated by the chief rabbi gave his permission.[83] He also stipulated that those children still resident at 95

Stamford Hill, an Orthodox school and hostel, not be controlled by the CBF. 'We could not be a party to their removal and we propose handing the full responsibility for these children to the Shavas Tora School, leaving no charge or responsibility for them with the CBF.'[84]

In addition, Schonfeld's own Jewish Secondary Schools Movement was to assume the education of all Orthodox refugee children, while income from 'the Deeds of Covenant' from widely scattered points such as Egypt, Montevideo and Santiago, among other places, was to be allotted to the Jewish Schools Movement to pay for this expenditure.[85]

Dr Schonfeld continued to be concerned about the future welfare of 'his' children. In a letter to Chief Rabbi Brodie, he asked who would assume responsibility for children returned to the CRREC by their sponsor? Or, for those already in the work force, who would look after them should they become ill or have an accident? Furthermore, he did not wish these Orthodox children to be integrated with children that other relief organizations sponsored, but directed that they remain in hostels or schools 'as they were'.[86]

So ended this phase of one of the refugee movement's most active, colourful and defiantly controversial leaders, but a man that now ageing Schonfeld children remembered with great affection many years later, for they felt that they owed their lives to him.[87] Indeed, Dr Schonfeld never lost contact with many of these young refugees. They visited him at his home and, as they married and started families, the rabbi raised funds for schools and synagogues to ensure access to the religious tradition that he, and they, cherished so highly.[88]

It seems, from studies done after the war and from anecdotal evidence that, on the whole, Orthodox children survived the ordeal of separation and new beginnings better than any other group. They knew who they were; persecution was not unknown in their own lives and certainly not in their history, and they had this unshakable belief in a God whose children they were.[89] Karl Overton (Oberweger) a *Kind* not raised in the Orthodox tradition, goes even further. He writes:

If it had not been for the orthodox Jews, we would have disappeared long ago. ... It [orthodoxy] is a huge force for civilization, not just for the preservation of monotheism but also for Jews to survive as Jews, and remain as an identifiable group in the world. They have been a tremendous influence for good.[90]

Youth Aliyah, Hechalutz and the Young Pioneer Movement for Palestine also contained Orthodox constituents, but they were open to any young people with Zionist interests. They also sponsored many children for whom they arranged agricultural programmes and farm training schools in the hope of early re-emigration to Palestine.[91] Children and Youth Aliyah, for example, assisted young people between the ages of ten and sixteen to train as 'farmers, craftsmen, or skilled workers in those occupations for which they show special aptitude. ... It maintains and educates them in the spirit of group life and in the full understanding of the history and tradition of their people.'[92] Funds to support these programmes came largely from Hadassah, the Zionist women's organization in the United States.[93] One of the larger schools was established for a time at Whittingehame, the late Lord Balfour's estate near Edinburgh.[94]

The CBF, which catered for Zionists, non-Zionists, Orthodox and non-Orthodox children alike, collaborated with all the refugee organizations. In the end, however, there was so much internal dissension that this particular aspect of the refugee movement (the Zionist training schools) was closed down. Fred Dunstan (formerly Fritz Deutsch), a youth camp worker, wrote in December 1940 that in the agricultural camps 'ideology and indoctrination often took preference over smooth cooperation. ... The effect on the children was predictable, and many of them turned away from Zionism as soon as they had an opportunity.' Dunstan further maintained that the children 'lost all confidence' in the adults who were to have been their leaders, and became 'completely demoralized'. 'The project ultimately ended in chaos and the children were sent to various youth hostels all over the country.'[95]

Obviously, the road to rescue was strewn with many unforeseen adversities, even for those with the best of intentions.

7

JEWISH CHRISTIAN CHILDREN

THE Nuremberg laws and other anti-Semitic legislation did not only target Zionists, the Orthodox, or even solely practising Jews. Completely assimilated Jewish families that had converted to Christianity decades earlier, as well as Christians with only some Jewish ancestry, which might be as far removed as 1815, eventually became victims as well. The children of these Jewish Christians were called *Mischlinge*, or by the English 'non-Aryan Christians' or 'crossings'.[1] 'Non-Aryan Christians' had four full Jewish grandparents whereas 'crossings' had only one or two Jewish grandparents. The situation became more complicated when the regime instituted several more levels of discrimination: first-degree *Mischlinge* did not practise Judaism and were not married to a Jewish spouse, but had two Jewish grandparents. A second-degree *Mischlinge* need only have one Jewish grandparent to be stigmatized. All the groupings had restrictions imposed on them, especially in relation to marriage. As sociologist Marion Kaplan points out, 'while the April laws and boycotts had attempted to reverse economic integration, the Nuremberg laws intended to reverse assimilation ... through marriage and conversion.'[2]

'Crossings' initially had some rights in German law, especially in the area of education, but these privileges were soon eroded[3] and they were subjected to the same humiliations and injustices as the rest of the Jewish population. Children from mixed marriages were in an especially difficult position. In addition to being ostracized at school and in the community, they were often unwanted at home as well. When marriage to a non-Aryan spouse became a crime against the state, many marriages were dissolved. Hugh Schramm was one of the *Kinder* greatly affected by this legislation. Divorce was forced on his Aryan father by the father's family and by peer pressures, and Hugh's mother and her three sons were abandoned to fend for themselves as best they could.[4] Henry K's Aryan father also left his non-Aryan wife and their six-month old son.[5] Marion Kaplan observes that 'anecdotal evidence suggests that it was more likely for an Aryan man to divorce his Jewish wife than for an Aryan woman to divorce her Jewish husband.'[6] This seemed to be confirmed when, in February 1943, the Berlin Gestapo rounded up several thousand Jewish men in Berlin who were still married to Aryan women. Approximately 3,000 of these Aryan wives and other relatives gathered in front of the building in which their husbands were incarcerated (Rosenstrasse 2–4) and demanded their release. After a week, during which they refused to leave the street, the wives saw their husbands freed and most of them survived the war.[7] 'The Rosenstrasse Protest', as this demonstration came to be called, appears to have been the only successful recorded mass public demonstration against the Nazi authorities.[8]

There were, of course, cases of Gentile men declining to leave their Jewish wives. Rudolf Horstmeyer refused to divorce his Jewish wife and when warned that the Gestapo were about to arrest both of them, they fled and were successfully hidden. Peter Gruner also remained with his wife, while Paul Saloschin was transported with his Jewish wife and both were murdered at Łódź.[9] While these and others like them provide heroic examples of love and loyalty, unhappily they were the exceptions.

The law was not necessarily satisfied with a divorce. Ingeborg Hecht's Aryan mother remained close friends with her divorced Jewish husband. When on 27 September 1938 an executive order pertaining to the Reich Citizenship Law announced that 'the profession of attorney is closed to Jews', Ingeborg's father, a lawyer, was without income. Without hesitation, Ingeborg's mother went to work in 'a frightful sewing room a long way from home' and also cleaned house for a doctor's wife to support the family.[10] Finally, Frau Hecht was arrested and gaoled, threatened and bullied for allegedly committing an 'act of racial disgrace' with her former husband. She was required to sign a statement promising never to see him again, and agreeing that she would be held responsible to ensure that neither of her children would form relationships with Aryan partners. The shock of imprisonment seriously affected her health. Ingeborg reflects, 'my mother never shook off her terrible fears and has since required constant medical attention.'[11]

As Aryan women were required to answer for their half-Jewish children's relationships, so the children of these mixed marriages also suffered. The Inter-Aid Committee for Children from Germany reported the story of a 16-year-old Protestant girl whose Aryan father, a doctor, had married her Jewish mother before the Nuremberg laws came into effect. The mother died not long after the child's birth and the father remarried, this time to an Aryan woman. The children from this second marriage were ashamed of their half-sister and 'psychologically abused her', while the father did nothing to protect his daughter.[12] Such cases were not uncommon, but the stigma of being unwanted scarred these children for life. As Mrs Skelton of the Inter-Aid Committee summarized:

> The Non-Aryan child might find the cruelty of the racial bar even within its own home if the 'Aryan' parent was ashamed of the Jewish mate – sometimes indeed of his or her own 'non-Aryan' children – or if divorce were demanded by the 'Aryan' parent and the children of the detested marriage repudiated.[13]

Sometimes, a child who was not allowed to join the Hitler Youth along with his or her contemporaries would attempt to identify with the Nazis by such behaviour as hanging out the swastika or being violently anti-Semitic in speech and conduct.[14] Curiously, a few *Mischlinge* actually managed to enrol in Hitler Youth organizations, such as the *Jungvolk* (literally Young People), which catered for boys aged between ten and fourteen. Attracted to the parades, uniform and music, Hugh Schramm, who was barely ten, applied to and was accepted by the *Jungvolk*, possibly because of his Aryan father. When he was summarily expelled some time later, it was likely that the *Streifendienst*, the Hitler Youth secret police force, had exposed him as a 'crossing' to the leadership.[15]

Teenaged *Mischlinge*, especially, often had a very difficult time, excluded as they were from Aryan activities, including those of the church, yet also not identifying with their Jewish peers.[16] As Leon Levison wrote to Bishop Bell: 'the German Government treats them as Jews while the Jewish people look upon them as Christians.'[17]

Helen Bentwich was among the first to draw the Church of England's attention to the plight of Christian Jews. She wrote to Bishop George Bell of Chichester as early as 19 September 1933 to inform him of these 'people of partial Jewish ancestry who are today, many of them, orthodox and practising Christians. Their position seems almost more tragic than anyone else. The Jews belong to a community. ... But these non-Aryans are veritable pariahs and belong to no corporate body which unites them.'[18] Sir Leon Levison, president of the International Hebrew Christian Alliance in Edinburgh, estimated the number of such people to be approximately 1.5 million, or more 'Christians of Jewish descent in Germany than the total Jewish population of Germany'.[19] These figures seemed unrealistic, and even Bishop Bell thought them to be exaggerated, especially in view of Helen Bentwich's estimate of '260,000 persons likely to be affected by the investigation of Jewish parentage and grand-parentage in Germany'.[20] Whatever the actual number, the Nazi decrees obviously affected hundreds of thousands of individuals and families.

The compliance of the German Evangelical Church, to which many Jewish Christians belonged, with the state's anti-Semitic legislation compounded the tragedy. By applying these laws to its own members, the Church afforded them 'little if any protection'.[21] On 19 December 1933 Reichsbischof Müller signed a contract that amalgamated the evangelical youth organizations with the Hitler Youth, an organization that proudly sang: 'We are cheerful Hitler youth, we need no Christian virtue, Adolf Hitler is our leader, our saviour and our mediator.'[22] Or again: 'We give our souls to the devil, our love to the League of German Girls, and our worship to Hitler.'[23] Small wonder that it was said that 'the Germans have a new God called Race, and they sacrifice human lives to him.'[24]

The situation continued to deteriorate. In an interview on 31 January 1937, Dr Spiero of the *Paulus-Bund* mentioned that in the city of Magdeburg:

> It is impossible to have a funeral for a Christian non-Aryan. The crematorium is closed to such, though it is open for Jews. When a non-Aryan Christian dies, the corpse is left in the house. No undertaker will have it. The Prefect of the Police is sent for by the relatives, and it is for him to decide whether the body is to be buried in the Jewish or the Christian cemetery.[25]

As early as 1934, a radical group called the *Deutsche Christen* (German Christians) demanded the removal of the Old Testament from the biblical canon, together with all hymns that contained any reference to Jehovah, Hosanna, Zion and the like, because 'of the racial inferiority of the Jews'. Its memorandum stated that 'the local group of the *Deutsche Christen* [of Dortmund] feels compelled to join the holy war against the divisions in our faith and ... the disastrous Judaizing of Christianity. ... Our first aim must at least be "unjudaizing" and cleansing our Church.'[26] Such a Church would obviously make no effort to protect non-Aryan Christians and, indeed, could be expected to implement anti-Semitic legislation vigorously.

By 1938 it had become obvious to theologians such as Karl Barth, that 'Christianity, in its teaching and what it demands, is no longer in harmony with the German character as it has been discovered in the empire of Adolf Hitler ... and Germany, from the religious point of view, has taken the place of Christianity.'[27]

Fortunately, the German Church was not unanimous in its anti-Semitic stance. The German Protestant Church's governing body cooperated actively with the World Alliance, based in the Netherlands, which protested with 'profound emotion' about both the state's and the synod of the Old Prussian Church's treatment of all people of

Jewish origin. It condemned such anti-Semitic actions as 'altogether in contradiction to the teaching and the spirit of the Gospel'.[28] The pastor of Saint Hedwig's Cathedral in Berlin, Bernhard Lichtenberg, openly prayed for Jews who were being deported. He was denounced, sent to Dachau and 'died' on the way there. Pastor Heinrich Gruber, dean of the Protestant Church in Berlin, organized a rescue operation for Jews to cross into the Netherlands. And there were others, but far too few. Yet, even these few too often retained some of the traditional anti-Jewish attitudes so deeply ingrained in Lutheran theology.[29]

The German Confessing Church (*Bekennende Kirche*) was formed in 1934 as a protest against Nazi attempts to control the Protestant Church, which included efforts to exclude all Christians with any Jewish heritage from the church. Leaders such as Martin Niemoeller, a highly decorated First World War submarine captain who later became a pastor, and Dietrich Bonhoeffer, a theologian from a distinguished German family, saw the danger to the larger community if persecution of the Jews were to be enforced without protest. The vicar of Gross Kiesow, who hid a pharmacist from Berlin in his vicarage for five years, was another example of someone who actively worked against the Nazi regulations. So closely was the Confessing Church identified with its support of the Jewish community, though it must be said that Christian Jews were its main concern, that during the 1936 Olympics, when the authorities discouraged overt anti-Semitism,[30] a placard was prominently placed in a shop window near St Paul's Church where Bonhoeffer was preaching:

Nach der Olympiade
Hauen wir die BK zu Marmelade;
Dann schmeissen wir die Juden raus,
Dann ist die BK aus.

After the Olympiad
We'll beat the Confessing Church to pulp;
Then we'll throw out the Jews,
And that will be the end of the Confessing Church.[31]

Dietrich Bonhoeffer was executed in a concentration camp during the last month of the war for conspiracy to commit crimes against the Nazi regime. Niemoeller was imprisoned in 1937 and later also sent to a concentration camp. Some other leaders of the Confessing Church shared a similar fate. While the Confessing Church did more than its fellow religionists to support non-Aryans, it was obviously suspect in the eyes of the regime, which clearly limited its effectiveness in assisting its Jewish members.[32]

The Roman Catholic Church acted in accordance with the dictates of its bishops and, generally speaking, non-Aryans were 'not afraid for the Catholic members amongst them as the Catholic Church does care for them.'[33] Richard Downey, the Roman Catholic Archbishop of Liverpool, for example, was the first British Christian leader to appeal publicly to Germany 'for a change of heart'.[34] There were exceptions, however, and Bishop Bell commented that James McDonald, the high commissioner for refugees, 'is finding it very difficult to get much help from the Roman Catholic Church'.[35] One reason for this, of course, was that the Vatican signed a papal concordat with Germany in 1933, by which the Church sought to protect its own members. The collaboration, however, was short lived. Sir John Hope Simpson, in a review of the refugee situation, noted that 'a letter from the Vatican Secretariat circulated to the Catholic episcopate dated 9 January 1939 expresses the opinion that about 200,000 "non-Aryan" Catholics will have to leave Germany.'[36] By the 1940s 'Vatican relations with Germany were very tense and little remained of the Concordat.'[37] The extent of the Vatican's helplessness, at this point, is exemplified by its inability to protect even clergy who were of Jewish extraction. Edith Stein, a Carmelite nun who died at Auschwitz in 1942, is perhaps the best known of these victims.[38]

The safety of Jewish members of the exiguous Society of Friends (Quakers) in Germany – with just over 200 members in 1939 – 'caused acrimonious dispute within the Society itself'.[39] Finally, the society decided to continue its rescue work for Jews and political dissidents, but to cede the administration of this programme 'solely [to] foreign Friends',[40] thus relieving some of the political pressure on the German society. Quaker relief programmes had had a presence in Germany since the end of the First World War when the *Quakerspeisung* (Quaker meals) provided a meal a day for many thousands of German children at 11,000 feeding centres,[41] thus making the Quakers one of the oldest of all relief organizations in that country. Even the Nazis recognized their long-standing service.

Despite the Germans' appreciation for such substantial assistance, however, the Society of Friends' attempts to mitigate the appalling conditions of the then contemporary Jews and political prisoners met with little success.[42] Bertha Bracey, a British Quaker activist, began pleading the cause of non-Aryan German children soon after the first anti-Semitic legislation came into effect, but it was Helen Bentwich who suggested to Bishop Bell in October 1933 that a fund administered by the Save the Children Fund should be organized to assist all children 'irrespective of race, creed or political affiliation'. She added with complete candour that, since 'I am both Jewish and a known Socialist and Pacifist ... my name would probably be quite harmful in connection with any such appeal.'[43] The fund was established as requested (without Mrs Bentwich's name appearing) and more than 400 children, both Jewish and non-Aryan Christians, were admitted to Britain under its auspices.

These youngsters represented only a token of the hundreds of thousands in need, for urgent pleas for aid were coming from many organizations and individuals in Europe. German Pastor Furell wrote to Bishop Bell lamenting 'the hopelessness of the [non-Aryan Christians], hopelessness for their children and youngsters in general'.[44] German Protestant women sent the following memorandum to the World Ecumenical Congress meeting in Stockholm. 'We Mothers of Christian non-Aryan children beg [the] Oecumenical [*sic*] Congress to save at least a small part of the non-Aryan youth from death' by allowing the young people to work in Christian homes and businesses outside Germany.[45]

Slowly the Christian Church in Britain, prodded by the indefatigable Bishop George Bell, began to take seriously the gravity of the Jewish situation in Europe, including that of non-Aryan Christians. A national appeal for 'Non-Aryan' refugees was launched in 1936 and the Church of England Committee for 'Non-Aryan' [*sic*] Christians was organized in 1937, with a subcommittee especially designated to deal with children.

These organizations soon joined forces with the International Christian Committee for German Refugees, of which Bertha Bracey was an active member. In 1938, on Bishop Bell's initiative, the Christian Council for Refugees from Germany and Central Europe was formed as a coordinating body for the refugee work of Christian churches, rather than as a case-working organization.[46] Various churches, including the Roman Catholic, Church of Scotland (which also sent a mission to Prague), Methodist and Free Churches issued statements strongly condemning anti-Semitism at home and abroad. The Archbishop of Canterbury, speaking on behalf of the Anglican communion, declared, 'I should wish to make it quite clear that Anti-Semitism is quite plainly contrary to the spirit of the Gospels; Christians ought to unite in resisting it to the utmost of their power.'[47]

In June 1939, Dr Hinsley, the Roman Catholic Cardinal Archbishop of Westminster, who co-chaired the Christian Council with the Anglican Archbishop of Canterbury, took another major step towards uniting the Christian response when he requested the Quakers to deal with Roman Catholic non-Aryan children who were being evacuated from the Greater Reich on the Kindertransports.[48] This was a complete reversal from his position only a year earlier when he was 'anxious that the Catholic body (which is no smaller than the body of Friends) should assume responsibility for its coreligionists in the refugee problem'.[49]

Despite the ever-increasing efforts of Christian churches in Great Britain, they acknowledged that their undertaking on behalf of refugees, especially children, 'cannot be compared with those of the Jewish community'.[50] Indeed, it was reported that Sir Wyndham Deedes, chair of the Inter-Aid Committee, commented unhappily:

The Jews who had to bear the burden of their suffering communities not only in Germany but in Poland and Romania as well, had, he believed, given more help in respect to Christian children from Germany than had the Christian community itself … little could be done for the adults but it should be possible to salvage the lives of some of the children.[51]

The situation of non-Aryan Christians was reported in law to be no better than that of Jews, but 'morally and spiritually it was worse'.[52]

The question of who qualified as a 'Jew' received attention within both the Christian and Jewish communities. In Germany the official designation 'non-Aryan' was put forward in 1933, and included every person who had at least one Jewish grandparent, though a distinction was made at this time between non-Aryans and *Mischlinge*. In 1935 this classification was extended to include converts to Christianity, as well as the children of converts.[53] British refugee organizations finally agreed that the term 'Jew' should include all 'those persons who were affected by the Nuremberg laws'.[54] This, then, indisputably included those whom the Nazi regime labelled as non-Aryan Christians or *Mischlinge*, a term the German Jewish–Christian community regarded as pejorative and many in the Jewish community viewed as an anomaly.

Protestant rescue efforts for these Hebrew Christians were spearheaded in Germany by *Paulus-Bund*, which Dr Spiero directed, and Fräulein Friedenthal, secretary of the department of the provisional church government dealing with non-Aryan Christians that a Dr Albert headed. Their primary goal was to send any endangered children out of Germany and, after the occupation of Austria in 1938, they expanded their effort to include Vienna, which was at the centre of Jewish life in Austria. Since the *Paulus-Bund* was only legally entitled to assist people with no more than 50 per cent Jewish ancestry, Bishop Bell sent his sister-in-law to Hamburg and Berlin to organize aid, with the help of the Quakers, for those precluded from the *Paulus-Bund*. 'It's our business because we are human beings,' he told those detractors who questioned the need for such an organization.[55]

The Roman Catholics organized the *St Raphaelsverein*, which set up offices in Hamburg, Vienna and Prague to advise non-Aryan Christians on emigration.[56]

When leaders of these relief movements became discouraged at how few children were receiving safe placements outside the Greater Reich, Mrs Skelton of Save the Children Fund reminded them that 'at the end of his life', St Paulinus of Nola 'sold himself into slavery to redeem one single child from captivity'.[57] Jewish theology also teaches that one child's life is worth more than a king's ransom. This, however, was scant consolation when tens of thousands of youngsters were in need and only a very few hundred were receiving assistance. Fortunately, the Council for German Jewry, the Christian Council, and the National Council of Scotland all were adamant that they would not discriminate against children who professed neither the Christian nor the Jewish faith, but would seek to provide refuge for those most in need, whatever their background.[58]

The Kindertransport programme greatly increased the movement of children from German-controlled territories to safe havens elsewhere, and non-Aryan Christians, along with a small number of children of political prisoners or dissidents, made up approximately 15 per cent of the total number of the refugee children.[59] Most of these Christian youngsters were completely assimilated into their local culture. They had never considered themselves Jewish and now to find themselves refugees because of an unacknowledged or sometimes even unknown family history, exacerbated the child's trauma tremendously. As an anonymous writer for the Kindertransport collection at the London's Museum of Jewish Life writes, 'Christian children of Jewish descent had a particularly difficult time adapting to their refugee status. … They often had no idea why they had been sent away. They knew nothing about Judaism, did not feel Jewish and could not readily enter the Jewish community in Britain.' The same writer went on to say that, 'watching a small fair-haired girl with a cross hanging from a silver chain around her neck, [one] wonders whether the little non-Aryan Christians, in these strange surroundings, are not even more to be pitied than their Jewish play-fellows, who already take persecution for granted.'

As with other Jewish youngsters, many of these children's parents had told them that they were merely going to England on a holiday.

Esther Baumel states that, 'upon learning the truth in the reception camps, many suffered psychological breakdown and trauma. ... Indeed, many of them continued to use the Nazi salute in the reception camps.'[60] Margarete recalls two 'Nazi boys, aged 16 and 11, who were so infuriated at being sent out of Germany that they wrote letters to [the] German authorities denouncing their parents as "anti-Nazi".'[61] This group of assimilated German Jewish Christians often had the most difficulty adjusting to their refugee status and resisted being integrated into their British foster families.

While most of the non-Aryan Christian children were placed in private homes, there were also hostels at, among other places, Stoke Newington, Micklepage and Eastbourne, which were especially adapted to teenagers' needs. The situation that David (Arwed) Lewinski and Hugh (Horst) Schramm faced, however, was unique. An Anglican Church worker from Canada, Monica Storrs, who happened to be home in England on holiday when she heard about the refugee children's plight, agreed without hesitation to sponsor two boys around the age of ten or twelve because she had heard that boys this age were the most difficult to place. Storrs actually used the term 'adopt' instead of sponsor, but this was incorrect because both boys still had living parents and were not available for adoption. Miss Storrs greeted the boys at Harwich when they arrived on a Kindertransport and expected them to accompany her on her imminent return to Canada. This was not to be. The Canadian immigration officials refused to issue passports to the boys and, after several weeks of wrangling, Storrs reluctantly returned alone to the northern Canadian settlement where she worked. Canadian immigration laws were being interpreted very narrowly at this time and Jews, even Jewish refugee children, were not welcome.[62] It seems likely that Storrs suspected this might be the cause for the refused visas. She wrote to a friend that she was going 'straight to Ottawa for another attempt at close quarters to obtain their [the boys'] admittance. If this fails, I shall be very anxious for the soul of Canada, which can close its doors to such harmless immigrants.'

Under some duress, Storrs placed the boys with a friend in London in what she hoped would be a temporary solution. In Ottawa she

1. Refugee children arriving in England.

FACING PAGE:
2. David Lewinski (*left*)
and Hugh Schramm
(*right*) Berlin, 1939,
leaving on a Kinder-
transport.

RIGHT:
3. David Lewinski,
May 1939.

BELOW:
4. Hugh Schramm (*left*)
and David Lewinski
(*right*) settling in after
arrival in England.

ABOVE: 5. CRREC appeals for food for continental Jewry *c.*1946.

BELOW: 6. Kindertransport youngsters at lessons.

FACING PAGE: 7. Rabbi Dr Solomon Schonfeld in British officer's uniform *c.*19

ABOVE: 8. Little refugee tots in CRREC care.

BELOW: 9. Arriving in England.

ABOVE:
10. Postwar children
arriving in England.

RIGHT:
11. Sign in restaurant
window, Vienna.

LEFT:
12. Anti-Jewish sign, Germany.

BELOW:
13. Members of the Bielski Otriad family camp, Naliboki Forest, Belarus (then Belorussia).

personally met the governor-general and the minister responsible for immigration. Her brother, Sir Ronald Storrs, wrote letters to the highest levels of government, as did influential friends. Finally, in 1940, Storrs received word that David and Hugh would be allowed to enter Canada with a group of evacuated British school children. They arrived in October of that year to live in Fort St John, at that time a frontier settlement of approximately 100 people. It was, indeed, a unique experience and one that both boys thoroughly enjoyed.[63] The Canadian government's attitude at the time remains a source of shame.

When the United Kingdom government decided to intern all German and Austrian citizens aged 16 or more, the non-Aryan Christian children were not spared. Three boys were taken from boarding schools. The Bishop of Chichester intervened on their behalf because they were preparing for examinations, but the report fails to mention whether or not he was successful.[64] The bishop then suggested asking the Home Office to reconsider interning any students just before an important examination, which seemed only reasonable, but again there appears to have been no follow-up on this matter. Four other non-Aryan Christian boys were interned from the Eastbourne hostel and one from Stoke Newington, but there is no indication that any girls were ever sent to the camps.

When it was discovered that several of the older children wished to train for service with the Confessional Church in Germany after the war, or overseas as missionaries, a house in Wistow near Leicester, which Lord and Lady Cottesloe offered, was prepared as a home and study centre for 15 residents[65] and named the Wistow Training Centre for Post-War Christian Service. The house had no central heating or electric power, but was partially furnished and had beautiful grounds.[66] Spartan circumstances were likely considered conducive to building character. One girl decided to become a deaconess and entered the Southwark and Rochester Deaconess House for her training, while two boys entered theological colleges to prepare for Holy Orders.[67]

A certain Leo Lipmann put forward a scheme for training young German Christian non-Aryans for consideration by the Society for the

Protection of Science and Learning to assist in the preparation of young refugees for life in the British workforce. It suggested that since these children came mostly from upper-middle-class homes, they should be trained in 'semi-technical professions such as designers, compositors, engineers, opticians, teachers, librarians [and] chiropodists'.[68] The scheme was implemented in conjunction with the Quakers, who already had the necessary framework in place.

Although various Protestant and Catholic organizations sponsored most of the Christian Jewish children financially, generally speaking they received very little emotional support. Eleanor Rathbone noted in the House of Commons that 'Christians have shown themselves less generous towards Christians than Jews have shown themselves to either Christians or Jews.'[69] Many influential Church of England leaders, including the Archbishop of Canterbury, shared this view.[70] Revd Dr J. W. Parkes went so far as to say that 'there never has been such a time when Jewry looked upon Christianity with so much longing and with so much contempt as today. We send missions to convert the Jews and [then] we leave them to look after refugees who are members of our own faith.'[71] Fortunately, this attitude of non-involvement changed dramatically with the onset of war and the chair of the Christian Council for Refugees, Revd W. W. Simpson, went on record as saying that the Christian Council 'would wish to be treated on the same basis as the Jewish organizations'.[72] In other words, no favouritism was to be shown to Christian children but neither was there to be a bias against them.

When concentration camp children began arriving in 1945, only nine of the first 300 were Christian, though 11 were registered at Butcombe Court in Somerset later that year and 30 more were expected from Vienna.[73] Some of these children were sent to Darleith House in Glasgow, with the comment, 'very poor discipline', attached to their report. This complaint became common once the children were in better physical condition[74] and able to exert themselves, which is understandable given their horrendous experiences. It is unclear why the percentage of Christian children from concentration camps is so much smaller than in the Kindertransports of 1938–39. There seems to be no awareness of this discrepancy in reports or other documents available at the time.

Just as the Jewish community was not homogenous, so the Christian community had its differences. Many of the problems the refugee organizations faced, whether they were Jewish or Christian, were in fact surprisingly similar. Roman Catholic clergy, for example, sought to have children who had been initially placed in Protestant homes removed to a Catholic environment; the Barbican Mission's conversionary activities caused great uneasiness and the Bishop of Barking was asked to investigate; Christadelphian and Unitarian homes, while very welcoming to the refugees, were suspect; when a Catholic boy wished to become a Quaker, Cardinal Hinsley reminded the Society of Friends that the principle of religious affiliation must be adhered to. Pastor W. Buesing of the conference of German-speaking congregations, however, resolutely put the children's welfare above denominational priorities. He informed the Revd Henry Carter:

> I fully realize the difference between Roman and non-Roman children as far as supervision through committees is concerned … [but] assuming that at least some of the children still belong to the Lutheran Church though they may be unaware of the fact and its implications … it is not our intention to indulge in missionary activities which could only complicate for those children a situation already precarious enough.[75]

In the end, a consensus was reached and a Miss Eccles was hired to be responsible for the religious welfare of all Christian children, although, as in the Jewish community, church leaders complained that the number 'of refugee young people not interested in Church activities is still large'.[76]

Despite their differences, in crisis situations the various denominations could and did cooperate, in much the same way as they did within the Jewish community. The Christian Council was composed of all major groups. Cardinal Hinsley, the Archbishop of Canterbury, Canon George Craven (a Catholic), Bishop George Bell, the Revd

Henry Carter and the Revd W. W. Simpson, among others, all chaired or co-chaired joint organizations and committees. The Quakers were involved everywhere. In the pre-Vatican II denominational climate, such cooperation was indeed remarkable.

Many Catholic and Protestant churches offered the refugees, both adults and children, 'frequent services' in both German and English. In 1941 Revd Father Edward Quinn was appointed to set up the Commission for Post-War Settlement, designed to assist all non-Aryan Christian children in their anticipated return to Europe.[77] This return, of course, did not materialize and, as the need for assistance gradually declined, the various Christian refugee organizations began to terminate their activities.

The Church of England Committee for 'Non-Aryan' Christians closed its doors in 1949. This committee had cared for 170 children, most of whom completed their education to the matriculation level while nine took university degrees. Eleven boys served in the British army, with three obtaining commissioned rank; three girls served in the ATS; two boys qualified as engineers and another as a research chemist; four boys and five girls became teachers; and ten girls trained as nurses.[78] This small number of children seems incongruous when compared with the large number of Anglicans in England until one remembers that many thousands of Church of England adherents became foster parents for children from organizations other than the Church of England committee.

The Friends Committee for Refugees and Aliens also began gearing down its work in 1949 and had completed all its activities by April 1954. The committee records show that it rendered assistance to 8,000 refugees, but how many of these were children is not indicated.[79]

After the closure of the Refugee Children's Movement in 1948, 131 Protestant children were placed under the guardianship of Sir Herbert Emerson, while 37 Roman Catholics were assigned to the care of the Roman Catholic Children's Committee. When this was brought to the home secretary's attention, it was decided that one guardian for all Christian children was most expedient. Officially, therefore, the Catholic children also remained wards of Sir Herbert, though in practice they were still under the wing of the Catholic committee.[80]

All the Christian committees, with the exception of those designated to conclude operations, ceased their activities some time during 1951. A 'Continuation Committee' was formed to take care of all remaining responsibilities, and this group met as late as 19 February 1954.[81] The Christian Council, the Catholic Children's Committee and the Riversmead Methodist Committee had together assumed responsibility for approximately 1,100 refugee children, and now, at their closure, they made a 'permanent settlement' for those few cases that still remained their responsibility.[82]

It was the end of an era that had seen remarkable growth in cooperation between churches and, perhaps even more importantly, between Christians and Jews who submerged their differences in the interests of endangered children. Already in 1933, the high commissioner for refugees J. G. McDonald noted, 'Jewish efforts on behalf of the refugees have been by no means limited to Jews. Protestants, Catholics and refugees of no religious faith at all have in many instances been and are being relieved by Jewish charity.'[83] The Christian Council expressed its 'keen appreciation of the harmony and good fellowship' that existed between the CBF and the council, a harmony that, alas, had not filtered down to some segments of the general populace.[84]

8

HIDDEN CHILDREN AND CAMP SURVIVORS: THE POSTWAR REFUGEES

As far as the public record is concerned, Kindertransports ceased with the arrival on 31 August 1939 of the last transport, although 40 children (some records say 80)[1] arrived from the Netherlands on 14 May 1940 on a ship carrying adults as well as children. Gertruida Wijsmuller, a Dutch woman active in the rescue of refugees who had commandeered half a dozen motor coaches in Amsterdam and accompanied the occupants to the port of Ijmuiden, had arranged this unscheduled rescue. The refugees were at sea when the Dutch government capitulated and all on board reached England safely, but it is a moot point whether or not this can be called the last of the Kindertransports.

Rabbi Schonfeld, however, continued to use the term in relation to children brought from Europe after the war, whether to refer to those who had been in concentration camps or to those who had been in hiding.[2]

This, then, was the second wave of refugee children, also spoken of as arriving on 'children's transports', though they were never officially designated as Kindertransport children. In many respects, these children's stories differed substantially from those of the 1938–39 groups that had arrived in Britain under different legislation, yet there were also many similarities.

The Jewish community's first concern at the end of the war was to help children from the concentration camps.[3] Most children did not survive the camps, though the British community could not have known this at the time. The Nazis regarded children under the age of ten as 'unproductive eaters', so they were almost immediately exterminated. As historian Michael Berenbaum stated succinctly, 'the ultimate crime in the Holocaust was the murder of children.'[4] Older children were spared only if they could work. Gerda, for example, aged 15, was assigned to clean machinery or unload coal. At one point she worked in a textile mill, shredding clothing taken from prisoners that was then recycled into cloth for German use. Werner had to carry stones and take care of horses, while David cut stones for road work.[5] These youngsters, mostly boys, 'mastered lifesaving skills with breathtaking speed'.[6] Most survivors also eventually endured the death marches and the notorious open railway cars, when prisoners were moved to avoid liberation by the Soviets and sometimes by Western armies. Gerda, on a death march in January 1945, remembers that only 120 of approximately 2,000 girls survived. David marched with a group of boys on a two-month trek that began in February 1945. Fewer than half lived.[7] Some children witnessed not only starvation and inhumane treatment, but also even cannibalism.[8]

Although the British Jewish community had been anticipating such relief work since before 1943,[9] it was unprepared for the unexpected immensity of the task. At first it was feared that no children at all had survived the camps. However, when Leonard Cohen and Leonard Montefiore travelled to Paris just before the end of the war in Europe to consult with other Jewish organizations, they learnt that some youngsters had indeed survived. Montefiore immediately wrote to Anthony de Rothschild of the CBF in London, outlining a plan whereby 'a few hundred children from Bergen-Belsen or Buchenwald' could be brought to Britain to be cared for by the CBF.[10]

Initially, during the 1930s, conditions had not been too difficult in Bergen-Belsen. There was some medical help and enough food.

Although barracks inspections could be frightening – little Dorien's first word was *Achtung* – the prisoners generally remained hopeful. This changed dramatically in 1944 when Bergen-Belsen was officially designated a concentration camp.[11] By the time British troops arrived on 15 April 1945, conditions were beyond imagination. Approximately 10,000 unburied bodies, many of young people and some already decomposing, were stacked in the yards and most of the prisoners were 'living skeletons'. One newspaper correspondent with the British troops began his report by saying: 'it is my duty to describe something beyond the imagination of mankind.'[12] Yet, some children survived even these horrors.

The British Home Office approved a proposal Otto Schiff put forward and granted permission to bring 1,000 camp children under the age of 17 to the United Kingdom for recuperation on the understanding that they would re-emigrate within two years.[13] The postwar orphans committee, or Committee for the Care of Children from the Camps (CCCC), chaired by Leonard Montefiore and with experienced refugee workers such as Elaine Blond and Lola Hahn Warburg among its members, was quickly organized to finalize details of the relief effort. Rabbi Maurice Swift of the CRREC represented the Orthodox community.[14] The Central British Fund was to be financially responsible for all maintenance and other expenses incurred on behalf of the children. Otto Schiff wrote in the *Jewish Chronicle*:

> The Jewish Refugees Committee, in conjunction with the Friends Committee for Refugees and Aliens has received permission to bring to this country 1,000 children from the concentration camps … at least 80 per cent will be Jewish children. … What is to happen to them when convalescence has been completed need not be discussed at this moment though it can assuredly not be far from the mind of all concerned.[15]

Certainly, convalescence was uppermost in the CCCC's mind. Immediately after its inception, the committee set to work by renting a hostel near Windermere for accommodation, and by hiring the German refugee psychologist, Oscar Friedman, in preparation for the arrival of the first children, whenever that might be.

In August 1945, the United Nations Relief and Rehabilitation Administration (UNRRA) informed Montefiore that there were youngsters from Theresienstadt (Terezín) and other camps, now gathered in Prague, who needed medical attention but who were fit enough to travel, and that the Royal Air Force (RAF), repatriating Czech airmen, had agreed to carry these children on the return flight to England. On 14 August, therefore, with only 24 hours' notice, 305 children were driven to Ruzyně airfield, in Prague, from where they were airlifted to Crosby-on-Eden, near Carlisle.

George and Edith Lauer, who had also been interned at Terezin, remember the details of that journey. At the Czech government's request, they had remained in the camp to care for the sick children and when the evacuation was announced, they were selected to accompany the children to Britain. George Lauer vividly recalled the half-hour walk to the railway station and how difficult it had been to keep all the youngsters under control, for they were unimaginably excited about being outside the camp for the first time in many years. When they arrived at the airport there was a two-day delay before the planes arrived and then, Lauer recounted, there were only nine planes instead of the expected ten. Everything had to be rearranged so that no one was left behind. The bombers had no seats, 'the facilities were two buckets behind some old blankets', and many of the children became air sick. However, on arrival, when people lining the streets cheered the buses carrying the children to their destination, it all seemed worthwhile.[16]

On 25 August 1945 *The Times* reported that 150 of these 'orphaned Czech and Polish refugee boys from Prague arrived last week at the Troutbeck Bridge Hostel ... where they will be educated and cared for by the Jewish Refugees Committee and the Friends Committee for Refugees and Aliens ... all boys ... from three to sixteen years'. Of the younger boys, six three-year-olds were billeted at Bulldogs Bank, a home offered by Lady Clark, and four nine-year-olds were sent to Weir Courteney, Sir Benjamin Drage's estate in Lingfield, Surrey.[17]

The criteria for age selection in all the camps were not vigorously enforced – selection by appearance seems to have been the predominant method – and of course, no one had identity papers. At the same time malnutrition caused many internees to look much younger than their actual years, so on arrival the actual age of the boys was found to be between 3 and 23 years, far beyond the legal age limit of 16.[18] Nevertheless, the authorities allowed all of them to remain in Britain. As noted in the committee report and, as Norman Bentwich later commented:

> It may well be that no group of immigrants has ever entered this country with a more sympathetic welcome or with fewer formalities. The Immigration authorities made everything easy – no questions asked. ... We took the good with the bad, the sick with the healthy, the whole with the maimed and there were many maimed in mind and body – it was completely unselective immigration and therefore stands out from all the subsequent schemes.[19]

In December 1945 the committee learnt that about 200 children still in Bergen-Belsen could no longer remain in the unsuitable camp conditions. This was especially true of those who were ill, some with serious conditions such as tuberculosis.[20] Some time before liberation, conditions in Bergen-Belsen had deteriorated to the point where rations were reduced to one piece of bread a day, one pint 'of water containing turnips and potato peels, a so-called soup'. Under such circumstances, many of the children weakened and became ill.[21] Consequently, these sick and malnourished Bergen-Belsen survivors were also accepted for immigration, as were 150 more children from Czechoslovakia in January 1946, and still more from various other points on the continent, until the last camp survivors arrived in England in June 1946. And still the British government's quota of 1,000 children was not reached. Only 732 children from the camps were finally located and brought to Britain for medical help and rehabilitation.

The refugee committees had expected young children from the camps and were shocked when on occasion they were faced with some survivors already sporting beards. The *Daily News Bulletin* explained that these youths had been utilized for forced labour, whereas younger children were usually killed on arrival in the camps, as were most girls. This explains why, among the 500 children brought to France from Buchenwald, for example, there were only ten girls. The ratio of girls to boys for those arriving in Britain was approximately the same.[22]

For concentration camp survivors who were minors, the Home Office insisted on the appointment of an official guardian. Not unexpectedly, Lord Gorell, already guardian for the 1938–39 *Kinder*, was chosen for this office, with Revd Ephraim Levine as guardian of children under the auspices of the Jewish Refugees Committee.[23]

While the efforts of the Committee for the Care of Children from the Camps were exemplary, they were not accomplished without acrimony and resistance from within the Jewish community. The minutes of the CCCC's working committee for November 1945 note 'a great deal of unrest' at Bergen-Belsen, where 'the Zionists in the Camps were endeavouring to prevent the children from leaving, attempting to influence them by stories of non-Jewish homes in England'.[24] The Central Committee for Displaced Persons, the organization the Allies had entrusted to provide for the thousands of stateless Jewish people in Europe, was strongly Zionist in orientation and determined to ensure that all the camp children went to Palestine, then a British mandate destined to become the state of Israel. The committee therefore resisted all efforts to bring the children to Britain, regardless of the conditions in the camp. Only after the personal intervention of David Ben-Gurion did the committee reluctantly allow children from Bergen-Belsen to be flown to the United Kingdom, and then only on condition that once there they would be placed in Zionist hostels.[25]

In October 1946, Rabbi Dr Schonfeld, certainly no radical Zionist, also personally visited the camps as a delegate of the CRREC and the

United Jewish Relief Appeal. The CRREC's executive committee minutes disclosed that 'arrangements have been made for him to go as an UNRRA delegate and in uniform.' Dr Schonfeld's uniform, that of a 'British Army Chaplain, with a badge of the Tablets of the Law on his Officer's cap'[26] gave him a certain authority not generally accorded to civilians.

Rabbi Schonfeld did visit the camps and made arrangements for some of the internees to go to England. He even recruited some of the older and healthier girls to assist him in various ways. Yet, his primary concern at this point seems to have been to locate and return to the Jewish community those children who had been hidden prior to the destruction of Jewish family life, especially in Poland. The CRREC, however, did not limit its efforts to Poland. The last of the children's transports organized by Dr Schonfeld, left Prague in 1948, carrying 138 child survivors gathered from various countries formerly occupied by Germany.[27]

Until 1941, several avenues were open, even in Nazi-occupied territories outside Poland, through which at least some Jewish families could send their children into hiding. After that, it became much more difficult, for on 19 September 1941, all Jews, including children over the age of six, were required to wear a yellow star on their clothing, which easily identified them. In Poland the 'star', or rather blue and white armband, was already compulsory in 1939. Still, the most common route for hiding a child was to entrust him or her to the care of a Gentile servant, colleague or friend. Marian's father, for example, transferred the title of his factory to a Polish employee, who then hid the child for the duration.[28] Such arrangements were often made hastily in the trauma and confusion of enforced movement. They rarely included provision for hiding the parents,[29] for it was obviously easier to hide a child or even several children than an entire family, and these parents were prepared to sacrifice their safety for that of their children. Edith's mother, with three small children, tried desperately to find a place where the family could stay together. When this proved impossible, she and her older daughter found a place where they could work (with false papers), while the two younger ones were sent into hiding in the country. Edith, the second youngest, felt abandoned and screamed 'you don't love me', until her mother rocked her into quietness by whispering, 'I'm doing this *because* I love you so much.'[30] These children and their parents were experiencing the trauma of separation that the Kindertransport families had already experienced in 1938–39.

Some children were truly hidden, unable to leave a house, room, attic or even a cupboard for long periods of time. Little Hynrik, for example, was kept in a cellar for 14 months, while Richard Rozen was hidden in a basement cabinet for over a year.[31]

Others were hidden 'openly', becoming part of a family or of many different families if the child was moved several times. Sara Spier, for example, was transferred to 32 different locations to ensure her safety.[32] Little Gerda had only one home and reported after the war that the Polish woman who hid her 'treated her as her child'. Alfred also remained with the same 'goyim' for three years until the end of the war.[33] Actually, it was not too difficult in wartime for any family openly sheltering a young Jewish child to come up with a cover story to explain the youngster's presence – a niece or nephew evacuated from a bombed city, a cousin's illegitimate child, or some similar story.[34] Older children were more difficult to hide, though they too could often be passed off as a relative come to help on the farm or in the house.

Sometimes a parent or parent's contact would bring the child to a religious institution, such as a convent or orphanage, where the youngster would be less isolated than in most private homes and yet quite safe.[35] Jadwiga, for example, was brought to an orphanage where she was raised as a Christian, while Margaret and Irene spent the war hidden in a convent among other children.[36] Some aimlessly wandering orphaned children might accidentally find themselves at such a place and consequently be saved, though they were at the same time usually exposed to Christian indoctrination.

While most children were placed in homes through personal contact or a network of personal contacts,[37] there were organizations that sought to rescue and hide Jews, especially children. These organizations, among others, included the Zegota in Warsaw, the Naamloze Venootschap (NV) in the Netherlands, the Comité de Défense des Juifs in Belgium, and the Oeuvre de Secours aux Enfants (OSE) in France.[38] In addition, there were various youth groups, often operating within the structure of a Christian church. The organizations included personnel as diverse as social workers who could use their position to aid the children, anti-Nazi youths working in the underground or priests with contacts within their parish. Some of these organizations were in a position to pay at least a minimal sum for the child's upkeep, although, as Eric Silver writes, 'not one of the [Dutch] villagers wanted to make money out of it, but there were a lot of poor people. … If the people who took the children were well-to-do, we didn't pay them. We used the money to pay someone else.'[39] In Belgium, the Comité de Défense des Juifs paid for the maintenance of children placed in private homes, while those in convents and other institutions were supported by these organizations.[40] A few Gentile families, as Rabbi Schonfeld was later to discover, sheltered a child with a view to possible future financial reward, but they were a very small minority.

Parents who still had money would of course gladly pay for their child's safety, but sometimes families were contacted by individuals whom they did not know personally and therefore could not be sure were trustworthy. It was an incredibly difficult situation for parents forced either to relinquish their child to strangers or put their offspring's life at risk by having him or her remain at home. Piet Meerburg, a Dutch student whose organization was instrumental in saving between 300 and 400 Jewish children, remembers that 'parents cried tremendously most of the time', yet at the end of the day, 'driven to desperation by the situation [they] were willing to give their children to a strange goy.'[41] Holocaust scholar Deborah Dwork also points out how much courage it took for parents to part with their children:

> The act of giving up one's child, of surrendering one's own daughter or son – was the first and most radical step in the chain of rescue. … Whether one relinquished that son or

daughter to a personal friend or a stranger – that initial act of abdication was the fundamental beginning.[42]

This was of course true also of all those parents whose children had been sent to England in 1938–39 on the Kindertransports. The price parents paid in emotional trauma for their children's safety is indeed beyond comprehension and must never be ignored. Further study on this subject is needed.

For a child to be safely settled in a new home, it was essential for him or her to adapt as much as possible to the sheltering family's routine and habits. The child was given a new name and, if old enough to understand, even a new family history. False identity papers provided a new place of birth and the names of bogus parents. Most of the children could accept all this. What is seldom mentioned, however, is the difficulty some Orthodox children experienced when faced with the hiding family's dietary habits. One youngster commented, 'I said to myself, "I have to eat. If it does not please God, He has to open the sky and take me suddenly." I ate and nothing happened. Since then I do not eat kosher anymore.'[43] Some no doubt agonized more deeply. For others, again, not observing the rules of *kashrut* was no problem. One child commented, 'we ate pork. It did not disturb me. We were happy with what we had to eat.'[44]

Assuming the new family's identity included, of course, its religious observances. As Dwork and sociologist Diane Wolf pointed out, 'all hidden children had to bury their Jewish identities and backgrounds,' while 'the ultimate adaptation to living as a gentile among gentiles was in fact to become a gentile, either through simple attrition or by formal conversion. The adoption of a Christian faith was not rare.'[45] For younger children it was simply a matter of growing up in the church their sheltering family attended. Abraham Foxman, for example, was hidden by his Roman Catholic nannie, who had him baptized. 'Many hidden children resent having been baptized and converted by their rescuers,' he writes.

Not I. She raised me with faith and ritual. She did it with a good heart and for the benefit of my soul – she raised me with faith, allowing my father later to ease me away from that faith into our own faith – I never suffered any latter-day identity confusion or crisis over my early Christian upbringing.[46]

He was more fortunate than many.

The safest place for a child to be hidden was obviously in a convent, especially when the convent belonged to a teaching order. An orphanage was also considered secure. In such situations, additional children could come or go without attracting too much attention. Often the mother superior was the only person who knew that these children were Jewish, though many of the other nuns may have guessed. Sociologist Suzanne Vromen, in her very insightful study of hidden children in Belgium, points out that clergy – nuns and priests – were in a better and safer position to shelter children than families, or especially than individuals.[47]

It was more difficult for children who were older when they went into hiding, especially those who found themselves in Christian institutions that imposed considerable religious pressure on them, or those in the care of zealous families that might view the placement as an opportunity to proselytize. Older children often felt that it was a betrayal of their parents or even of God to attend a Christian church. The trauma this caused the child could in turn lead to exposure, with all its subsequent dangers to both the child and the sheltering family.

Many children, however, for a variety of reasons, did convert to Christianity, or at least acceded to baptism, especially those hidden in convents. Evelyn, aged 11, was 'slowly won over to Catholicism' when one of the nuns gently asked whether she would like to be baptized. Camille and her sister agreed because of the advantages that full membership of the community offered, such as walks outside the convent walls.[48]

Edith, on the other hand, had been hidden in an isolated Jewish country home. When the situation became too dangerous, she and the others hidden with her were instructed to say that they were Catholic orphans who had come to board at this particular school. Before arriving, they were given forged baptismal certificates and warned that they would be required to attend weekly church services. The refugee girls learned ritual Catholic responses by carefully watching other students. When Edith prayed, however, she said, 'God, you don't mind that I'm pretending to be a Catholic, do You?'[49] She remembered the last words her mother spoke to her – 'remember who you are.' Yet here she was with a new name, a whole new family history and now even a new God. Who, indeed, was she?

This problem of identity was one of the great postwar dilemmas that the hidden children had to face, and for some it presented a lifelong predicament. Emil, however, adopted a unique approach to having to attend church services: 'I integrated Jesus, the Apostles – these were Jews – and the Virgin. I integrated them into my religion and I accepted them rather fast.' After liberation, 'as rapidly as I had integrated them, I let them go, just as fast'.[50] His experience was exceptional, as was Abraham Foxman's, but for most such children the identity crisis, especially if it involved baptism, proved to be more traumatic.

Postwar research has suggested that children were generally more likely to be given sanctuary in countries with the fewest number of Jews,[51] while areas with high concentrations of unassimilated Jews were more likely to cooperate with the Nazis. This research appears questionable. For example, Rabbi Schonfeld found that Poland harboured more hidden children than any other country. This, he held, was partly because there was a much heavier concentration of Jews in Poland than elsewhere and therefore much more contact with the non-Jewish population, and partly because the Jews there believed the Nazi threats and acted accordingly.[52] And, despite the dangers and the small Jewish population there, even German families hid children.[53] Edgar Gold, for example, was hidden in the home of German family friends when both his parents were sent to the camps.[54] Martin Gilbert records that 'perhaps thousands' of ordinary Germans hid Jews, especially children. Yad Vashem awarded 'righteous' recognition to more than 300 Germans, which meant that they risked their lives to save Jews and did so without receiving payment of any kind.[55] It should be pointed out that, irrespective of the dangers, more than 6,000 Poles also received the same recognition.

What was it then that, regardless of a family's financial position or geographical location, prompted Gentiles to harbour Jewish children when the cost of discovery would mean loss of possessions, imprisonment or even death? It was certainly not generally for financial gain. For some it was a strong humanitarian impulse, an empathetic need to assist a helpless human being. Social psychiatrists Eva Fogelman and Samuel and Pearl Oliver ascribe such actions to 'a case of solid humanitarian values and compassion acquired in childhood'.[56] For some, whether Catholic or Protestant, there was strong religious motivation. Eric Silver notes that in France, 'the motivation of the plateau-people is to be sought in their Huguenot descent, their Bible-based culture and their long history of persecution'.

Miriam Whartman, who was hidden in the Netherlands, believes that her protectors saved Jews because of their strong Calvinistic mores.[57] Roman Catholic institutions, Catholic families and individual priests were responding to similar motivations. Suzanne Vromen notes that 'within convents and orphanages the nuns had the potential to combine fundamental goodness with Christianity. The war offered them an extraordinary opportunity to do this; fortunately, they seized it.'[58] It seems safe to conclude, then, that, for some, religious conviction was indeed a strong inducement for sheltering Jewish children.[59] Suzanne Vromen, however, found that by and large, at least in Belgium, children were hidden 'predominantly for humanitarian reasons and not purely for conversion purposes, even if after the war there was scattered reluctance to return rescued children to their Jewish heritage.'[60]

But, for whatever motive – whether loyalty to a friend or employer, religious conviction, humanitarian concern or some other reason – hundreds, possibly thousands, of people throughout Europe opened their homes to Jewish children and thus made it possible for a remnant to be saved. As Martin Gilbert comments, 'we hidden children have a mission. ... For each of us is living proof that even in hell, even in that hell called the Holocaust, there was goodness, there was kindness, and there was love and compassion.'[61]

Besides all those children who were hidden, there were also some who hid themselves. If a child was blond and blue eyed it was possible to pass as an Aryan and, although the older, more self-sufficient children were the most likely to survive, children as young as eight or even six years of age wandered the countryside as refugees, finding food and shelter as best they could.[62] Bluma, for example, who was just seven years old, went from town to town with her sister and brother 'begging as gypsies' until they were caught. The brother was killed but the girls survived and 'lived in the fields' for three months until they were 'liberated'.[63] One boy remembers jumping out of the lorry that was taking his family to a camp: 'I was very tired and a farmer let me sleep the night in the hay loft – for some months I looked after the sheep for a farmer – I was nine years old.' A little girl whose parents were killed writes that she lived by begging. 'After that – I hid myself with a farmer who let me live in the cellar. No one knew I was there.'[64] If a child spoke Polish fluently, it was possible to pass as a national. Leah, for example, got a job in a hospital kitchen where, 'all of a sudden, I had to become a Polish girl, with all the Polish mannerisms.' This proved to be very unsettling for her. 'I felt like an actor on a stage, playing a role that I hated.'[65] Some of the older girls, one of whom was called Rachela, passed themselves off as 'Ukrainian' housemaids not only in Poland but also in Germany. Esther, a 'very beautiful girl', was taken to Krakow to live with a Polish officer.[66]

Still others joined partisan groups in the dense forests of Poland and Russia. At the age of nine, Jacob hid in the forests with his brothers, while another child 'jumped from a death train' and then found himself with a Jewish group in a forest.[67] Marila fought with the partisans and a notation in her file comments, 'she shoots well'.[68] Another such teenager was Faye Schulman. She remembers that joining a partisan group was not always simple, especially for Jewish children who might face anti-Semitic hostility unless they happened upon a largely Jewish encampment. The composition of the group, the continuous search for food and weapons, and being constantly on the move for fear of discovery destroyed any childhood these children would normally have experienced.[69] Children as young as 14 were accepted as active fighting partisans, but younger children, sometimes entire families, were also sheltered in 'civilian' camps deep in the forests, protected and supported by Jewish partisans.[70] One such camp was Bielski Otriad in the Naliboki forest in Belarus (then Belorussia). It is said that they 'turned no one away, including older men, women and children, whom other groups would not take in.' In addition to the civilians, there were close to 1,300 fighters, both male and female, in the camp.[71] After the war many of these young fighters returned to their former homes in search of family. But, on finding only desolation, they eventually entered camps for displaced persons. From here, a large number of them entered Britain in the second wave of the child refugee movement.

Naturally, the Jewish community made every effort to ensure that these hidden children – as well as those who lived and fought in the forests – were returned to their heritage. An editorial in the *Jewish Chronicle* challenged, 'we have lost our millions to the bloody hate of anti-Semitism. Dare the civilized world suffer us to be robbed also of these, our children?'[72]

Because so little has been written about the actual dynamics of any rescue operation, it is of interest to examine briefly Dr Schonfeld's experiences and his methods.

To assist in the search for hidden and hiding children, Rabbi Schonfeld organized a project called 'the Eastern Rescue', in which he was assisted by a man named Chil (Chiel) and initially also by Mizrachi, Agudas and Zionist groups.[73] Although the CRREC's Postwar Religious Reconstruction Programme, the Jewish Committee for Relief Abroad, set up by the Board of Deputies, as well as the Anglo-Jewish Association, had been planning strategy since 1943, Dr Schonfeld's first visit to Poland, aimed specifically at locating Jewish children, occurred only in November 1945.[74] It seems that he was assisted at this time by several Polish camp survivors, although this is not specifically noted in his diaries. Rozalia, however, remembers that after liberation she worked closely with Rabbi Schonfeld, 'identifying Jewish children and facilitating their emigration to England'.[75]

This was often a daunting task. Diane Wolf points out that 'most Jewish children had been given another name, identity and family background ... and a new religious identity.'[76] Added to this, the political situation in Europe was still unstable and not conducive for such a search. On his arrival in Poland, for example, the rabbi found the population 'excitable and anti-Semitic', 'still complaining [about] too many Jews'.[77] Indeed, Michael Etkind, a camp survivor, wrote that he was terrified of the Poles: 'I had never known such fear. Not even in the camps.'[78] There was reason for such fear. As historian Michael Steinlauf pointed out, 'in Poland from 1944 to 1947, between 1,500 and 2,000 Jews were murdered, most of them specifically because they were Jews.' He then cites a memorandum to a counsellor at the United States embassy. 'Until this very day those [Jewish] children are kept in the garret of the house, hidden away from the neighbors for fear that the neighbors discover that the Christian family saved the Jewish children and vent their vengeance on the whole family, and this one year after liberation.'[79] Holocaust historian Martin Gilbert states that 'child survivors of the Holocaust were murdered on 4 July, 1946, in Kielce, Poland during the pogrom there.'[80] Although the children were among those killed and not specifically targeted, Rabbi Schonfeld had good reason to act quickly.

Armed with block visas provided by the Home Office, Dr Schonfeld set out to rescue as many of these Polish Jewish children as possible, children who had survived the war but whom he correctly believed now again to be in mortal danger. He issued the following handwritten instructions to his colleagues:

(a) There are visas for those, born between 1928–1933, coming to relatives in England; they must have passports and 'must all arrive here [Warsaw] in their proper names.'

(b) Eighteen *yeshiva* students 'can come out on other names but must arrive on their own names i.e. proper identity cards'.

This matter of 'their own names' reveals the uniqueness of the situation. Many of the children hidden as infants did not remember their names and frequently there was no one left to provide this information. Many older children had knowingly assumed Gentile names and consequently all their personal papers provided a false identity. Then, also, a few children already accepted on a transport, for whatever reason were unable to leave and their visas and other documents were simply transferred to another child who thereby assumed an identity that was not his or her own. Thus, Ruben Katz arrived in Britain on one of Rabbi Schonfeld's transports as Adolf Bader. He later commented that 'what Rabbi Schonfeld did may not have been strictly speaking legal, but those were not normal times, and that helps to illustrate the measure of the man, who would "bend the rules" and never miss a chance to rescue another child.'[81] Dr Schonfeld's instructions continue:

(c) Orphans: 50 visas for children 14 and under, 'chosen by me. All accompanying transport must have been examined with a doctor's certificate and identity cards to be shown to the British Consul before departure.'[82] All children should, 'if possible' also be dusted with DDT powder.[83]

The instructions then go on to warn that 'the Central Committee in Warsaw will do everything to stop us. If they are now ready to send the children [to Israel or South Africa] act quietly and quickly. Take the children to Zabr'[84] where the Rabbi had a gathering place for them and felt they would be safe.

Dr Schonfeld then mentioned two lists, one containing the names of orphans and the other the names of children with at least one parent still living. Those on the second list were to wait for the 'next transport as parents must sign a witnessed affidavit giving the children over to the CRREC and this [affidavit] must first be submitted to London. If no division [of the lists] is possible, bring the lot.' Often a parent, still living but in dire circumstances, would apply for the child to be sent to England. As one mother wrote to the rabbi, 'I will be very happy to give my only child better conditions of living.'[85]

The names that family members in Britain supplied were not the only source of information about hidden children.

Information concerning rescued children reaches the Jewish Relief Committee in Lublin almost every day. Polish families bring Jewish children to Jewish organizations, and relate how they sheltered the child all through the Nazi occupation. There are also instances of Catholic priests informing Jewish organizations about groups of Jewish children who had been hidden in monasteries.[86]

It seems that Christian institutions that had hidden children were generally more willing than individuals to return them to the Jewish community. As Vatican representative, Monsignor Arthur Hughes, promised:

> All Jewish children in Europe who have been sheltered by Catholic institutions during the Nazi extermination hunt will be restored, not only to their parents but also to any Jewish institution or individual prepared to receive them. The Catholic Church … will not procure the conversion of children entrusted to its care.[87]

Monsignor Theas of Montauban wrote in a similar vein to Chief Rabbi Hertz:

> With regards to the Jewish children that the Catholic Church sheltered in its religious houses, be fully assured. These children will be rendered to the Jewish communities as soon as these will be able to take them. We deny all indiscreet proselytism. … As to the outlay which has been made for the maintenance of Jewish children in the religious houses, there is no question for you to pay back.[88]

While most Catholic authorities declared their willingness to return Jewish children, there were exceptions, especially if the child had been orphaned. In Belgium, for example, a Father Reynlers and Bishop Kerkofs determined that orphans who had converted and been baptized should remain Catholic and not be returned to the Jewish community.[89]

The general readiness of Christian institutions to return hidden children is hardly surprising. Quite simply, to begin with there were usually a number of children already in a convent or orphanage and the addition of one or more did not ordinarily impact emotionally on the nuns in charge. There was, of course, always the danger of discovery, but a caregiver in an institution did not ordinarily become as emotionally attached to an individual child as a caregiver did in a private home. In a private home there was usually only one hidden child who would become part of the family. A baby hidden for several years would come to feel like one of their own and any idea of surrendering that child would become unthinkable. Love between the hidden and the hider was often mutual. The psychiatrist Robert Krell admits that, as a hidden and much loved child, after the end of hostilities he wanted to stay with his hiders rather than return to his parents.[90]

On the other hand, there was a greater chance of persuading children to convert if they lived in an institution and, unfortunately, not all clergy respected the dictates of their superiors with regard either to surrendering a child or to proselytism. Proselytizing could continue even once the child was in Britain. In fact, as Dr Grunfeld wrote to the Revd Canon L. G. Craven, 'we had to invoke the help of the Archbishop of Westminster and the Bishop of London ... in order to stop the conversion by a Catholic priest of a seven-year-old Jewish child in one of the camps in England.'[91]

Despite such lapses, most European countries attempted, at least on an official level, to restore the approximately 100,000 hidden children who survived to the Jewish community. The Netherlands enacted a law stating that its citizens must declare or bring forward adopted children, while a Belgian court ruled that when non-Jews concealed a Jewish child, 'they were merely fulfilling their duty as good citizens' and thus were not entitled 'to adopt or retain the child if restoration' was claimed.[92] France followed a similar course.

Defying such legislation, newspaper reports concluded that, while

Orthodox children were generally returned, children from non-observant families 'whose association with the Jewish faith has been nominal, the decision [usually] is given [by the War Orphans Commission] in favour of keeping the child in the Christian fold'.[93] The Jewish leadership in Belgium sometimes resorted to producing bogus family members in the hope that a judge would rule blood ties of greater significance than a hiding family's emotional attachment and from time to time this tactic worked. All across Europe, though, families that had hidden children for many years argued that the child, especially when orphaned, should remain in the family where he or she was loved and not be placed in Jewish institutions until they reached the age of 18. These institutions, which the American Jewish Joint Distribution Committee mostly financed as an alternative to care for children when a surviving extended family member might be unable to do so, were called 'homes' rather than orphanages.[94]

Arieh Handler, returning from a tour of the Netherlands, France and Switzerland on behalf of Youth Aliyah and the Bachad movement, contended that the number of Jewish children still in non-Jewish homes in 1946 'is greater than any of the official or semi-official figures that have been given out'. He advocated that Jewish youth leaders personally go out into the villages and organize actual house to house search expeditions to ferret out such youngsters.[95]

Even drastic measures such as forceful removal were considered when it became obvious that not everyone who had hidden a Jewish child was ready to relinquish him or her to the Jewish community, even under legal duress. The Schonfeld papers document the case of a child who was removed 'by force' from the care of a Christian maid.[96] Finding such children became a priority, especially for Rabbi Schonfeld. As he noted in his diary, 'there appear to be 72 children among the Polish peasants [in the Auschwitz area] and it is becoming increasingly difficult to get them out.'[97] He felt that the CRREC had a sacred duty since 'no other organization has, so far, brought to safety – any of these children from Poland, although Poland is the only country in Europe where the children are faced daily with danger of being murdered.'[98]

It was with this sense of urgency that, aided by a Captain Drukker as well as Charles Ullman from the United States, Dr Schonfeld initially looked for Jewish children in Poland rather than elsewhere in Europe.[99] As a last resort the rabbi decided to offer money to buy the children back from the recalcitrant families. Times were very difficult in Europe and many families in Poland and elsewhere were on the brink of starvation. Dr Schonfeld assured sheltering families that the sum offered was in repayment for the child's maintenance throughout the war, though in his reports he calls the money a 'ransom'.[100]

The amounts that Schonfeld offered to foster families differed with each individual case. For Gertie, an orphan in Staszow, he offered 'the man who has her at the moment', 'up to one million [*zlotys*]. I can get them at two and a half thousand to the pound.' In another case the Polish guardian wished to emigrate with the child, 'but agreed to accept payment for her' instead.[101] So Schonfeld's organization searched for and found approximately 300 children for whom a ransom was paid.[102] On 4 October 1946 Dr Schonfeld summarized: 'In a very large number of cases children have been taken out of non-Jewish homes in Poland and on the average a ransom of £50 has been paid.' The expense of preparing transport to bring the child to Britain added to the cost, as did an additional amount for maintenance, so that the total cost per child amounted to approximately £80.[103] With deep sorrow, he declared, the 'rescue work is only hampered by lack of funds'.[104] Dr Schonfeld personally made five trips to Germany and Poland in the interests of these children.

An account by Ruben Katz, an adolescent whom Dr Schonfeld rescued, contains the most detailed information available on one of the rabbi's rescue operations,[105] though the rabbi's methods differed according to time and place. On this particular occasion, the children were gathered at a location central to the area where they were found, then moved to Gdynia, a port city. Here Dr Schonfeld chartered a ship to bring them to England. According to Ruben Katz, the ship carried no cargo 'except barrels of salt herring stored on deck, which we "tucked" into'. The journey took one week. *En route* the rabbi instructed the young refugees in Judaism. He also taught them to say 'thank you' and 'please' in English and to 'behave politely'. He had such a 'great love of country', which he sought to share with these adolescents, that he even included patriotic songs such as 'Land of Hope and Glory', and 'God Save the King' in his instruction.[106] Dr Schonfeld appeared to have been the only adult on board, apart from the crew, while his charges were in many cases boys from the forests, 'like wild animals', according to Katz. He commented that the few girls on the ship were from convents or private homes and that they were much better behaved. 'Rabbi Schonfeld taught us to sing and laugh, and tried to restore our faith in humanity,' remembered Ruben Katz.[107]

When the ship arrived in London, 'nurses were waiting, soap and tooth brushes were distributed, items most of us had forgotten existed', and a delicious meal was laid on. 'Rabbi Schonfeld had thought of everything and taken care of all our needs.'[108] Small wonder these children, along with those of the 1938–39 Kindertransport, developed such an affection for him that they began calling themselves the 'Schonfeld *Kinder*' and kept in contact with him in later years.[109]

Rabbi Schonfeld had assumed that the relatives in Britain who instigated his search for an individual child would pay the cost of the ransom, but this was not necessarily so. By August 1946 he confessed to 'finding it extremely difficult to meet my obligations undertaken during my visit to Poland. These monies were advanced in the expectation that relatives and friends will be glad to refund these sums.' Again, in January 1947, he wrote to a Mr F that 'I personally still have debts to settle arising out of my borrowing in order to redeem your son and send him to England.'[110] To meet his obligations and continue his rescue operations, the rabbi finally appealed yet again to the larger Jewish community. 'Without your help many of these children may be left in Poland lost to their people. This is not what their parents in poverty and danger hoped and prayed for when they hid them on the eve of entering the Gas Chambers and Crematoria.'[111] It was indeed a poignant appeal and Rabbi Schonfeld was not exaggerating the precarious financial position of the relief organizations, including his own, which were supported solely by voluntary donations.

The CBF alone was sponsoring 26 hostels, some of which still housed prewar Kindertransport children. Since most of these hostels were Orthodox in orientation, space and staffing must be found for the non-Orthodox postwar adolescents now on their way to Britain. The urgency of separate accommodation was clearly demonstrated when open hostility surfaced between the two factions.[112] Private homes were not considered an option at this point since the children were to receive 'constant supervision' for the first three to six months.[113] A special house, Weir Courtney in Lingfield, Surrey, was set aside for children under seven years of age, while those who were tubercular were sent to Quare Mead, Ugley, in Essex, for medical care.[114] Initially, most children spent at least a night or two at the Jews' Temporary Shelter on Mansell Street in London, where they were registered with the police as required and where an attempt was made to clothe them adequately, for most barely had even the necessities.[115] And so the expenses mounted.

In October 1946 the CBF was on the verge of collapse 'owing to the lack of money and support' and, by 1947, it was facing bankruptcy.[116] The *Jewish Chronicle* reported in March of that year that there were funds 'only until the summer' and strongly supported the CBF appeal for one million pounds while lamenting that the community suffered from 'a deplorable lack of public interest – a most distressing inertia'.[117] This seems to be an exaggeration of the facts, given the continuing generosity of guarantors still supporting prewar refugees and the strictures of the postwar economy. Be that as it may, the funds required for this rescue mission were received over time and the work to search for hidden children was able to continue.

Other problems also had to be addressed. As earlier at Bloomsbury House and Woburn House, there were complaints about organizational inefficiencies. A case in point was Youth Aliyah, accused of not properly preparing the detailed reports the government required – in fact they were 'very inadequate, very often not fully completed and moreover, inaccurate'.[118] Youth Aliyah could only plead lack of time and the exigency of the situation. As legitimate as this explanation surely was, it offered scant consolation to the over-worked administrators whom government bureaucrats were confronting about shoddy reporting.

To complicate matters further, those involved in the rescue were not necessarily of common mind and purpose, especially in religious matters. As Joan Stiebel, a refugee, later reflected, 'there was a competition to win souls.' Ben Helfgott remembered that 'several organizations – vied with one another to offer us care – like missionaries. Some were really very disappointed that not more attached themselves to them.'[119]

Not all religious tension, however, originated from within the organizations. In an interview with historian Martin Gilbert, Israel Taub remembered that he and a group of about 20 other survivors, all of them 'very Hassidic', were 'not satisfied with the *kashrut* in the Shelter [The Jews' Temporary Shelter in London]. We started a revolution!'[120] Then there were problems with a group of Aguda-sponsored children who refused to sit down to meals with the others on a transport, and even the rabbi could not persuade them to soften their stance.[121] These young rebels were often children who came from ultra-Orthodox homes 'in the strictest and narrowest sense, orthodox in the sense that US orthodoxy would seem a very wishy-washy sort of orthodoxy', children who were 'clearly happy in reverting to traditional Jewish observances and customs'.[122] Commendable as this surely was, it still made life difficult for the relief organizations and for the many children who did not share these convictions.

Among the refugees there was also a considerable amount of anger and bitterness towards organizations and individuals who sought to put pressure on the survivors to conform to Jewish laws and practices, an anger beyond the awareness of the competition that Stiebel and Helfgott expressed. 'I can't be religious, not after what happened to me,' admitted Fela Drybus, while Kitty Hart stated bluntly, 'all Judaism has ever done for me is destroy my life.'[123] Theirs were not isolated voices.

Dr Schonfeld and the CRREC seemed to be at the centre of much of the religious controversy, for the rabbi longed desperately to restore these children to full communion with their Jewish heritage. To him, however, this meant Orthodox observance and no other. Not only did he distrust secular Zionists, but he also had no kind words for the CBF, which nominally represented all segments of Judaism. 'We are having our rows with the Central British Fund and other major relief organizations,' he wrote to his brother Moses, 'all of whom naturally object to our existence'.[124] When the Aguda claimed credit for having formed the CRREC, the reply was prompt and defensive: not only was the council not formed 'by the Aguda or any party – it is most damaging to try and drag our non-party religious and relief work into the arena of party strife'.[125]

In another instance Rabbi Schonfeld admitted that members of the Jewish Welfare Board were excellent organizers but '*kalte Yiden*' (cold Jews) and therefore should leave religious work to the Orthodox.[126] Such altercations between Dr Schonfeld and other Jewish organizations spread to the Youth Aliyah and the Keren Hayesed, even to the CRREC's attitude toward the South African Jewish community, which it labelled 'smug' and 'incorrect in its statements'. Dr Schonfeld's conflicts with Sir Robert Waley Cohen were legendary.[127] Incredibly, despite such in-fighting, the work of rescue proceeded unabated.

Unfortunately, organizational, financial and religious problems were not the only difficulties that the people responsible for this postwar influx of refugee children into Britain faced. Although the first group from Theresienstadt was recognized for good behaviour and good manners, the press quickly reported a hard core of difficult cases in other transports. In its editorial, the *Jewish Chronicle* wrote that some children are

> near to the jungle level, for no other qualities but utter hardness mixed with animal cunning were of any use to enable them to survive. ... No one else, they imagine, has suffered as they have ... [this] has rendered them 'a real social menace', 'wild children', 'impossible to shock'.[128]

Some of these boys afterwards admitted to such behaviour. Martin S, for example, reflected in later years that he managed to survive the camps as a child by becoming 'too inhuman'.[129]

On a more sympathetic note, Mrs Lionel de Rothschild reasoned that it was 'not so much the poor physical condition of the children as their expressions. Those children had seen and experienced at eight, ten or twelve years of age, more than anybody present had, whatever their age.'[130] L. G. Montefiore, who visited the camps, acknowledged that after six years in such conditions, many 'have formed what one may call adult tastes'.[131] It was small wonder that the CBF reported that 'the boys are being more difficult than ... expected'.[132]

Not unnaturally, initially some of the children were desperately depressed, did not eat and wanted to die. Such youngsters needed not only loving care and unlimited patience but also professional counselling and, to the credit of the hostels' staff and the Jewish Refugees Committee and their planning, this help was available. Yet, for some even this was insufficient. 'They never felt we did enough,' wrote Helen Bamber who worked with Oscar Friedman in the counselling programme. 'All we could produce for them was very mediocre from their point of view. The young people did not feel that we could give them what they needed – and how could we?'[133] Kitty Hart exemplified this anger and frustration from the point of view of a camp survivor when in later years she wrote:

> What I find particularly hard to forgive is that there was no programme [for rehabilitation] even within the Jewish community. In fact, I cannot mix properly with the Jewish community because I cannot forgive this. They did not want to know what had happened to survivors.[134]

Rena Zabielak also suffered from the Jewish community's reticence. In 1946 nobody wanted to hear her story. 'We also had a war,' was her Jewish hosts' response.[135] It was an experience that most survivors shared. Ann Sore, a hidden child, has written that 'we are not like others. No one could understand our past. We, the children of the

Holocaust, had been overlooked, our words too faint to be heard …
we carried our burden in silence and alone.'[136]

As these women pointed out, what many of the survivors
desperately needed and what even the sympathetic Jewish community
was obviously often unable to provide was an understanding attitude
and a listening ear to hear of the horrific experiences that left many of
them with terrible nightmares and a great need to regain a measure of
healthy self-respect. It was an incredibly difficult time and often, for
many, it seemed there could never be a happy ending. This is a major
issue that deserves special study.

Gradually, however, with much help, many of these problems were
sorted out, though for most the nightmares continued well into their
adult lives and, for some, forever. In October 1947, two years after the
first camp survivors arrived in Britain, the *Jewish Chronicle* reported that
the majority of them were now in good physical health and so the task
of integrating them into the community could proceed with greater
dispatch. By December 1945, the Westmorland camp had already been
closed and the adolescents moved to more suitable hostels in larger
centres, such as London and Manchester. Here an effort was made to
adapt each hostel to meet the needs of the various religious factions
represented. In the end, there were nearly twenty hostels scattered
around the United Kingdom.[137] Children were by now also being
placed in private homes, as boarders, with the refugee organizations
bearing the cost.[138] In 1946 the age limit for orphaned or abandoned
refugee children allowed to enter Britain was officially raised to 18,
from the previous 17.[139] This legislation was rather late in coming, for
many of the camp survivors who entered as 'children' had exceeded
even that age.

As they matured, the majority of young people left the hostels that
had been their homes and either continued their education, entered the
work force or emigrated. The Committee for Children from the
Camps' 1951 report stated that from the 700 orphans, 93 had
emigrated, 90 were supported by relatives, while 'about 450 are in work
but still need occasional help'. 'Money played quite a part' in their
choice of work, which was perhaps not surprising given that they had

been destitute for most of their short lives and, perhaps also not surprisingly, some simply refused to take up work placements.[140] The remainder were either still at school, in vocational training (those in the ORT school were especially successful), at university, or attending a *yeshiva* (several wished to become rabbis). A few were still in hospital recovering from tuberculosis. Of these, four were 'very ill'. Three of the camp children had died, and one was 'absent'.[141]

The camp committee's report also noted that by now all the young people spoke English and that most had 'progressed on the road to normality', despite their experience of the 'suppression of every instinct except survival'. While some had 'arrived with a prejudice ... against any form of manual work', most had gradually begun to realize that 'sooner or later they must become self-supporting'. Those in places of learning had studied so diligently that they passed the London matriculation and credits in the school and higher certificate examinations. The report acknowledged that many of the adolescents had arrived in England with a 'general consciousness that they were martyrs, and that Jews in general and the Anglo-Jewish Community in particular owed them a debt,' and that while the 'virtues' of most 'are many and of a very high order, ... to lads who have successfully bamboozled and deceived the SS and the Camp Commandant, to hoodwink a Jewish Community and its Welfare Officer must seem mere child's play.'[142] Sadly, the report acknowledged that efforts to rehabilitate the boys resulted 'in certain cases in failure'.[143]

Yet the failures were surprisingly few. 'Special funds had been set aside for those who would be unable to cope with life. We assumed there would be many, but there were very, very few ... only one or two who became welfare cases,' noted the report.[144] It goes on to speak of 'their relatively excellent record – which confounded all the prophets about the probable effect of four years of prison life on adolescents'.[145] The hunger for education and a determination to succeed, rather than a welfare mentality, marked their lives, as it did those of the earlier Kindertransport refugees. 'A most striking quality about this diverse group is their affirmation of life ... and its members' ethical and spiritual involvement,' marvelled Sarah Moskovitz in her study.[146]

Much credit for the resettling and progress of the postwar transport children must be given to the excellent care most of them received on arrival in Britain. As the young people left their secure hostels or home environment for work or education, many of them were drawn to London. The Jewish Refugees Committee (JRC), as well as the boys, quickly recognized the need for a meeting place in the capital. The JRC chose Paul Yogi Mayer, a prewar German refugee youth worker, to head this new project, which was to be a meeting place in the form of a club. He believed that 'if the club was leading those boys and girls away from the horror of the camps into a personal development and realization of their potential, then the club had to be "open," i.e., encouraging local Jewish boys and especially girls to become members as well.'[147] The club, named the Primrose Club because of its location, was an immediate success and, among other activities, it organized dances, football teams, table tennis tournaments and cricket. As hoped, the club attracted many of the 1938–39 *Kinder* as well as local youth. And Mayer's programmes, plus his policy of allowing girls as members, 'accelerated the integration of the boys into British society'.[148]

Partly because they had no other family and partly because the Anglo-Jewish community was less than enthusiastic about accepting them socially, the Primrose Club fostered a strong sense of loyalty within the group. Ben Helfgott, an active member, noted many years later that 'we have gone from strength to strength. Today we are not only concerned with helping each other – but we give financial and moral help wherever required.'[149] All this was despite the survivor guilt that 'haunts even some of those who were infants at the time of the Holocaust and which seems to remain forever'.[150]

In 1958 the CBF announced that 'the time has now come ... to absorb [the special needs camp children] into the general care which we give to all the young people we brought over from the camps, the majority of whom are now self-supporting and in need of periodic assistance or advice only.'[151] Lingfield House, therefore, one of the last hostels housing postwar refugee children to remain open, closed in 1962.

It had initially been intended that the camp children would emigrate within two years of arrival in Britain and some, indeed, did so. The majority, however, remained in the United Kingdom and, when the government passed the necessary legislation, they became citizens. The last verse of a poem by Michael Etkind, who was one of 'the Boys', expresses the feelings of love and appreciation for their adopted country that characterized this 'lost generation' of European Jewry:

> You made so few demands upon my
> cunning and skill.
> You never cared if I succeeded/failed,
> loved you or not.
> England, you took me in your stride.[152]

9

IN LATER YEARS

I N 1947 the British government passed legislation that allowed
Kinder between 15 and 21 years of age, who had arrived in Britain
before the war and were now orphans, to apply for British
citizenship.[1] This offer was extended shortly thereafter to all remaining
prewar refugee children. In 1950 the same opportunity was extended
to concentration-camp and postwar refugees, and the great majority
from both groups gladly accepted the provision.

The need to share experiences with others who understood how
they felt led the now adult refugees to form various organizations,
though the time lapse between the end of the war and organizing such
associations is significant. One of the first groups, however, was the
world gathering of Holocaust survivors in 1981, at which, according to
psychiatrist Robert Krell, many of those attending were reluctant to
speak. It was not until 1991 that Krell, who had himself been hidden
as a child, witnessed a greater willingness among those who had been
hidden to identify themselves as Holocaust survivors and to share their
stories.[2] In 1983 Sarah Moskovitz organized the first child survivor
group in Los Angeles from among survivors who had immigrated to
the United States. The movement expanded to become the
International Network of Child Survivors, meeting in various cities,
including Jerusalem.[3]

The first such gathering for Kindertransport children occurred in
1985 when Vera Gissing and a few of her friends organized a reunion

for Czech *Kinder* who had been billeted in the Welsh village of Llanwrfyd Wells; 70 former students and staff came for the weekend. They presented the town with a mayoral chain of office to show their gratitude and left a plaque that reads: 'Llanwrfyd Wells, the smallest town in the land, remains for ever the greatest in our hearts.'[4]

In 1989 Bertha Leverton, a *Kind* originally from Munich, took the initiative to plan a fiftieth anniversary reunion for all 1938–39 Kindertransport children. They too commissioned a plaque, which was placed in the town of Harwich where most of them had disembarked. 'This plaque is a gesture of thanks to the town from the children for the hospitality received at that difficult time, erected by the Harwich Society for Reunion of Kindertransports to mark the 50th anniversary of their arrival.'

Not all former refugee children were anxious to attend such reunions. Susie Bradfield admitted later: 'I was not particularly keen to attend, largely because my memories of that grim journey were something I had been doing my best to forget. I remembered the fear, the uncertainty, the loneliness. ... There were too many ghosts and I did not wish to disturb them.'[5] There were others who shared her apprehensions.

Despite the reluctance of a few, the Kindertransport reunion was, however, an overwhelming success. More than 1,000 people attended and it, in conjunction with the child survivor conferences, provided stimulation for the release of autobiographies, memoirs and various studies on the *Kinder*. These gatherings, augmented by material from subsequent reunions and conferences, have contributed hitherto unknown and invaluable information related to the later lives and experiences of the unaccompanied refugee children.

Kindertransport reunion records reveal that the majority of *Kinder* stayed in Great Britain, though as many as could, especially those the Youth Aliyah sponsored, emigrated to Israel. 'We want to go to Palestine [now Israel] not to throw bombs but to do real constructive work,' said a spokesperson for one of the trainee groups that left England in 1947.[6] Approximately 25 per cent of the *Kinder* eventually left for the United States, Canada or other parts of the world.

Very few returned to their country of origin, even though there was some encouragement to do so. One exception was Werner Fisher, who believed that German refugee youths were in a unique position to make a contribution 'to help shape future relations between Germany and World Youth'. This was possible, he held, because 'German is our native tongue. Our parents once lived there as free citizens. … We do not flee and leave the country for good.'[7] There were also personal reasons for returning. Vera Gissing's foster parents offered to adopt her, but she 'wanted to go home [to Czechoslovakia]. There was no question of my staying in England.'[8] As she wrote in her autobiography, quoting from her diary: 'It will be hard … but I am young. I want to help rebuild my country.' She added, 'I could not envisage a future anywhere but in Czechoslovakia.'[9]

The CBF supplied these returning refugees with warm clothing and 75 per cent of their return fare. On seeing the destruction the war had wrought in their homeland, some of the young people returned to Britain almost immediately.[10] Others, like Vera Gissing and Joe Schlesinger, remained on the continent, idealistically hoping to contribute to the physical and moral reconstruction of Europe.[11] Both Gissing and Schlesinger, however, eventually also left, Gissing to return to England and Schlesinger to emigrate to Canada. A number of the *Kinder* returned to Europe in the course of their work, usually as translators or interpreters for an allied branch of the services, or for the United Nations. Hedy Epstein and David Goldberg, for example, were attached to the American government and served as interpreters at the Nuremberg trials.[12] Paul Sutton (Sontheimer) was still in the British army when his unit liberated Bergen-Belsen. His obituary states that he knew his father had perished in the camps and therefore it gave him 'a personal sense of retribution' to arrest Gustav Krupp, the industrialist and armaments manufacturer, and the employer of slave labour. Sutton also later served as an interpreter at Nuremberg.[13]

Some, like Jacob Spinrad who studied Jewish law at the Tree of Life College in London, were determined to return as rabbis to assist in the spiritual rebuilding of the European Jewish remnant.[14] Various non-Aryan Christians sought to bring healing to the German Church, which had so largely failed them. Several of the Barbican Mission boys became ordained ministers and at least one of them went to Africa as a medical missionary. His brother, ordained in the Church of England, became adviser to the Archbishop of Canterbury on matters of inter-faith dialogue.[15]

Only a few hundred of the 10,000 *Kinder* were reunited with parents located outside the United Kingdom, a task for which the Jewish Refugees Committee took responsibility.[16] Rabbi Schonfeld lists children who had been five, seven or one-and-a-half years old in 1939, now teenagers or preteens, going to Belgium in 1947 to join their parents.[17] This was not necessarily a happy time for the *Kinder*, parents or assisting agencies. Some children still had deep feelings of anger towards parents who, they felt, had abandoned them.[18] Others felt their parents' 'foreignness'. 'It was our saddest time', wrote Dorothy Hardisty of the RCM, 'when children went home to be miserably unhappy'.[19] Ruth remembers when her mother came to Britain after the war. 'She was a total stranger to me. I did not want to be associated with her.' Moreover, her parents served Ruth's beloved foster parents with a legal writ to get her repatriated to Germany, so Ruth was 'displaced all over again', except now she was no longer 'a frightened four-year-old but an angry, stubborn 14-year-old.' After six unhappy months, her parents allowed her to return to England where she eventually became a psychotherapist working with adolescents.[20]

Parents who had parted with a toddler or six-year-old often found it impossible, as in Ruth's experience, to accept a teenager. Kurt Fuchel also was angered by his family's attitude. 'My parents treated me, especially my mother, as if I were still seven, in a year when I was 16 or now 17, 18, whatever,' he remembered.[21]

Hugh Schramm's mother and younger brother, Hans Peter, had been evacuated from Shanghai to the United States in 1946.[22] A Swedish philanthropist paid for the middle brother, Heinz Dieter, to be flown from Sweden (where he had been sent on a children's transport) to meet his family and the Salvation Army facilitated the arrangements. Hugh arrived from Canada and the family reunited briefly in San Francisco. Sadly, like so many meetings between parents and long-separated children, it was a reunion of strangers.[23] David Lewinski's experience was rather similar. His mother had perished on the way to the camps but his father survived Auschwitz and, in 1953, David and his wife, Nora, flew to Germany for a reunion with his father, who had by now remarried. However, although they remained in contact, there was no close relationship.

Other *Kinder*, reunited with their parents, found language a formidable barrier. Hugh Schramm's mother spoke some English but his brother, Heinz Dieter, who only spoke Swedish, needed an interpreter to converse with his mother and brother.[24] Inge Sadan and her sister Bertha rushed to greet their parents. 'And then another realization dawned. They were speaking to my sister in German, and I couldn't understand a word!'[25]

Many perceived their parents' cultural and social values as 'strange and irrelevant', which the children of camp survivors found especially difficult to handle. It seemed impossible to adjust to their 'harassed, tormented and nervous parents, the mere sight of whom conjured up disagreeable associations of hostile and dangerous surroundings'.[26] As one child remarked, 'how does one relate to a mother who has been to Auschwitz? I got a different mother back.'[27] Not only were their parents strangers, but they were strangers 'broken in spirit and body, unable to respond' to their children's needs.[28] There were also some entirely unexpected reactions. Bertha Leverton, for example, remembers, 'I didn't want my [refugee] friends to know my parents had survived. I felt so guilty.'[29]

Children who had converted to Roman Catholicism faced a uniquely stressful situation. Renée would try to slip off to attend Mass on Sundays, but when her mother realized what was happening, she tore the girl's prayer book to shreds.[30]

Most *Kinder* eventually became reconciled to the strangers who were their parents and later developed an understanding, respect and 'even admiration' for them.[31] Inge Engelhard summed it up beautifully:

It was a strange experience getting to know our parents again … they were foreigners! They didn't speak English, my father wore a long coat and used a purse, and my mother counted the change she was given in a store [a teenager's sense of the appropriate!] … it was a very difficult period of adjustment all over again, but we made it, and became a loving and loved family again.[32]

Many *Kinder*, whether reunited with their parents or not, experienced deep trauma. Most experienced survivor guilt and depression. Hugo Gryn, a camp survivor, commented, 'I know that it is not my fault that I survived, but guilt is not always a rational thing.'[33] Vera Gissing, upon receiving her mother's letter of farewell, cried out to an aunt who had survived the camps, 'I should have been with her. I shouldn't have let her go through all this suffering on her own.' Whereupon her aunt chided: 'how dare you say that! Don't you realize that the knowledge that you were in safety was the only consolation, the only happiness that she and your father shared to the end?'[34] This comforted young Vera and, in response to the gentle admonition in her mother's farewell letter, 'remember your home and us, but do not grieve,' she wrote in her diary, 'I am so proud to be the daughter of such parents. … I shall try not to be sad.'[35]

Parents who survived to be reunited with youngsters whom they could not recognize and with whom they now had no rapport must undoubtedly have suffered just as intensely as did their children.

Interestingly, when Kindertransport refugees became parents, some also faced problems communicating with their children, especially in connection with their war experiences. Max Dickson attended the 1994 Kindertransport reunion in Jerusalem, as did many second-generation *Kinder*. After a meeting with both first and second-generation *Kinder*, he wrote:

This was really an eye-opener. How they felt about the way they tried to protect us, the lack of communication between us. I think this was the crux of the matter. We who always wanted them to have a better life, shield them from the agonies we went through but also, to bring all the past up again is quite a painful experience. ... Something very good should come out of all this.[36]

Relationships with people outside the family could also become difficult. Several survivors mentioned that they no longer trusted non-Jews. After all, they felt, they could never trust a Christian because the Germans were Christians, as were those who sheltered Jewish children during the war and then refused to release them to the Jewish community. Franklin Littell, a Protestant American theologian, acknowledges that the murder of 'circa six million Jews ... by baptized Christians in the heart of Christianity ... puts the credibility of contemporary Christianity to the question'.[37] It is not surprising, therefore, that for religious or other reasons, intermarriage with non-Jews was very unusual among the now adult child refugees, although it became more common among their children.

The pain of many survivors, whether hidden children, concentration camp internees or Kindertransport refugees, goes beyond an intellectual, rational assessment of culpability. One woman, for example, a camp survivor whose son had married a '*shikse*' – a derogative Yiddish term for a female Gentile – went so far as to hope, when her daughter-in-law became pregnant, that the young woman would lose the baby. 'I don't want to have grandchildren who are *Goyim*,' she confessed.[38] And William Helmreich observed, 'Is it really possible to trust a Gentile? Isn't anti-Semitism something that has been with Jews since the beginning of time? Given their own experiences, such suspicion and hostility are quite understandable.'[39]

Other *Kinder*, by contrast, expressed great appreciation for the Christians who had fostered them and for England as a Christian country that had given them asylum.[40] John Fieldsend is a case in point. His foster parents, the Cumstys, 'were a wonderful family and I was very happy there'. To this day he continues to speak of the warmth and happiness found in their home and how their influence eventually made him decide to become a Christian.[41]

Ambivalent feelings also surfaced among survivors whom Gentiles had hidden, for they might feel mistrust and resentment as well as appreciation and sometimes love. A few regularly even sent money to their benefactors, 'out of gratitude to them for their assistance'.[42] Such opposing positions may well have their roots, at least in part, in the individual's focus and on the treatment received. Sociologist Diane Wolf concludes that survivors' reactions 'are a reflection of age, personality, and culture, among other factors'.[43]

There is a close association between attitudes towards non-Jews and relationships with other minority groups. Many *Kinder* claim that their experiences served to increase their understanding of and tolerance for minority groups, so it was rather surprising to learn that Berghahn found an 'unexpectedly high' degree of antagonism towards Britain's black community among the refugees.[44] One survivor whom Helmreich interviewed in the United States, however, commented that, 'as a survivor I have a strong affinity for blacks. ... I know they did not participate in the Holocaust. ... The other factor is that blacks don't have a tradition of anti-Semitism the way whites have had for centuries.'[45]

Marrying and raising a 'family of normal, healthy children' became an ideal for many children who were happily reunited with their parents or whose foster homes were loving and affirming. Sarah Moskovitz found that even among child survivors who had no memory of loving parents or even of caring foster parents, the 'most fundamental motivations' were to have their own families.[46] William Helmreich's research confirmed this. He observed: 'Most survivors, rich or poor, religious or irreligious, educated or not educated, famous or anonymous, identified raising a nice family as their chief accomplishment.'[47] Suzanne Vromen, who focused her research on hidden children in Belgium, found that 'though they were robbed of childhood, they became competent adults' and caring parents.[48] An exceptionally strong urge for parenthood was also transferred to many survivors' children. As Eli, for example, explained:

I really feel that my raising a family has cosmic significance. I feel I have a sacred duty to have children. I feel it's the only way to respond to the evil of the Holocaust and to ensure that the death of my family and the Six Million was not in vain.[49]

Those who married within the Jewish faith in England frequently chose a spouse from among fellow refugees rather than from within the Anglo-Jewish community. Where refugees chose an Anglo-Jew, the marriage was surprisingly often looked down upon and in-law relationships were frequently strained. The cause of this tension may well have been rooted in the extended delay of the assimilation of refugees into the Anglo community, which, in turn, the age-old stereotyping of 'German Jews' as arrogant and 'Eastern Jews' as inferior perpetuated.[50] The child refugees had too frequently felt unwanted and now, as adults, they disclosed their hurt and angry feelings: 'they resented our coming'; 'we were even worse than the Goyim for them.'[51] German Jews viewed themselves as more cultured, more cosmopolitan, and saw British Jews as 'obsessed' with religion and 'orthodox in a strangely narrow-minded way'.[52] Marion Berghahn believes that these cultural differences 'reflect a genuine and substantial ethnic differentiation between German and English Jews' and thinks that this dichotomy will likely continue for some time to come.[53]

This tension within the Jewish community was reflected in the refugees' attitudes toward the non-Jewish British population as well. For example, marriage with Gentiles was unusual for survivors, but more common among their children. While not readily open to marriage with British non-Jews, most of the *Kinder*, especially the younger ones growing up in English homes, felt accepted and comfortable in England. They became British subjects as soon as they were qualified to do so. Many, and not only those who served in the armed forces during the war, Anglicized their names and tried to emulate English ways. Bertha Leverton, for example, laughingly remembers that her greatest wish as a young person was to become 'more English than the English'.[54] Some refugee leaders, such as the confirmed Anglophile Rabbi Dr Schonfeld, vigorously rejected marriage to non-Jews but nevertheless nurtured a love for all things

English. One may recall that he even went so far as to teach refugee children *en route* to the United Kingdom polite forms of English usage and patriotic British songs.[55]

Any assimilation into the British community, however tenuous, created a source of division within the Anglo-Jewish community. While Professor S. Brodetsky, the Zionist president of the Board of Deputies, for example, saw assimilation as 'an abandonment of a [Jewish] sense of history', Anthony de Rothschild believed that assimilation was not only the 'civic ideal' but also the 'true fulfilment of the Jewish ideal at its best'.[56] Ursula Rosenfeld agreed with the latter view. As she remembers, 'I was as entirely accepted as everyone else. And I gradually felt that I had somewhere I belonged. ... I like the British way of life.'[57] Rosenfeld served as a magistrate in the city of Manchester and she and her husband were presented to the queen. 'When I look back now', she commented, 'strangely I see a similarity between my fierce defence of the British way of life and my father's fierce defence of the German way of life.'[58]

Many *Kinder* and other child survivors, however, had more ambivalent experiences than Ursula Rosenfeld did of the acceptance they so greatly desired. Too often they felt like outsiders, stigmatized by their experiences and unsure of their personal identity. In later years, this question of identity frequently resurfaced, even among those who had apparently adjusted well to their environment. Some refugees questioned whether a Jew could 'ever become English', though most felt that it was possible to become 'British' – a more ethnically-inclusive term that allowed one to be different, 'accepted as a person in [one's] own right'.[59] One boy touchingly revealed his ambiguity:

> I came to England at the age of three-and-a-half. I was brought up in the Midlands. I went to a Christian school. I was no longer considered German. I was not considered English. I certainly wasn't Jewish – my Jewish background wasn't nurtured. I am neither German nor English; neither Gentile nor Jewish. I would like to know what is my identity.[60]

Among those who were either Christians before arriving in Britain, or who converted to Christianity while in England, the question of identity could become increasingly complex. John Fieldsend, for example, gladly converted and yet, he remembers, 'I never forgot that I was Jewish, but something in me died.' After receiving counselling, his 'innate Jewishness burst through the barrier of suppressed memory' and he found his identity as a Messianic Jew.[61] Others, like Peter Schneider, 'never disclaimed his Jewish background; all his life he felt as much a Jew as a Christian.'[62] Among child survivors, especially among the hidden children, a few deliberately chose Christianity and rejected Judaism. Sometimes this was partly because of fear of renewed persecution, sometimes because their 'hiders' had been much-loved Christians and occasionally because Christianity 'provided a rightful place among humanity'.[63] Simone, who had been hidden and baptized in a convent, decided to remain a Catholic after the war, despite her family's strong objections. 'She feels her Jewish origins are stigmatizing. In fact, she has never been able to tell her children and grandchildren about them. She thinks it would be dangerous for her grandchildren to know about their Jewish roots,' writes interviewer Suzanne Vromen in her comprehensive study of hidden children in Belgium.[64]

Vromen, by contrast, came across some able to integrate their Christianity with their Jewishness and, like John Fieldsend, perceive themselves as belonging to both communities. This was considerably easier for those whose entire families had perished in the Holocaust, for there were then no relatives to object strongly to any Christian orientation, no one to recite *Kaddish* (the prayer for the dead) with all the attending grief and ostracism. 'The common thread between the experiences of the hidden children who remained Catholic,' Vromen concludes, 'is their rejection by Jewish relatives after the war. In a sense, they acquired a pariah status.'[65]

Even for those who returned to their Jewish roots, the transition could be slow and very difficult, especially for children who were hidden at a very young age. Vromen points out that Christian holy objects, such as medals, pictures of saints and rosaries had become a way of life. 'The children had become attached to these holy objects and felt protected by them. ... Some confrontations [with parents or relatives] were abrupt and painful. ... It was difficult to flip identities again so rapidly and give up instantly what one had been taught to consider significant and comforting.'[66]

When it seemed that love might be withheld because of an immediate inability to give up what had been 'significant and comforting' or for any other reason, the child suffered intensely. Lorraine expressed this so poignantly. 'Did I need love? Very desperately ... I am left with a legacy that I am oversensitive ... and still in desperate need to be loved. ... I'm still very insecure, and I'm an old lady by now.'[67]

Education was often seen as a means of assimilating into British culture and, among the *Kinder*, especially those placed in university centres, the numbers attending university and obtaining secondary school diplomas were far higher than in the general population. In Cambridge, for example, 'a great many of the boys and girls who were refugees got Leverhulme Scholarships and were able to study at the [London School of Economics, which had been evacuated to Cambridge].' Of the 2,000 refugee children in that area, 77 became 'university teachers and academics, professors, fellows of the Royal Society, judges, et cetera', while 31 received teaching positions in technical colleges, according to Greta Burkill, the socially active wife of a Cambridge don.[68] Burkill is credited with 'somehow' always finding finances for degree courses for the Cambridge *Kinder*, and doing 'everything in her power to give him or her the best possible education'.[69] This paid huge dividends.

Kinder have won some of the world's most prestigious awards. Walter Kohn, with a fellow researcher, received the Nobel Prize for Chemistry in 1998. Arno Penzias, who arrived in England with his younger brother as an unaccompanied six-year-old and later emigrated to the United States with his parents, was awarded a joint Nobel Prize for Physics in 1978 for his 'Discovery of Cosmic Microwave Background Radiation'.[70] The stories of success, not only in the professions, academe, science and business, but in other areas as well, are truly remarkable.[71] One boy became a successful Newmarket jockey. Joe Schlesinger became an award-winning senior news journalist and executive director of the Canadian Broadcasting Corporation (CBC) television news, while Lord Alf Dubs was made a Labour Party 'working peer' and appointed as parliamentary under-secretary of state for Northern Ireland.[72] 'We just had to succeed', acknowledged one respondent, a survivor.[73]

From his interviews with survivors who eventually emigrated to the United States, William Helmreich concludes that those who went on to lead successful and useful lives displayed ten general traits or qualities. These were flexibility, courage, assertiveness, tenacity, optimism, intelligence, group consciousness, an ability to distance themselves, the capacity to assimilate the knowledge that they had survived and to find meaning in life.[74] Although Helmreich's interviews were largely with concentration camp survivors, his findings would seem generally applicable to *Kinder* as well.

A sense of gratitude at having been spared the fate that befell their families ties in closely with these stories of success. Over and over again someone voiced sentiments such as, 'I don't take my life for granted. … [It] was a gift so I don't waste it.' Or 'I feel lucky that I got the opportunity to live.'[75] To those who have become parents the enormity of their own parents' sacrifice in sending them to safety has become very real. 'When I became a mother I often used to imagine what a heartache our parents suffered having to send us away not knowing where to and whether we would ever meet again.'[76] When asked whether they would do the same for their own children should a similar situation ever arise, the response was invariably slow in coming, but for the most part, it was in the affirmative. 'Yes, if it would save their lives as mine was saved.'[77] Only occasionally does a respondent feel that it would have been better to have perished as a family.[78]

Gratitude to Britain for having offered a safe haven is a very common response from the now adult *Kinder*, as well as from camp survivors. As Bertha Leverton wrote on the occasion of the fiftieth anniversary of the Kindertransport movement: 'We think of the tremendous effort made on our behalf by total strangers of all denominations, of a government moved by our plight.'[79] In the mid-1960s various Jewish refugee organizations launched a 'Thank-you Britain Fund'. They raised £90,000 and decided to use the proceeds for 'research and lectures in the field of human studies'. On presenting the money to the British Academy, Sir Hans Krebs said:

> No sum of money can adequately and appropriately express our gratefulness to the British people. Perhaps the only proper way for us to try and repay the debt is to make a continuous effort to be useful citizens ... fully identifying ourselves with the communal life of the country and offering our services whenever the occasion arises.[80]

At another public acknowledgement of their appreciation in June 1999, the *Kinder* unveiled a plaque in the House of Commons that reads: 'In Deep Gratitude to the People and Parliament of the United Kingdom for Saving the Lives of 10,000 Jewish and other Children who fled to this Country from Nazi Persecution on the Kindertransport 1938–1939.'

Not everyone shared this deep sense of gratitude. Gerti, whom three elderly ladies who never really showed her any affection sponsored, concluded that they regarded her 'as their way to heaven' and that she therefore felt she had paid her dues.[81] Another woman whom Berghahn quoted expressed a similar reaction: 'England and I are even,' she declared. 'They have opened their doors for me, but I have enriched them.'[82] Such attitudes, however, seem to be very much in the minority. As the Kindertransport reunions, written memoirs and recorded interviews reflect, the overwhelming majority of refugee children, however painful their own experiences may have been, express deep gratitude and appreciation for having been saved from the worst aspects of the Holocaust. Sigmund Gestetner of the Board of Deputies summed up the relief agencies' attitude:

> Thanks to the openheartedness of people in this country, we were able to bring this large number of children over in such a

short time. The response of the Anglo-Jewish community was not as great as we anticipated and we were more than grateful to accept the hospitality of those true Christians who felt it their duty to save these persecuted Jewish children.[83]

As the *Kinder*'s attitudes to Britain differed, so too did their attitudes to Germany and the Germans, especially to older Germans who might have been involved in the anti-Jewish persecutions. How much did the average German know about what was happening to his or her Jewish friend, neighbour, doctor or dentist who suddenly disappeared? Did no one notice vandalized synagogues or confiscated stores and shops? As Adam LeBor and Roger Boyes put it, 'few knew everything, millions knew something. ... It was not necessary to be aware of gas chambers in Auschwitz to see that German Jews ... were being treated systematically like animals.'[84] Why then was there so little protest? Certainly, there were people who offered resistance, including the White Rose Group of Munich university students, some members of the Church and even some members of the military,[85] yet historians Matthew Hughes and Chris Mann conclude that 'the vast majority of Germans were indifferent to the fate of Jews who had been around them until recently.'[86] However, indifference and being a bystander involve a measure of implication, so if one accepts Hughes and Mann's findings, then the suspicion many *Kinder* felt towards older Germans appears to have been wholly justified.

In their antipathy to Germans and Germany, some *Kinder* and other child survivors went so far as to boycott all things German, including household appliances, food products and cars, and to feel an aversion to Germans *per se*, not only to the older generation.[87] Most remained 'cautious' about Germany and Germans, while a few felt no resentment at all. 'Life is too short to carry the heavy burden of hate.'[88] Lory Cahn expressed her reactions with great poignancy:

> Little by little, I said, what am I going to do? Am I going to hate everything that has to do with Germans? ... I realized that if I wanted to hate ... I would not be able to live a normal life, and

definitely not a happy life ... nobody should ever, ever, forget what they have done to us. But I don't want to hate for the rest of my life.[89]

The research of child therapist Sarah Moskovitz also reveals that among survivors, 'there is a general absence of conscious anger or bitterness toward Germans. ... Perhaps there is the ultimate humane lesson learned ... that hating an entire group can lead to the creation of yet more innocent victims such as themselves.'[90]

As the daughter of survivors living in America, Deborah Oppenheimer reflected on the ambivalence many *Kinder* felt towards Germany and the Germans.

My parents didn't want to perpetuate the German culture. They did not teach us German. They boycotted German products and wouldn't think of buying a German car. Yet we grew up on German nursery rhymes, children's songs and books. ... And whenever my parents didn't want us to understand anything, or when they were angry with us, they spoke in German. In a house of three children, there was a lot of German spoken. ... For first generation Americans, we turned out awfully German.[91]

Yet, in one aspect at least, writes John Dippel,

Hitler won a victory in spite of his military defeat: he made Germany and the rest of the continent free of Jews ... in Germany today the Jew is no longer at home, no longer a citizen among other citizens, to the extent that he once was. For better or worse, they were thrust onto other worlds, to forge new souls.[92]

Many *Kinder* and survivors have visited Germany and Austria for holidays or to see their old homes, but very few have returned there to live. The need to see their former homes seems to stem from the 'vaguely reassuring feeling that they can walk through their hometown with some semblance of safety, a privilege denied them during those horrible years,' or 'I went because I just wanted to convince myself that all these stories and places which I thought about, I truly remembered rather than fabricated.'[93]

Truly remembering their heritage did not, to a greater or lesser extent, prevent them assimilating into non-Jewish British society, but by and large many of them still felt most comfortable with their coreligionists. Not many were convinced Zionists, but most expressed pride in their Jewish history, traditions and culture.[94] Vera Schaufeld put this succinctly:

I am not religious, I don't have any religious beliefs, I'm an agnostic, and I've never felt any religious need to be Jewish, but I'm a hundred per cent sure of my Jewish identity. And the fact that my parents died because they were Jewish, made me very strongly want to remain Jewish.[95]

As in Vera Schaufeld's case, this sense of Jewishness did not generally translate into a renewed religious interest and the question of God's presence (or absence) in their experience was rarely raised among the *Kinder* or other child survivors. Even Orthodox Rabbi Schonfeld gave no indication that he agonized over this matter.[96] As his son pointed out, he would never have questioned God over this matter. Dr Schonfeld would have maintained that 'we cannot challenge God's ways or understand his intentions, echoing that Talmudic Rabbi's view that "All is for the best". He could neither justify nor criticize – only accept the will of God.'[97]

Not everyone could accept his or her experience as the will of God. One respondent, for example, began attending synagogue because 'we have to forgive God for what happened to us'. Others admitted to losing their faith completely in the face of what happened to their families in Europe.[98] 'If you ... had seen your father and your mother shot before your eyes, would you still believe in an omnipotent and merciful God?' asked one lad.[99] One woman habitually dropped a bit of milk into her chicken soup, defying the rules of *kashrut*, saying, 'this is to punish you, God, for what you have done.'[100] Eli, the son of survivors, thought it blasphemous to give the traditional answer that human beings should not question God's ways. 'I have found that answer very hard to accept. I don't think that someone who lives in the twentieth century can be satisfied with it.' His questions led him to study philosophy at university and into an active search for answers.[101] The majority of *Kinder* and other child survivors, however, seem to have given the matter of God's involvement only a passing thought. Raul Hilberg sums up the various responses when he writes:

> Although many victims rediscovered and embraced half-forgotten Jewish traditions, a number of others attempted to jettison precisely those customs as ballast. A few changed their religion, detaching themselves from fellow victims as much as possible. Yet in their private lives the Christians of Jewish background could not always find new anchors. ... Only one certainty might arise in their thoughts: the recollection of humiliation and anxiety was not to be passed on to the next generation.[102]

John Fieldsend has been so successful in finding 'new anchors' as a Messianic Jew and in passing this self-assurance on to his children that one of his sons has reverted to the Jewish family name of Feige, but this seems to be the exception.[103]

According to a study by Reeve Robert Brenner, *The Faith and Doubt of Holocaust Survivors*, children from an Orthodox background seem to have come out of their experience with less trauma than others and Rabbi Dr Solomon Schonfeld's papers substantiate this conclusion.[104] Sarah Moskovitz concludes that 'religion was undoubtedly a stabilizing force' in the lives of the child survivors in her study, regardless of any particular religious orientation, and feels that this aspect deserves more attention.[105] Rabbi Schonfeld would agree.

Being a child refugee had psychological as well as sociological and religious implications. Some struggled with an inordinate fear of anti-

Semitism, going so far as to send their children to Roman Catholic schools in an effort to hide their Jewishness in case of a resumption of pogroms or other forms of persecution.[106] Many suffer from nightmares and 'bad memories'. They feel unexplainable 'pain', anger and a sense of 'loss and emptiness'. Trying to come to terms with their parents' deaths might leave them in a protracted state of mourning and they are likely to suffer from an inability to establish deep personal relationships through fear of being separated from someone they love.[107] The memory of being separated from their parents seems to be the main cause of the emotional trauma. 'The trauma accompanying ... separation from their families is very deep – perhaps the most difficult trauma to cure,' writes Dina Wardi.[108] Aaron Haas agrees. 'People who were children ... during the war appear to have more internal obstacles to establishing emotional ties with others. ... The younger a child when persecuted and separated from parents, the higher is his/her risk of later personality decomposition.'[109] That many of the *Kinder* were very young when they were uprooted may account for the higher suicide rate among refugees as a whole than among the general British public.[110] However, since no separate statistics for Kindertransport suicides are available, this is pure conjecture. Also, rather surprisingly, Sarah Moskovitz found no suicides at all among the postwar child survivors of her study.[111]

Many *Kinder*, as well as hidden and camp children, grieved the loss of their childhood and lamented the need to become mature and independent at an age when most youngsters could still be carefree and reliant on their parents. This was especially true of an older sibling made responsible for a younger child, either by their parents upon leaving or in their foster home. Yet, there was also 'powerful survival value ... in looking out for others'. Judith Stern, for example, interned at 15, 'took the courage to go on only when she remembered her mother's charge to look after her sister'.[112] Still, as the dramatist Tom Stoppard has Herzen say in *The Coast of Utopia*, 'a child's purpose is to be a child ... later is too late.'[113]

As Robert Krell has pointed out, 'it is widely known that survivors overwhelmingly have avoided seeking help from any type of mental health professionals, largely because of fear that they will again be "categorized and be made to feel inferior".'[114] Bertha Bracey noted as early as 1942 that, despite their reluctance, 'the increasing incidence of mental disorder among refugees was causing concern to all the caseworking organizations ... [and] it was clear that the problem was a serious one.' A 'rest home' for these individuals was consequently proposed,[115] but it is not known how many of the refugees requiring this type of assistance were *Kinder*, though anecdotal evidence seems to indicate that the number was very small.

Old age, however, seems to bring back many painful memories. As Eli, whose parents were survivors, commented: 'as my parents get older I'm beginning to sense that everything isn't quite in order, that what they went through just can't be suppressed. ... The past comes through in subtle ways now. Uncertainty about the future. ... My parents feel they can't be too secure.'[116] Helen's mother will occasionally 'fall into one of those deep, seemingly bottomless depressions that terrified me as a child'.[117]

Increasingly, there were those who could not deal with these 'bottomless depressions' and so, in 1987, the CBF opened another Jewish mental health centre in London to provide support for survivors of all ages.[118] Fred Dunstan, who worked with refugee children, wrote that, on the whole, how they coped 'depended on the intelligence, education, knowledge of English, and the capacity of each child to adapt to their different situation'.[119] Most coped remarkably well. Ruth Michaelis, a *Kind* who became a psychotherapist and worked especially with former Kindertransportees, wrote that she believed

three issues ... made a big difference to how the individual child was able to deal with the Kindertransport experience. ... [These were] the amount of stability in the family prior to separation (and many families suffered horrendous persecution), the developmental stage of the child at the time, and most importantly whether they continued to have contact with someone who represented a link with the past, the old familiar world.[120]

The adult *Kind* largely reflected the experiences of the younger refugee.

Sharing an experience can often bring healing and many *Kinder*, as well as other child survivors, have found that reunions such as those the Kindertransport associations and child survivors' conferences organized are not only therapeutic but also soul satisfying. They provide the occasion to tell their stories to people who listen with understanding, thus forging that important link with the past that Michaelis mentioned.[121] Many have found it a relief to share their survivor guilt or childhood feelings of anger toward parents who had 'abandoned' them. At these reunions some share their experiences more openly than others. While interviewing Holocaust survivors who emigrated to the United States, Dr Helmreich encountered some who not only shared their stories gladly but who also 'found release in public speaking and writing'. They recorded their stories on tape and volunteered to speak in schools and synagogues.[122]

This is true also of *Kinder* such as Rudi Lowenstein of Winnipeg and Bertha Leverton of London. Mrs Leverton, although in her eighties, still travelled widely, not only in Britain but also on the continent, in Israel and even in South Africa. Others, as noted, speak of their experiences reluctantly or not at all.[123] As the survivors age, however, there seems to be a greater openness to share. Rozalia, who came to England as one of Rabbi Schonfeld's children at the age of 14, saw terrible things in the camps. For years she tried to bury them, 'to hide it very deep inside'. She did not speak about the Holocaust at all until 1980, when she admitted, 'I have to live with this memory. I dream about it. It's in me and I really want history to know about it.'[124]

Whether they speak about their experiences or not, it seems safe to say that all child refugees will, in Bertha Leverton's words, 'never forget all that we had and lost, all that should have been and never was and all the grit and determination necessary at a tender age to reshape our lives.'[125] Yet, remarkably, Sarah Moskovitz, exploring the adult lives of child survivors, found that:

> Despite the severest deprivation in early childhood, these people are neither living a greedy, me-first style of life, nor are

they seeking gain at the expense of others. None express the idea that the world owes them a living for all they have suffered. On the contrary, most of their lives are marked by an active compassion for others.[126]

It must be emphasized that these refugee children were neither superhuman nor extraordinarily gifted, but ordinary children that an accident of history had uprooted. William Helmreich writes with insight:

The story of the survivors is one of courage, and strength, of people who are a living proof of the indomitable will of human beings to survive and of their tremendous capacity for hope. It is not a story of remarkable people. It is a story of just how remarkable people can be.[127]

10

EPILOGUE

B Y 1950 most of the *Kinder* and other child survivors were in their teens or older, and the organizations that had brought them to Great Britain were being dismantled. Sir Alexander Maxwell of the Central Committee for Refugees wrote to Sir Herbert Emerson as early as 28 September 1948 that, since responsibility for all destitute refugees and those unable to look after themselves had now been transferred from local authorities to the National Assistance Board, there was no good reason why refugee committees should not wind down by March 1950,[1] and most of them had done so.

The Refugee Children's Movement had already closed its files in December 1948, because of financial difficulties, and also relinquished its lease of Bloomsbury House. The Jewish Refugees Committee and the Christian Council took responsibility at that time for any minors who remained in the care of the RCM.[2] When these latter organizations also disbanded, the CBF, renamed World Jewish Relief and organized initially only as a fund-raising organization, now assumed responsibility for all refugee children who were still minors or attending school, as well as those unable to function in society for whatever reason. There were surprisingly few *Kinder* or even child survivors in need of long-term assistance, yet the need did remain. In Manchester, for example, a new hostel housing 18 to 20 young people opened its doors in February 1950, partly in response to the closing of Laski House, which had sheltered adolescents and 'difficult' children.[3]

There was a very small minority of children who were too damaged emotionally ever to live independently and Jewish voluntary agencies took responsibility for this group as well as for those incapacitated through illness.[4]

There were also a few 'difficult' children, but nowhere is it fully explained why they were classified as such. It is known that several became involved with the law, and that the Home Office had revoked several certificates of naturalization without explanation.[5] Sarah Moskovitz found that among the child survivors in her study, there was only one person 'who came of age during the 1960s' who had been involved with drugs, and only one 'who lived for a time outside the law'.[6] In the context of the total number of refugee children, these numbers are insignificant.

What is truly remarkable, however, is the 'magnificent ability' and energy of the great majority of these uprooted children to rebuild their lives. They succeeded in overcoming horrendous memories, bitter loss and lack of parental love, care and the security of a home.[7] What Suzanne Vromen writes so succinctly about hidden children would apply to most child refugees. 'They were cheated out of their childhoods, suffering losses and sacrifices impossible to evaluate.'[8] With such a scarred background, one could have projected that these children would all become dysfunctional, but that was not so. The 'social and familial success' of children from both waves of the children's exodus have amazed critics. A disproportionate number entered the helping professions. The German philosopher Nietzsche once commented that 'what does not kill us makes us stronger'. This is not to say that there were no wounds. At the inaugural address for the Belgian Hidden Children Association, the speaker noted:

The wounds recalled were not those of bombardments or earthquakes, but injuries to the soul. ... These ex-hidden children talked about the separation from their parents, the entrance into another milieu in which the religion, the customs, and even the language were often different. They talked about fears, hidden tears, forbidden prayers, also about a conversion not always forced, and the guilt of having called 'mom' some-body who was not their mother.[9]

Thousands of Kindertransport children who preceded the second wave of refugees also experienced such 'injuries to the soul'.

Unlike the concentration camp survivors, many *Kinder* did not initially think of themselves as Holocaust survivors. After all, they had neither been incarcerated in a camp (except for those interned briefly on the Isle of Man) nor suffered the awfulness associated with forced migrations or death marches. David Lewinski, for example, saw himself simply as a refugee fortunate enough to be sent to Canada with a group of British school children at a time when no Kindertransport youngsters were being admitted to that country.[10]

Hidden children were also cautious about calling themselves survivors.[11] Only in 1979, when amateur film makers Myriam Abramowicz and Esther Hoffenberg made a documentary, *As If It Were Yesterday*, about the Committee for the Defence of Jews, was the plight of the hidden children in Belgium brought to public attention. Suzanne Vromen praised the film highly and commented that it 'remains to this day the most historically significant and compre-hensive film about the rescuers'.[12] The film led to the eventual formation in 1991 in New York City of the first international gathering of children hidden during the Second World War. Thus, the hidden children were finally recognized as a distinct category of victims.

Even before this, however, the American Gathering of Jewish Holocaust Survivors clarified the ambiguity of who was a survivor of the Holocaust by issuing the following statement:

Generally speaking we define a Holocaust Survivor as a person who due to Nazi persecution had to leave home between 1933 and 1945, irrespective if the person was or was not in a concentration camp, Ghetto or in hiding or not [*sic*]. In the case of the Kindertransport children, we believe that the majority of them left after *Kristallnacht* which is usually considered the beginning of the Holocaust.[13]

Just how many unaccompanied children were actually brought to Great Britain is difficult to determine. According to its records, the Refugee Children's Movement brought in 9,354 children. Youth Aliyah sponsored approximately 500 for its agricultural programmes and 431 arrived under the auspices of the Inter-Aid Committee.[14] If to these we add those whom Rabbi Schonfeld and the CRREC sponsored, both before and after the war, the number rises to somewhere around 12,000 children, though figures from the various organizations may overlap. The number also may be even higher than 12,000. Norman Bentwich placed it at 13,000 in 1943, which was before the postwar influx of hidden children and concentration-camp survivors.[15]

Sadly, had the war broken out only one day later, another transport from Czechoslovakia would have arrived in England with its young passengers. Vera Gissing's two cousins were on that train. 'It wasn't until years later,' she wrote, 'that I found out they were already seated on the train, ready to depart, but that was the day war broke out, and the train was not allowed to leave … none of the children on that transport, including our cousins, survived the war.'[16]

The organizations that brought these children out of Europe have been subjected to intense scrutiny from both within and outside their own ranks. The Quaker Charles Carter, for example, gives due credit to the Friends' 'unique and splendid' effort but deplores 'our numerous lamentable errors'.[17] Other refugee organizations would doubtless say the same of their own efforts. Yet, given the circumstances under which they laboured, the emergencies they faced in connection with the huge numbers of children who had to be moved and placed, usually at very short notice, the financial crises that on more than one occasion threatened to overwhelm them and, perhaps above all, the differences in the rescue organizations' ideologies, one must conclude, along with Charles Carter, that the relief efforts on behalf of children were indeed 'unique and splendid' despite the 'numerous and lamentable errors'. Of these 'errors,' possibly the most lamentable was the high level of contention and discord displayed within the Jewish community and its relief organizations. Yet, even this did not prevent the rescue of thousands of children.

The Anglo-Jewish community's response to the child refugees is complex and difficult to assess. Comments to the effect that the community gave generously of its money but not of its hospitality are commonplace. It is beyond doubt that the Jewish community was more than generous with its wealth, for it is estimated that upwards of six million pounds sterling were donated to relief organizations at a time when working-class wages could be as low as £5 a month.[18] Not everyone in the community, however, thought that even the donations were as generous as they could have been. Ben Moss, for example, writing in the *Jewish Chronicle*, dismissed the avowed concern and generosity of his coreligionists as 'just cant and hypocrisy'.[19]

The Anglo-Jewish community has been criticized more harshly for its lack of hospitality than for its lack of financial generosity. In 1939 it had approximately 350,000 members, which equates to roughly 87,000 households. Surely these could have fostered all 10,000 *Kinder*? Yet, at a Board of Deputies meeting, Jacques Cohen declared that 'only about 1,000 Jewish homes had offered hospitality to the children brought [to Britain] since 1933 by the Refugee Children's Movement.'[20] Cohen's argument, however, fails to take into consideration the total number of refugees, adults as well as children, for some of these were financially independent and, at least to some degree, the Jewish community was helping many of them. In 1943 Norman Bentwich estimated that approximately 55,000 adults and 13,000 children had come from Germany and Austria, and about 10,000 from Czechoslovakia,[21] and this excludes those from Poland and other European countries. In the light of these statistics and the relative poverty of many British Jews, it seems unfair to castigate the Anglo-Jewish community, yet the chief rabbi is recorded as having said that the 'feebleness of the response fills one with despair' and had wondered how to 'rouse London Jewry from its apathy.'[22]

One segment of Jewish society that escaped overt criticism of any kind but that has also not received its deserved recognition is the network of women's organizations that served the refugee children and took responsibility for most of the day-to-day operations. Hadassah (a Zionist organization), the Women's Appeal Committee, the Federation of Women Zionists, and the B'nai B'rith Care Committee for Refugee Children, to name but a few, as well as countless synagogue sister-hoods, worked together in greater harmony than their male-dominated counterparts and were, arguably, the mainstay on which the happiness and well-being of the refugee children largely depended. For example, in 1947, which was a difficult postwar year in Great Britain, WIZO (Women's International Zionist Organization) appealed to the women of Britain to raise £100,000 for relief purposes and they did.[23] Such was the wonderful spirit of concern and generosity among Anglo-Jewish women!

People in Europe who hid Jews during the Nazi era, especially Jewish children, also embody a spirit of selfless concern. Under-standably, recognition of these non-Jewish individuals was not a pressing issue at the end of the war, but when the organization Hidden Children first met in 1991, some 46 years after the end of the conflict, it was felt that those who had hidden these children and thus saved their lives should receive appropriate recognition. It is important enough to bear repeating that hiding a Jewish person, even a child, could have tragic consequences, such as torture or even death, not only for the rescuer but also for his or her entire family. This was especially true in Poland. Yet, records show that more than 6,000 Polish Gentiles have been honoured for saving Jewish lives. Martin Gilbert records the names and stories of numerous Poles who were executed with their families for just such an act of compassion. In one case, which Gilbert describes, fifteen people were shot for trying to save three Jews.[24]

Despite the grave danger and potential cost, Rabbi Schonfeld and others found that hundreds of children had been hidden, not only in Poland but also in other parts of Europe. In his 1946 report he mentions that 'the Council's Prague office ... succeeded in rescuing Jewish orphans from Hungary and other East European countries.' Elsewhere he mentions the Netherlands and France.[25] Suzanne Vromen devotes an entire section of her study to how Belgian nuns hid youngsters from the Nazis.[26] The record shows that thousands of Jewish children were hidden across Nazi occupied Europe, and some for several years.[27] The reasons for such altruistic courage can perhaps best be summed up as predominantly a 'sense of decency' closely linked to humanitarianism and 'truly deep and pure religious feelings'.[28]

Already in the 1970s a serious search for non-Jews who saved Jewish lives was quietly underway on a small scale, initiated primarily by individuals, usually survivors, such as Judge Moshe Bejski. The Holocaust museum and archive in Jerusalem, Yad Vashem, conferred formal recognition on these 'hiders', naming them the Righteous Among the Nations. Martin Gilbert writes that by the year 2000, more than 19,000 such rescuers had been honoured, while more than 800 were being identified as righteous each year.[29] Who were these people? The nuns and priests of Belgium have already been identified as have other religious communities across Europe.[30] David Prital tells of being hidden by Baptists, a Protestant denomination, who viewed him as a visitor sent by God.[31] Yet there were also hundreds of ordinary families and individuals in all walks of life who risked their lives on a daily basis to save Jewish lives, especially those of children. Martin Gilbert expresses it so well:

> When the Holocaust is finally beyond living memory, the desire to remember and honour those who extended a helping hand will remain. This is a question not only of recognizing individual bravery, but of providing a reminder that it is possible for human beings, in situations where civilized values are being undermined, to find the strength of character and purpose to resist the evil. ... Long after the Righteous of the Second World War have died, they will serve as models of the best in human behavior and achievement to which anyone may choose to aspire.[32]

The story of the refugee children's transports would be incomplete without this recognition of the Righteous Among the Nations. Unfortunately, as one woman lamented, there were exceptions. 'I am so sorry I cannot give you any Righteous in my life. In my life, there have not been any Righteous Gentiles.'[33] This is the sad truth underlying much of the history of the Holocaust.

By the end of the war, long before the matter of recognizing the hidden children's rescuers became important, indeed before the hidden children's existence was general knowledge, the Jewish community had not only rallied to the cause of refugees but had also actively searched for means of mitigating the suffering of their coreligionists on the continent. Yet, relief workers reported that Jews in the camps harboured very bitter feelings towards British Jews, whom they considered to be living in the lap of luxury, for what they perceived as indifference to their plight.[34] The truth was that conditions in many parts of Britain were hardly short of desperate. There were crippling taxes, massive bombing damage to businesses, public buildings, people's homes and public utilities, severe rationing and a worrisome lack of many foods and other commodities. Despite this punishing regimen, the Anglo-Jewish community made many offers to share even such restricted items as tinned foods and soap with their beleaguered coreligionists on the continent. In 1947, the British government permitted its people to use their precious ration stamps to send parcels to Europe. It was a sacrifice many Jewish families made gladly and with great generosity.

Having said all this, the seriousness of the question that has surfaced regarding the Anglo-Jewish community's response to refugee children must be seen in its proper context rather than simply dismissed, though agreement on this issue will probably never be achieved. Despite much ambivalence, it seems evident that the Jewish community, for all its many faults and failures, deserves kudos and not harsh criticism for its generous response to refugees, especially to children, during a very difficult time in history.

It is imperative to remember that the Jewish community in the British Isles had itself experienced anti-Semitism in the recent past. The 1930s were replete with reports of discrimination and anti-Jewish agitation by labour organizations. Yet, when the need was greatest, the government and people of Britain, including the Jewish community, made possible a relief effort that saved thousands of Jewish children.

More could certainly have been done, and if Britain's doors had been opened earlier and with fewer restrictions, an additional unknown number of children might have reached safety together with their parents. It remains a fact, however, that the United Kingdom accepted more refugees than any other Western nation. While the American Congress vetoed a bill to allow entry to unaccompanied Jewish children, Britain's parliament offered hospitality to as many as the refugee agencies could care for. In their thousands, the people of Britain opened their homes and often their hearts to the 'strangers within their gates', and many millions of pounds sterling were donated without any thought of reimbursement. The prophecy of Mr Logan, MP, when addressing parliament in 1938, had been fulfilled, for by 'doing the things that [were] morally right', the country had indeed achieved something 'worthy of the name of the British nation'.[35]

Doing the 'morally right' thing had not been the response of the Western world in general. The refusal of Canada and the United States to accept any *Kinder* apart from those already on quota lists is a disgrace beyond apprehension.[36] Erich Loewy, the victim of such refusals, writes:

> I personally remember consulates telling my family and friends that American 'quotas were full', only to find out many years later that the US quota had never been filled except for one year; in fact, from 1933 to 1942, only 45 per cent of the quotas were actually used. During this entire time, except for regular quota admissions with their families, the United States allowed only 240 children into the country, and those were charged to the quota.[37]

A few South and Central American countries allowed entry for a selected number of children whose parents were already in the country. The shame of anti-Semitism vented even on innocent children remains a blot on humanity. Leonhard Friedrich, a German Quaker, wrote in a paper relating his own experience in Buchenwald that 'if ordinary, decent, thinking people had come to grips with the anti-Semitism which developed in the 1920s, though no one could then have foreseen the future, something might have been done many years earlier to prevent the Jews' tragedy.'[38] Virulent anti-Semitism was, unfortunately, not limited to Germany but was found among peoples and nations throughout the Western world. Where were the 'ordinary, decent, thinking people' who could have made a difference?

It must be said, however, that there were at least handfuls of such thinking, caring people in Germany and elsewhere. People who hid Jewish children on the continent at great risk to themselves have been considered. In Britain, Bishop Bell of Chichester, among others, laid advancement of his career on the line to advocate an unpopular cause. This sense of responsibility for one's neighbour, however belated, resulted in unprecedented cooperation between Jewish and Christian organizations, a hopeful portent for future amicable interaction between the two communities. A good beginning was made in 1949 when, in Birmingham, the Jewish and Christian refugee councils amalgamated.[39]

Leaders such as Neville Laski were acutely aware of the importance of mutual understanding and cooperation. He wrote:

> I maintain with all the fervour of which I am capable, that the phrase I use, 'the building of bridges between the Jewish and non-Jewish communities' is our only possibility of salvation in the postwar world, outside any possibilities which Palestine may hold, and I feel … and I believe … that the exclusionist policy, which so many have adopted in the past, has provided Hitler and his lot with their best arguments.[40]

The Kindertransport movement and the postwar rescue of child survivors served as important vehicles for such bridge building.

Unfortunately, old prejudices are difficult to eradicate. As early as 1947, Bishop Bell was alerted to 'the alarming spread of anti-Semitism'.[41] In 1949 the Jewish authorities were voicing grave concern about renewed anti-Semitism in Great Britain and urged even the refugee organizations to keep a low profile.[42] Anti-Semitism seemed to explode again all over Europe and the spectre of the possibility of another Holocaust became an urgent topic of discussion. Although the highly articulate Holocaust survivor Elie Wiesel initially argued that such an unthinkable tragedy could never be repeated, on observing the renewed racism he changed his mind.[43] Bombing synagogues in Paris, setting Jewish schools alight in Créteil in France, holding neo-Nazi demonstrations in Germany with the support of British, Dutch and French sympathizers, and Italian neo-Fascists marching on the streets of major cities are the sorts of events that not only characterized the 1930s but that also happened in the 1990s and are continuing to take place into the present millennium.[44]

Fortunately, the task of building bridges also continues, especially with the formation of organizations such as the Council of Christians and Jews. Not only organizations, however, but also tens of thousands of ordinary, decent people who seemed to be so silent in the 1930s are now standing up to be counted, active in their resistance to the evils of racism and xenophobia. Is it possible that we have finally realized, in Dorothee Sölle's words, 'that the role of the spectator, the bystander, is not acceptable'?[45] Yehuda Bauer sums it up as follows. 'Thou shalt not be Perpetrator; Thou shalt not be a Victim; And Thou shalt never, But never, be a Bystander.'[46]

The matter of reparations for the victims of Nazism is not generally considered to be a bridge-building area, but it could and probably should have that component, for, shortly after the war, it became an obvious and pressing issue. Most, if not all the refugee children in this study would be eligible for financial restitution, especially those whose parents had been murdered. The complexities involved in the whole area of reparations, however, places it beyond the scope of this present work. Suffice it to say that, according to Christian Pross, the word 'reparation' is 'an umbrella term covering restitution of stolen property, compensation for damage to health, professional harm, and so on'.[47] A brief overview reveals that the victims of Nazi persecution organized immediately after the war and, in March 1947, a council was established for victims of persecution. The Council of Jews from Germany formed the United Restitution

Organization in London in 1949, the same year that the Jewish Restitution Successor Organization, active in the American occupation zone of Germany, began its work. In a comprehensive study, Christian Pross, the medical director of the Berlin Center for the Treatment of Torture Victims, writes:

> The German people did not like the victims, and they certainly did not like paying for them. Reparation was a burdensome duty imposed by the victors. In 1952, the allies, the state of Israel, and the Conference on Jewish Material Claims Against Germany, representing millions of murdered and victimized Jews, forced the Federal Republic through international treaties to pay reparations.[48]

In June 1957 Rabbi Schonfeld applied for £26,500 in reparations to help defray the costs of the three schools that were primarily teaching refugee children. He argued that the grant would 'assist in the cost of maintaining and developing the Jewish day schools which we provide for refugee children in place of those destroyed in their home towns by the Nazis'.[49] The chief rabbi supported his claim. Despite this, Dr Schonfeld was refused a hearing at the (Jewish) claims conference arbitration (or *Din Torah*) and was also denied any compensation.[50] Dr Schonfeld unsuccessfully claimed an anti-Orthodox bias.

While Jewish organizations vetted Dr Schonfeld's applications, the German reactions that Christian Pross described changed over time. Pross writes that while Germans surviving the war seemed reluctant to pay reparations, Germans living at the turn of the twenty-first century are more open than their parents and grandparents were to healing the sins perpetrated under the Nazis, 'to make good again' (*Wiedergutmachung*). Germany has thus made great progress in this area since the 1950s. While reparations were not mentioned during the interviews I conducted, I hope that the children in the Kindertransport programmes have by now received just and equitable compensation for what is rightfully theirs, though at the time of writing not all the claims had been satisfactorily resolved.[51]

One can but hope that some lessons have been learnt from the child refugees' experiences. Among Rabbi Schonfeld's papers there is a handwritten page on which he considers this question. He writes:

> Every child and mother, every man and woman and those millions that died unburied served a purpose, if only to demonstrate to the world the depths to which unethical western civilization can sink. Every corpse in that great mountain of the dead, every grain in that heap of human ashes ... is part of the terrific monument warning mankind it must not happen again.[52]

As Michael Berenbaum points out, 'the Holocaust offers no happy ending, no transcendent meaning, no easy moralism ... the overriding theme of the Holocaust is evil perpetuated by individuals, organizations, and governments.'[53] The 'evil' in this study has focused on evil perpetrated against children. Madeleine Albright muses that 'whether war is especially cruel to children depends on the particular case. Sometimes it is easier when we are young and do not fully understand. Sometimes it is harder because the young cannot protect themselves. Either way, war is tragic.'[54] One of the tragedies is that we shall never know what future 'musicians, philosophers, physicians, and rabbis we lost – who would have eradicated cancer, controlled the use of nuclear energy, liberated the oppressed and fed the hungry'.[55] We *do* know, however, that there *are* musicians, philosophers, physicians, Nobel Prize winners, rabbis and people who liberate the oppressed and feed the hungry among the thousands who were rescued.

One further question remains. Was the painful uprooting of these thousands of children in the first wave of the Kindertransport movement a wise and positive operation, or was it not? John Presland had already answered that question in 1944, before the child survivors arrived in Britain:

> In the appalling total number of refugees with which postwar Europe will be faced, the figure of ten thousand is a small one, but each one of these ten thousand is a sentient human being

and but for the work of the [Refugee Children's] Movement –
imperfect in many aspects like all human endeavour – those
children must have suffered death, or a fate far more horrible
than death, if they had been left within the frontiers of the
Greater Reich. It is not a small thing, in these years of suffering
without parallel, to have given ten thousand children the
opportunity to grow up in an atmosphere of decency and
normality, to work, to play, to laugh and be happy and to
assume their rightful heritage as free men and women.[56]

What was true about the first wave of Kindertransport children was
also true of the second wave of child refugees. These hundreds too
were given the opportunity to 'assume their rightful heritage as free
men and women'. It is a story to be told and remembered, for, as Baal
Shem Tov put it, 'forgetfulness leads to exile, while remembrance is
the secret of redemption.'

NOTES

Preface

1. Bishop George Bell, *Papers*, vol. 27, pp. 9–10.
2. Sarah Moskovitz, 'Making Sense of Survival: A Journey with Child Survivors of the Holocaust', in R. Krell (ed.) *Messages and Memories: Reflections on Child Survivors of the Holocaust* (Vancouver, Deskside Publishing, 1999) p. 19.

1. Descent into Darkness

1. A very brief overview of the background of anti-Semitism in Germany seems mandatory for a book of this nature, if for no other reason than to provided a bibliography of sources for those readers interested in pursuing a more comprehensive and analytical study of a complex and multi-faceted subject.
2. Ilse Haas quoted in Bertha Leverton and Shmuel Lowensohn (eds) *I Came Alone: The Stories of the Kindertransports* (Sussex: The Book Guild Ltd, 1990) p. 133.
3. John V. H. Dippel, *Bound Upon a Wheel of Fire: Why So Many German Jews Made the Tragic Decision to Remain in Nazi Germany* (New York: Basic Books, 1996) p. 269, footnote 6.
4. Ingeborg Hecht, *Invisible Walls and to Remember is to Heal*, translated from German by J. Brownjohn and J. Broadwin (Evanston: Northwestern University Press, 1999) p. 8.
5. Marion A. Kaplan, *Between Dignity and Despair: Jewish Life in Nazi Germany* (New York: Oxford University Press, 1998) pp. 11–12.
6. Dippel, *Bound Upon a Wheel of Fire*, p. 31.
7. Author interview with R. Lowenstein, 1998; Dippel, *Bound Upon a Wheel of Fire*, pp. 17, 20.
8. Although Jews were not officially allowed in the Officer Corps, many served in posts throughout the army. Saul Friedlander, *Nazi Germany and the Jews*, vol. 1, *The Years of Persecution 1933–1939* (New York: Harper Collins, 1997)

offers a very detailed and well-annotated discussion of the subject. See also Raul Hilberg, *The Holocaust: The Destruction of the European Jews*, 3 vols (New York: Holmes & Meier, 1985); Zoe Josephs, *Survivors: Jewish Refugees in Birmingham 1933–1945* (London: Institute of Jewish Affairs, 1988) pp. 9ff; Nora Levin, *The Holocaust: The Destruction of European Jewry 1933–1945* (New York: Schocken Books, 1968); Bernard Wasserstein, *Britain and the Jews of Europe 1939–1945* (Oxford: Clarendon Press, 1979). While Germany had a relatively small number of Jews, Poland in 1939 was home to 3.3 million, 85 per cent of whom were later killed. See Judah Pilch, 'Jewish Life in Europe between the Two World Wars (1919–1939)', in Roselle Chartock and Jack Spencer (eds) *Can It Happen Again? Chronicles of the Holocaust* (New York: Black Dog & Leventhal, 1995) p. 94.

9. David Cesarani, 'Introduction to Children's Transport', collection housed in the Wiener Library.

10. Author interview with Henry K.; author interview with H. Schramm; Margaret cited in Leverton and Lowensohn, *I Came Alone*, pp. 111; Olga cited in Leverton and Lowensohn, *I Came Alone*, p. 69.

11. Lambeth Palace Library, Bishop George Bell Papers, vol. 27, p. 23. The interview took place on 1 October 1933.

12. L. Steiman to V. Fast, 2009.

13. Hilberg, *The Holocaust*, vol. 1, pp. 5, 21.

14. Quoted in Friedlander, *Nazi Germany and the Jews*, p. 81.

15. Friedlander, *Nazi Germany and the Jews*, p. 34; Hilberg, *The Holocaust*, vol. 2, p. 19.

16. Dippel, *Bound Upon a Wheel of Fire*, p. 4.

17. Ibid.

18. Friedlander, *Nazi Germany and the Jews*, pp. 83ff, offers a very comprehensive analysis of the subject, including the 'Protocol of the Elders of Zion' fabrication.

19. Thanks to D. Stone for this qualification.

20. Hecht, *Invisible Walls*, p. 22.

21. Mark J. Harris and Deborah Oppenheimer, *Into the Arms of Strangers: Stories of the Kindertransport* (London: Bloomsbury, 2000) p. 3.

22. In Nazi ideology the term 'Aryan' pertained to Caucasian Gentiles, especially those of Nordic extraction.

23. Hecht, *Invisible Walls*, p. 21.

24. Adolf Hitler, *Mein Kampf*, translated from the German by Ralph Manheim (London: Hutchinson, 1969) pp. 52, 64–5.

25. Quoted in Hilberg, *The Holocaust*, p. 20; anti-Semitism, however, also proved to be the forerunner of anti-Christian diatribes against any in the Church who failed to support National Socialism. A 'New Song of the Hitler Youth'

contained the following: 'We need no Christian virtue, Adolf Hitler is our Leader, our Saviour and our Mediator … I am no Christian and no Catholic' (Lambeth Palace Library, Bell Papers, vol. 6, p. 452).

26. Friedlander, *Nazi Germany and the Jews*, vol. 1, p. 33; François Furet (ed.) *Unanswered Questions: Nazi Germany and the Genocide of the Jews* (New York: Schocken Books, 1989) p. 21.

27. Author interview with Henry K, September 1994.

28. Kaplan, *Between Dignity and Despair*, p. 6.

29. Dippel, *Bound Upon a Wheel of Fire*, pp. 87–8. See also Kaplan, *Between Dignity and Despair*, pp. 17–49.

30. Karen Levine, *Hana's Suitcase: A True Story* (Toronto: Second Story Press, 2002) p. 23. These laws were not uniformly enforced. For example, Margaret Goldberger remembers going to films with her friends in Berlin during this time (Goldberger to Fast, 2009).

31. Author interview with D. Lewinski; author interview with S. Wasserman; author interview with R. Lowenstein.

32. Marisabina Russo, *Always Remember Me: How One Family Survived World War II*, unpaginated booklet (New York: Atheneum Books, 2005).

33. D. Nicholson, *Remember World War II: Kids Who Survived Tell Their Stories* (Washington: National Geographic, 2005) p. 14.

34. Suzanne Vromen, *Hidden Children of the Holocaust: Belgian Nuns and their Daring Rescue of Young Jews from the Nazis* (New York: Oxford University Press, 2008) pp. 10, 12.

35. Levine, *Hana's Suitcase*, p. 24.

36. Chartock and Spencer, *Can It Happen Again?*, pp. 48–9; interviews, V. Fast with David Lewinski and Rudi Lowenstein.

37. Dippel, *Bound upon a Wheel of Fire*, p. xxiii.

38. Kaplan, *Between Dignity and Despair*, pp. 62–70.

39. Author interview with D. Lewinski, 1992.

40. Harris and Oppenheimer, *Into the Arms of Strangers*, p. 23.

41. Ibid., pp. 27–8.

42. Lambeth Palace Library, Bell Papers, vol. 27, p. 47.

43. Andrew Chandler, *Brethren in Adversity: Bishop George Bell, the Church of England and the Crisis of German Protestantism 1933–1939* (London: Church of England Record Society, 1997) p. 12; see also Raul Hilberg, *Perpetrators, Victims, Bystanders: The Jewish Catastrophe 1933–1945* (New York: HarperCollins Publishers, 1992).

44. Adam LeBor and Roger Boyes, *Seduced by Hitler: The Choices of a Nation and the Ethics of Survival* (Naperville, IL: Sourcebooks, Inc., 2000) p. 8.

45. Quoted in Wolfgang Gerlach, 'When the Witnesses Were Silent: The Confessing Church and the Persecution of the Jews', in Jörg Wollenberg

(ed.) *The German Public and the Persecution of the Jews, 1933–1945* (Amherst, NY: Prometheus Books, 1996) p. 71.

46. Levin, *The Holocaust*, p. 124.

47. Quoted in Robert M. Seltzer, *Jewish People, Jewish Thought: The Jewish Experience in History* (New York: Macmillan Publishing Co., Inc., 1980) p. 703.

48. Central British Fund (CBF), Reel 28, 153/6.

49. Bodleian Library, Ms SPSL 99/5, 'Interstate Refugee Conference in Evian, 6–15th July', p. 145.

50. Friedlander, *Nazi Germany and the Jews*, vol. 1, pp. 241ff; see also, London Metropolitan Archives, Board of Deputies, Acc 3121/A/30, Report 11 May 1938.

51. E. Loewy quoted in Christian Pross, *Paying for the Past: The Struggle Over Reparations for Surviving Victims of the Nazi Terror*, translated by Belinda Cooper (Baltimore: Johns Hopkins University Press, 1998) p. 191.

52. The Evian Conference and the Madagascar Plan as well as several other emigration schemes are discussed in Hilburg, *The Holocaust*, vol. 2; Levin, *The Holocaust*; Wasserstein, *Britain and the Jews of Europe*, and many other texts dealing with this period. On German emigration policy see also Karl Schleunes, *The Twisted Road to Auschwitz: Nazi Policy toward German Jews, 1933–1939* (Chicago: University of Illinois Press, 1970) pp. 198ff; A. J. Sherman, *Island Refuge: Britain and Refugees from the Third Reich, 1933–1939* (London: Frank Cass & Co. Ltd, 1994) pp. 264ff. Hansard, HCD, 341, 21 November 1938, records that Tanganyika and British Guinea were also considered as options for immigration.

53. Interview V. Fast with Hugh Schramm. Between 16,000 and 20,000 Jews entered Shanghai between 1937 and 1939. See Barry Turner, *The Long Horizon: Sixty Years of CBF World Jewish Relief* (London: CBF World Jewish Relief, n.d.) p. 17. By 1944 more than 7000 destitute Jewish refugees were starving and completely dependent on charity. See David Kranzler, *Thy Brother's Blood: The Orthodox Jewish Response During the Holocaust* (New York: Mesorah Publications Ltd, 1987) p. 76, which deals with the Orthodox community and the Japanese; and Marvin Tokayer and Mary Swartz, *The Fugu Plan: The Untold Story of the Japanese and the Jews During World War II* (New York: Paddington Press, 1979) p. 256.

54. Quoted in Rebekka Gopfert, *Der jüdische Kindertransport von Deutschland nach England, 1938–39* (Frankfurt: Campus Verlag, 1997) p. 42.

55. Mitchell Bard, *48 Hours of Kristallnacht: Night of Destruction/Dawn of the Holocaust: An Oral History* (Guilford, CT: The Lyons Press, 2008), pp. xii–xiii.

56. Author interview with S. Wasserman, 1998.

57. Quoted in Nicholson, *Remember World War II*, p. 14. Heidi later left for England on a Kindertransport.

58. Hecht, *Invisible Walls*, p. 58.
59. Quoted by Jörg Wollenberg, 'The Expropriation of the "Rapacious" Capital by "Productive Capital"', in Jörg Wollenberg (ed.) *The German Public and the Persecution of the Jews, 1933–1945*, English edition translated and edited by Rado Pribic (Amherst, NY: Prometheus Books, 1996) p. 140.
60. Sir Nevile Henderson, *Failure of a Mission* (London: Hodder & Stoughton, 1940) p. 172.
61. For the American response, see CBF Reel 1, 'Archives' booklet, p. 8, in which it is noted that cooperation with the American Jewish Joint Committee was very disappointing: 'political rather than humanitarian considerations were paramount among American Jewish lay readers.' British Jews, on the other hand, while divided on theology, were immediately united in their response to this present desperate need. See also Henry L. Feingold, *The Politics of Rescue: The Roosevelt Administration and the Holocaust, 1938–1945* (New Brunswick, NJ: Rutgers University Press, 1970) pp. 280ff, who speaks of 'bitter strife among the Jewish organizations in the United States'; and David S. Wyman, *Paper Walls: America and the Refugee Crisis, 1938–1941* (Amherst, MA: University of Massachusetts Press, 1968). For another view of the American Jewish response, see Yehuda Bauer, *American Jewry and the Holocaust: The American Jewish Joint Distribution Committee, 1939–45* (Detroit: Wayne State University Press, 1981).
62. *Encyclopaedia Judaica* (New York: Macmillan, 1972) vol. 6.
63. See Vivian Lipman, *A Century of Social Service, 1859–1959: A History of the Jewish Board of Guardians* (London: Routledge & Kegan Paul, 1959) for an account of the Board of Guardians. For a background to British Judaism, see David Cesarani, 'Great Britain', in David S. Wyman (ed.) *The World Reacts to the Holocaust* (Baltimore: Johns Hopkins University Press, 1996); CBF Reel 41, 'Introduction'.
64. For an outstanding analysis of Rabbi Dr Baeck, see Dippel, *Bound Upon a Wheel of Fire*, pp. 256ff.
65. Norman Bentwich, *They Found Refuge: An Account of British Jewry's Work for Victims of Nazi Oppression* (London: The Cresset Press, 1956) pp. 9–21; Amy Zahl Gottlieb, *Men of Vision: Anglo-Jewry's Aid to Victims of the Nazi Regime, 1933–1945* (London: Weidenfeld & Nicholson, 1998) pp. 8–10.
66. Neville Laski and Leonard Montefiore to Lionel de Rothschild, in Gottlieb, *Men of Vision*, p. 23; see also Turner, *The Long Horizon*. The Central British Fund for German Jewry changed its name to Central British Fund (CBF) and then to World Jewish Relief.
67. Gottlieb, *Men of Vision*, pp. 23–6, 213–14; and Turner, *The Long Horizon*, present pertinent biographical information on all the committee members.
68. The background history of Jewish diversity and its reasons is beyond the

scope of this study, but see Gottlieb, *Men of Vision*, p. 25; Hartley Library/Archives (HL), University of Southampton, Chief Rabbi Hertz papers, Ms 175/139/1 folders 1, 2.

69. Amy Gottlieb (*Men of Vision*, p. 216 note 48) estimates the £250,000 sterling raised in 1933 to be the equivalent of £7,750,000 in 1997.

70. John Presland, *A Great Adventure: The Story of the Refugee Children's Movement* (London: Bloomsbury House, 1944). By the end of the war Rabbi Schonfeld had listed the following Anglo-Jewish relief organizations – Agudas Israel, CRREC, Federation of Polish Jews, Jewish Agency for Palestine, Jewish Committee for Relief Abroad, JRC, Kadimah Society, Kring van Nederlandsche Joden in England, Polish Jewish Refugee Fund, CBF, The Mizrachi Federation of Great Britain and Ireland, United Jewish Relief Appeal, World Jewish Congress (HL, Schonfeld, 183/234/folder 1).

71. Elaine Blond, *Marks of Distinction* (London: Vallentine, Mitchell & Company, 1988) p. 74.

72. Imperial War Museum (IWM), Margareta Burkill, interview 4588/8.

73. Gopfert, *Der jüdische Kindertransport*, p. 52; see also Kathleen Freeman, *If any Man Build: The History of the Save the Children Fund* (London: Hodder & Stoughton, 1965).

74. Blond, *Marks of Distinction*, p. 24.

75. John Ormerod Greenwood, *Quaker Encounters: Friends and Relief Work*, vol. 1 (York, UK: Friends & Relief, 1975); while Greenwood speaks of the 'righteous among the nations', the phrase is used in other places as well; on the same subject see, Eric Silver, *The Book of the Just: The Silent Heroes Who Saved Jews from Hitler* (London: Weidenfeld & Nicolson, 1992). The name change for the Quaker Committee occurred in December 1942.

76. John Presland, *A Great Adventure*. Mrs Norman Bentwich is credited with providing the initiative for this committee, which was originally under the joint chairmanship of Viscount Samuel and Sir William Deedes, when for a short time, it was known as the World Movement for the Rescue of Children from Germany: British Inter-Aid Committee (Presland, *A Great Adventure*, pp. 1–2). Sir Charles Stead, originally chosen as executive director of the movement, resigned at the outbreak of war to join the service, and was succeeded by the redoubtable Dorothy Hardisty, a civil servant. A Catholic, Canon George Craven, and a Protestant, Revd William Simpson were elected to the central committee together with Rabbi Maurice Swift.

77. Kindertransport (children's transport), although a German word, almost immediately became part of English common usage and is therefore not italicized in these pages.

78. In 1942 the Central Office for Refugees, under the joint chairmanship of Henry Carter and Anthony de Rothschild, published a handbook with

Bloomsbury House. *The Care of German and Austrian Refugees* lists the 30 refugee agencies either housed in Bloomsbury House or closely related to it. See also Hansard, HCD, p. 740, which lists all the coordinating committee members.

2. Exodus and Arrival

1. Members of the committee, chaired by Neville Laski and Leonard Montefiore, included Lionel Cohen and Otto Schiff (Amy Gottlieb, *Men of Vision*, pp. 12–13).
2. Gottlieb, *Men of Vision*, pp. 13–19; Gottlieb discusses at some length this meeting and the responsibilities assumed.
3. Hartley Library University of Southampton, Schonfeld Papers, Ms 183/132/3, 23 May 1938.
4. See especially the *Jewish Chronicle* from mid–1938 to the end of August 1939.
5. John Presland, *A Great Adventure*, p. 1. Amy Gottlieb, *Men of Vision*, p. 103 also notes the 'major concern at this stage was the rescue of the greatest number'.
6. Members included Lord Bearsted, Chief Rabbi Dr Hertz, Chaim Weizman, Neville Laski and Lionel de Rothschild.
7. Sir John Hope Simpson, *Refugees: A Preliminary Report of a Survey* (London: Royal Institute of International Affairs, 1938) p. 69; see also Hansard (HCD, the British parliamentary record) vol. 343, 1 February 1939; vol. 344, 7 March 1939; vol. 345, 3 April 1939.
8. The delegation included Viscount Samuel and members of the Jewish Refugees Committee, a representative of the Inter-Aid Committee, and Bertha Bracey and Ben Greene of the Quakers. See Esther Judith Baumel, 'The Jewish Refugee Children in Great Britain, 1938–1945', unpublished MA thesis, Bar-Ilan University, Israel, 1981, pp. 1–3; Gottlieb, *Men of Vision*, pp. 106–7; Presland, *A Great Adventure*, p. 1.
9. Hansard, HCD, vol. 341, 21 November 1938; Hansard records many pages of speeches on this day, condemning Germany and asking asylum for all Jews, not only the children.
10. Hansard, HCD, vol. 341, 23 November 1938.
11. Hansard, HCD, vol. 351, 30 October 1939. There were actually to be four categories of immigrants: transit emigrants to leave within two years, children below the age of 18, persons between 16 and 35 for training with a view to emigration, persons over 60 (Bulletin of the Co-ordinating Committee for Refugees, p. 8).
12. Hansard, HCD, vols 341, 410, 577, 578, 579.
13. Elaine Blond, *Marks of Distinction*, p. 67.

14. Turner, *The Long Horizon*, p. 29.
15. Friends' House Library Archives (FHLA), London, Friends Committee for Refugees and Aliens/3, letter by Norman Nicholson.
16. Hansard, HCD, vol. 343, 9 February 1939, quoting 'The Adoption of Children Act 1926'. This restriction was lifted after the war.
17. Imperial War Museum, Margareta Burkill, interview 004588/08, reel 5, p. 38.
18. The advertisements were frequently heart-rending and, according to anecdotal evidence, helped to bring many children to the United Kingdom, although no figures are available.
19. Karen Gershon (ed.) *We Came as Children: A Collective Autobiography* (London: Papermac, 1989) p. 17.
20. Gottlieb, *Men of Vision*, p. 123; London Metropolitan Archives, Board of Deputies, Acc 3121/E3/525/1, p. 7.
21. Bulletin of the Coordinating Committee for Refugees, February 1939, pp. 11ff.
22. Muriel Emanuel and Vera Gissing, *Nicholas Winton and the Rescued Generation: Save one Life, Save the World* (London: Mitchell Vallentine & Company, 2001) pp. 74, 177. Emanuel and Gissing question whether this independent work could actually be called part of the Kindertransport, because it operated under different conditions.
23. Emanuel and Gissing, *Nicholas Winton and the Rescued Generation*, pp. 66–8.
24. Andrew Billen, *Evening Standard* (London), 14 November 2001, pp. 27–8, called him 'The bloody-minded hero who became our Schindler'. Glen Cooper, *Independent* (London), 20 June 1998, p. 5, referred to him as 'Britain's forgotten Schindler'. Some sources describe him as 'a clerk in the London Stock Exchange' (*London Free Press*, London: Ontario, 5 September 2009).
25. Emanual and Gissing, *Nicholas Winton and the Rescued Generation*, pp. 177, 70, 93.
26. Martin Gilbert, *Kristallnacht: Prelude to Destruction* (New York: HarperCollins, 2006) p. 207.
27. See Emanuel and Gissing, *Nicholas Winton and the Rescued Generation*, pp. 108–9; Karen Gershon, *We Came as Children*, pp. 22–5.
28. Emanuel and Gissing, *Nicholas Winton and the Rescued Generation*, pp. 111–12.
29. Nicholas Winton, *Saving the Children: Czechoslovakia 1939*, vol. 1, n.d., 'Report on a Witness in Czechoslovakia'. Winton's two volumes of undated notes, clippings and reports are housed in the Wiener Library, London and also contain handwritten notes on many of the children, including where they attend school and the names of their guarantors.
30. Emanuel and Gissing, *Nicholas Winton and the Rescued Generation*, p. 127.
31. Blond, *Marks of Distinction*, p. 74; Gottlieb, *Men of Vision*, p. 114; Mark Jonathan Harris, *Into the Arms of Strangers: Stories of the Kindertransport*

documentary film written and directed by Mark Jonathan Harris, released 24 November 2000; Barry Turner, *And the Policeman Smiled* (London: Bloomsbury, 1990) pp. 92–5.

32. Harris and Oppenheimer, *Into the Arms of Strangers*, p. 13.
33. Hartley Library University of Southampton, S. Schonfeld, Ms 183/264/folder 2.
34. Ibid.
35. *Jewish Chronicle*, 11 August 1939, p. 21.
36. Hansard, HCD, vol. 344, 2 March 1939.
37. Schonfeld, Ms 183/132/4, 18 April 1939.
38. CBF, Reel 65, p. 301.
39. The details of procedure are recorded in Baumel, 'The Jewish Refugee Children in Great Britain', pp. 84–5.
40. Friends Committee for Refugees and Aliens, minutes 1939; Imperial War Museum, London, Dorothy, interview 16600/2; Margarete, interview 17542/2, quoted in Leverton and Lowensohn, *I Came Alone*, pp. 144, 152, 297.
41. Gottlieb, *Men of Vision*, p. 115.
42. Author interview with R. Lowenstein, November 1998; Dorit Bader Whiteman, *The Uprooted: A Hitler Legacy: Voices of Those Who Escaped Before the 'Final Solution'* (New York: Insight Books, 1993) pp. 20ff.
43. Imperial War Museum, Walter, interview 17355/9 A.
44. Author interview with H. Schramm, June 1991.
45. Author interviews with D. Lewinski, September 1992, and S. Wasserman, 1998.
46. Edith Bowen-Jakabowitz, 'Memories and Reflections', unpublished memoir, Wiener Library, London, n.d.
47. Hana, interview 16975/2/1-2, Imperial War Museum, London, n.d.
48. Gershon, *We Came as Children*, p. 19.
49. Gershon, *We Came as Children*, p. 26; Ernest Pollak, 'Departure to Freedom Curtailed', unpublished memoir, Wiener Library, London, n.d.
50. Turner, *And the Policeman Smiled*, p. 37.
51. Harris, *Into the Arms of Strangers*; Turner, *And the Policeman Smiled*, p. 1.
52. Quoted in Gilbert, *Kristallnacht*, p. 196.
53. Leverton and Lowensohn, *I Came Alone*, p. 236; Diane L. Wolf, *Beyond Anne Frank: Hidden Children and Postwar Families in Holland* (Berkeley: University of California Press, 2007) especially pp. 132–3.
54. See Harris and Oppenheimer, *Into the Arms of Strangers*, p. 108.
55. Dorothy, interview 16600/2, Imperial War Museum, London, n.d.
56. Quoted in Leverton and Lowensohn, *I Came Alone*, pp. 217, 224.
57. Gershon, *We Came as Children*, p. 26.
58. Author interview with B. Leverton, September 1994, also Harris and Oppenheimer, *Into the Arms of Strangers*, p. 103.

59. Joe Schlesinger, *Time Zones: A Journalist in the World* (Toronto: Random House, 1990) p. 1.

60. Quoted in Gershon, *We Came as Children*, p. 26. See also unpublished Jewish Museum information leaflet by Lawrence Darton, Friends Committee for Refugees and Aliens (FHLA) p. 51.

61. Kati David, *A Child's War: World War II through the Eyes of Children* (New York: Four Walls Eight Windows, 1989) p. 2; Gershon, *We Came as Children*, p. 19; Leverton and Lowensohn, *I Came Alone*, p. 95.

62. Harris and Oppenheimer, *Into the Arms of Strangers*, p. 88.

63. Author interview with Margaret Goldberger, September 2009.

64. See Gopfert, *Der jüdische Kindertransport*, p. 74.

65. Author interview with B. Leverton, September 1994.

66. Picture in Gershon, *We Came as Children*.

67. Baumel, 'The Jewish Refugee Children in Great Britain', p. 85.

68. Whiteman, *The Uprooted*, p. 163.

69. Quoted in Harris and Oppenheimer, *Into the Arms of Strangers*, p. 119.

70. Author interview with D. Lewinski, 1992; Turner, *And the Policeman Smiled*, p. 99.

71. Quoted in Leverton and Lowensohn, *I Came Alone*, p. 16.

72. Turner, *And the Policeman Smiled*, p. 82.

73. Baumel, 'The Jewish Refugee Children in Great Britain', p. 19.

74. Hartley Library, Greenberg Collection, Ms 150 (AJ/110/7), 'The Hope Train', unpublished manuscript.

75. Gershon, *We Came as Children*, p. 28.

76. Author interview with S. Wasserman, November 1998.

77. Quoted in Leverton and Lowensohn, *I Came Alone*, p. 218.

78. Whiteman, *The Uprooted*, pp. 159–60.

79. Quoted in Harris and Oppenheimer, *Into the Arms of Strangers*, pp. 112–13.

80. Hartley Library, 'The Hope Train', unpublished manuscript, Greenberg Collection, Ms 150(AJ/110/7); also Harris and Oppenheimer, *Into the Arms of Strangers*, pp. 112–17.

81. Quoted in Turner, *And the Policeman Smiled*, p. 3.

82. Baumel, 'The Jewish Refugee Children in Great Britain', p. 91; Imperial War Museum, Colin Anson, interview 11883/5/A.

83. Baumel, 'The Jewish Refugee Children in Great Britain', p. 91; Gershon, *We Came as Children*, p. 27.

84. See Gopfert, *Der jüdischen Kindertransport*, pp. 66–7.

85. Turner, *And the Policeman Smiled*, p. 46; Whiteman, *The Uprooted*, p. 158.

86. Quoted in Gershon, *We Came as Children*, p. 29; Whiteman, *The Uprooted*, p. 157.

87. Herbert, Jochi and Hanna Najmann, 'A Tribute to our Brother', *60th Anniversary of the Kindertransport* (London: ROK, 1999) p. 123.

88. Quoted in Gershon, *We Came as Children*, p. 30.

89. Quoted in Gershon, *We Came as Children*, p. 2; Gottlieb, *Men of Vision*, p. 114; Jewish Museum 'Kindertransport' file.

90. Lucy V. Davidson and John S. Ross (eds) *For a Future and a Hope: The Story of the Houses of Refuge in Chislehurst* (Chislehurst: CWI Publications, 1989) p. 8; Gershon, *We Came as Children*, p. 22.

91. Gershon, *We Came as Children*, p. 25; Gottlieb, *Men of Vision*, p. 123; *Jewish Chronicle*, 20 September 1939, p. 1.

92. London Metropolitan Archives, Board of Deputies, Acc 3121/E3/286.

93. Blond, *Marks of Distinction*, p. 70.

94. Author interview with J. Fieldsend, September 1994; Blond, *Marks of Distinction*, pp. 70–1.

95. Anna Essinger, a Jewess who had become a Quaker, came to England with her sisters Paula and Bertha. Bunce Court was noted for its progressive and liberal educational policies (Josephs, *Survivors*, pp. 71–3).

96. Turner, *And the Policeman Smiled*, p. 58.

97. Gershon, *We Came as Children*, p. 37; Turner, *And the Policeman Smiled*, p. 58.

98. *Jewish Chronicle*, 23 December 1938, p. 18. One of the boys maintained that the weeks spent at the Salvation Army hostel 'were the happiest period for some time to come' (quoted in Gershon, *We Came as Children*, p. 37).

99. Movement for the Care of Children from Germany, *First Annual Report*, 1938–9.

100. Schonfeld, Ms 183/132/4.

101. Gershon, *We Came as Children*, p. 33; Gottlieb, *Men of Vision*, p. 117; *Jewish Chronicle*, 9 December 1938, pp. 14, 17.

102. Schonfeld, Ms 183/90/2/folder 1.

103. Hertz, Ms 175/139/2, 28 January 1939.

104. *Jewish Chronicle*, 5 May 1939, p. 23.

105. Schonfeld, Ms 183/90/folder 1. Statistics released on 21 March 1939, show there were 393 Orthodox children in the camps, 146 Reform, 32 Liberal and 27 'other synagogues'.

106. Gershon, *We Came as Children*, p. 32, states that Anna Essinger later 'did not want to be reminded of the camp … she maintained that it was a terrible experience for those who passed through it.'

107. Author interview with S. Wasserman, 1998.

108. Manchester Central Library/Archives, Misc/872.

109. Schonfeld, Ms 183/53/2/folder 2.

110. Manchester Central Library/Archives, After Care Committee, M533/Box 1 (2146).

111. Exodus 20:10.

3. Strangers in your Midst

1. Harris, *Into the Arms of Strangers*.
2. Hartley Library University of Southampton, Schonfeld, Ms 183/53/2/folder 1.
3. Schonfeld, Ms 183/53/2/folder 1, 6 January 1939.
4. Video cassette, 'Heroes of the Kindertransport'.
5. Schonfeld, Ms 183/641/folder 2.
6. Quoted in Gopfert, *Der jüdische Kindertransport*, p. 126.
7. CBF, Reel 72, 333/29–31.
8. CBF, Reel 69, 313/6.
9. Author interview with B. Leverton, September 1994, in which Leverton tells this story; also Jeremy Josephs and Susi Bechhofer, *Rosa's Child: The True Story of One Woman's Quest for a Lost Mother and a Vanished Past* (London: I.B.Tauris, 1996) p. 25.
10. *Jewish Chronicle*, 12 May 1939, p. 35.
11. Amy Gottlieb, *Men of Vision*, p. 118.
12. Hartley Library University of Southampton, Hertz, Ms 175/139/1/folder 1: Poppers to Stephany, 6 October 1944; Poppers to Hertz, 12 July 1943.
13. Schonfeld, Ms 183/53/2/folder 1.
14. Meeting of the Executive, 18 January 1939, CBF, Reel 1, 2/295.
15. Letter of 14 March 1939, CBF, Reel 10, 53/123; also quoted in Gopfert, *Der jüdische Kindertransport*, p. 92.
16. Elaine Blond, *Marks of Distinction*, p. 86.
17. Quoted in Leverton and Lowensohn, *I Came Alone*, p. 147.
18. Schonfeld, Ms 183/53/2/folder 1 lists the occupations of hundreds of guarantors.
19. Harris and Oppenheimer, *Into the Arms of Strangers*, p. 184.
20. London Museum of Jewish Life, Kindertransport folio, anonymous.
21. Schonfeld, Ms 183/53/2/folder 1.
22. Schonfeld, Ms 183/617/2/folder 1.
23. Dorothy Hardisty, RCM, CBF, Reel 28, 166/120–5.
24. 'Evidence and Suggestion of Mrs D. H. Hardisty, General Secretary, RCM', CBF, Reel 128, file 166.
25. Schonfeld, Ms 183/53/2/folder 2.
26. Schonfeld, Ms 183/53/2/folder 1.
27. Schonfeld, Ms 183/53/2 folder 1, where the six month period is mentioned; London Metropolitan Archives, Board of Deputies Acc 3121/E3/532/1. 'On no account can guarantees ... be accepted for a lesser period than three years, and even then only for limited numbers and under special circumstances.'

28. CBF Reel 72, 333/18–19. In 1939, there were 20 shillings to a pound; at the beginning of the war the pound dropped from US$ 4.61 to $3.99 within a month. In March 1940, the British government pegged the value of the pound at $4.03, where it stayed for several years.

29. London Metropolitan Archives, Board of Deputies, Acc 3121/E3286, p. 2.

30. *Jewish Chronicle*, 16 December 1938, p. 32; also Presland, *A Great Adventure*, p. 8.

31. Schonfeld, Ms 183/132/4, n.d.

32. Quoted in Whiteman, *The Uprooted*, p. 225.

33. Quoted in Harris and Oppenheimer, *Into the Arms of Strangers*, pp. 154, 156.

34. Imperial War Museum, Colin Anson, Interview 11883/5A.

35. Quoted in Emanuel and Gissing, *Nicholas Winton and the Rescued Generation*, p. 147.

36. Board of Deputies, Acc 3121/E3/532/1, 5 December 1938.

37. Blond, *Marks of Distinction*, p. 73; Emanuel and Gissing, *Nicholas Winton and the Rescued Generation*, p. 157.

38. Quoted in Leverton and Lowensohn, *I Came Alone*, p. 248.

39. Leverton and Lowensohn, *I Came Alone*, pp. 168, 174; Turner, *And the Policeman Smiled*, pp. 162–3.

40. Gottlieb, *Men of Vision*, p. 124. The acronym ORT, standing for *Obshestvo Remeslenofo zemledelcheskofo Truda* in Russian (Society for Trades and Agricultural Labour) has become synonymous with quality high-tech education from ORT America.

41. Schonfeld, Ms 183/53/2/folder 2.

42. London Museum of Jewish Life, anonymous, Kindertransport collection.

43. Whiteman, *The Uprooted*, p. 224.

44. Gershon, *We Came as Children*, p. 39.

45. Quoted in Leverton and Lowensohn, *I Came Alone*, pp. 236, 211.

46. Ibid., pp. 160, 293.

47. Baumel, 'The Jewish Refugee Children in Great Britain', pp. 105, 183–5.

48. Whiteman, *The Uprooted*, p. 224.

49. RCM, Meeting of the Executive Committee, 21 May 1941, CBF, Reel 28, file 166.

50. Leverton and Lowensohn, *I Came Alone*, pp. 123, 117, 142, 115, 214, 220.

51. Whiteman, *The Uprooted*, p. 235.

52. Quoted in Leverton and Lowensohn, *I Came Alone*, pp. 147, 155.

53. Harris and Oppenheimer, *Into the Arms of Strangers*, p. 230; Leverton and Lowensohn, *I Came Alone*, pp. 113, 180. See also Ben Wicks, *No Time to Wave Goodbye* (Toronto: Stoddart, 1988) pp. 203–7, for similar experiences of English evacuees.

54. Author interview with Henry K, September 1994.

55. Turner, *And the Policeman Smiled*, pp. 129–30.

56. Leverton and Lowensohn, *I Came Alone*, pp. 135, 289.

57. Author interview with J. Fieldsend, 1994; Harris and Oppenheimer, *Into the Arms of Strangers*, p. 130; Leverton and Lowensohn, *I Came Alone*, p. 170.

58. Harris and Oppenheimer, *Into the Arms of Strangers*, p. 213.

59. Harris and Oppenheimer, *Into the Arms of Strangers*, p. 266; also pp. 163, 167, 180, 210, 264, 266, and others.

60. Whiteman, *The Uprooted*, p. 234.

61. Schonfeld, Ms 183/53/2/folder 1, 10 January 1939.

62. Leverton and Lowensohn, *I Came Alone*, pp. 107, 109, 143, 306.

63. Harris and Oppenheimer, *Into the Arms of Strangers*, p. 147.

64. Leverton and Lowensohn, *I Came Alone*, p. 107.

65. Ibid., p. 393. In the interviews the author conducted some interviewees spoke with fairly pronounced accents, some with only a trace and others with no accent at all. Much depended on where the child had been placed and how old he or she was on arrival.

66. Whiteman, *The Uprooted*, p. 221.

67. Leverton and Lowensohn, *I Came Alone*, p. 109.

68. Ibid., p. 65.

69. Ibid., p. 112.

70. Author interview with David Lewinski; author interview with Hugh Schramm; conversation with F. Stambrook; Josephs and Bechhofer, *Rosa's Child*, p. 29.

71. Turner, *And the Policeman Smiled*, p. 178.

72. Lambeth Palace Library, Bishop George Bell, papers, vol. 35, part 1, p. 178.

73. Leverton and Lowensohn, *I Came Alone*, p. 51.

74. RCM, 'Instructions for the Guidance of Local and Regional Sub-Committees', in Gopfert, *Der jüdische Kindertransport*, p. 122.

75. Harris and Oppenheimer, *Into the Arms of Strangers*, p. 204.

76. Schlesinger, *Time Zones*, p. 35.

77. Vera Gissing, *Pearls of Childhood* (London: Robson Books, 1988) photograph on p. 80, also p. 81.

78. Gopfert, *Der jüdische Kindertransport*, p. 119.

79. Author interview with David Lewinski, September 1992.

80. Author interview with David Lewinski, September 1992, and with Hugh Schramm, 1991.

81. Turner, *And the Policeman Smiled*, p. 174. See also Imperial War Museum, Dunstan interview 13617/1/B.

82. Turner, *And the Policeman Smiled*, p. 175.

83. *Jewish Chronicle*, 15 September 1939, p. 22.

84. Schonfeld, Ms 183/234/folder 2: 'Extracts from a report of Activities for the

Period Ending 31 December 1941' notes that hostels have been established in Cardiff, Clapton, Croydon, Glasgow, Manchester, Northampton, Nottingham, Shefford, Whitechapel and Willesden, and 'lately Tylers Green Hostel'.

85. Author interview with S. Wasserman, June 1996.
86. Leverton and Lowensohn, *I Came Alone*, p. 158.
87. CBF, Reel 28, 153/22.
88. *Jewish Chronicle*, 15 September 1939, p. 8.

4. Evacuation and Internment

1. The priority classes included, besides the school children, young children accompanied by mothers or guardians, expectant mothers and physically-handicapped adults. See Jeffrey and Barbara Baum, *Never Before, Never Again! Evacuation in the Edmonton Hundreds* (London: Heritage no. 4, Jewish Research Group of the Edmonton Hundred Historical Society, 1993) p. 60.
2. CBF, Reel 68, 310/39.
3. There were in fact three evacuations: the one on 1 September, which included 62,000 school children; the second in August 1940 at the time of the Battle of Britain with 141,000 unaccompanied children; the third in mid-June 1944, during the time of the 'Doodlebug', with 101,000 children. See Ruth Inglis, *The Children's War: Evacuation 1939–1945* (London: Collins, 1989) pp. 1, 13.
4. Schlesinger, *Time Zones*, p. 31.
5. Hartley Library University of Southampton, Schonfeld, Ms 183/997/3.
6. Schonfeld, Ms 183/391/1/folder 1.
7. Baum and Baum, *Never Before, Never Again*, p. 66.
8. *Jewish Chronicle*, 22 September 1939, p. 16.
9. *London County Council Bulletin*, 5 July 1941; Schonfeld Ms 183/641/folder 3.
10. Turner, *And the Policeman Smiled*, pp. 142–3.
11. Margaret Goldberger to Vera Fast, September 2009.
12. Judith Tydor Baumel, *Twice a Refugee: The Jewish Refugee Children in Great Britain during Evacuation, 1939–1943* (Bloomington: Indiana University Press, 1983) p. 175.
13. Schonfeld, Ms 183/382/folder 2.
14. Schonfeld, Ms 183/391/1/folder 1.
15. *Jewish Chronicle*, 20 December 1940, p. 10.
16. The idea of canteens was raised as early as 29 September in the *Jewish Chronicle*, pp. 10–12.
17. Schonfeld, Ms 183/382/folder 2.
18. *Jewish Chronicle*, 28 June 1940, p. 12.
19. Hartley Library University of Southampton, Hertz, Ms 175/132.

20. Hertz, Ms 175/116/3; Ms 175/132.
21. Hertz, Ms 175/132.
22. Hertz, Ms 175/139/2.
23. Schonfeld, Ms 183/391/1/folder 1.
24. Blond, *Marks of Distinction*, p. 87.
25. Hertz, Ms 175/137/2/folder 2.
26. These regional committees were Sunderland, Leeds, Nottingham, Cambridge, London, Oxford, Gloucester, Cardiff, Birmingham, Manchester, Edinburgh and Tunbridge Wells (Hertz, Ms 175/139/1/folder 1).
27. Bulletin of the Co-ordinating Committee for Refugees, May 1939; see also Gopfert, *Der jüdische Kindertransport*, pp. 86, 89.
28. Hertz, Ms 175/140/1.
29. Blond, *Marks of Distinction*, p. 87.
30. Schonfeld, Ms 183/444/2.
31. Turner, *And the Policeman Smiled*, p. 142.
32. Schonfeld, Ms 183/382/folder 2, 8 November 1942.
33. Gottlieb, *Men of Vision*, p. 128; RCM, First Annual Report, 1938–39; Turner, *And the Policeman Smiled*, p. 143.
34. Inglis, *The Children's War*, pp. 147–53.
35. Ibid., p. 154.
36. Ibid., pp. 156–7.
37. Hartley Library University of Southampton, Christian Council, Ms 65 A755 1/1, Christian Council for Refugees report 1940, 'The Present Position of the Refugees', p. 4.
38. Josephs, *Survivors*, pp. 48–50.
39. Connery Chappell, *Island of Barbed Wire: The Remarkable Story of World War Two Internment on the Isle of Man* (London: Robert Hale, 1984) p. 45.
40. Quoted in Martin Gilbert, *Kristallnacht*, p. 205.
41. Katherine Whitaker and Michael Johnson, *Stoatley Rough School 1934–1960* (Watford: Archives of the Jewish Museum, 1995) p. 23.
42. Schonfeld, Ms 183/641/folder 1.
43. Interview Walter Kohn by Karin Hanta, *Kindertransport 60th Anniversary Book*, p. 12.
44. London Metropolitan Archives, Board of Deputies, Acc 2793/03/03/06–08.
45. Gershon, *We Came as Children*, p. 91.
46. Chappell, *Island of Barbed Wire*, p. 40, lists the largest mainland camps as those at Huyton, Kempton Park, Ascot, Prees Heath and Wartin Mill. There is, in the introductory section, also a sketched map of the Isle of Man internment area by R. D. Lloyd-Davies.
47. Lambeth Palace Library, Bishop Bell papers, vol. 35, part 1, p. 160.
48. Schonfeld, Ms 183/90/3/folder 1.

49. Board of Deputies, Acc 3121/B5/4/16, letter from Revd Dr J. Rabbinowitz, 25 April 1940; Turner, *And the Policeman Smiled*, pp. 150–1.

50. Bell Papers, vol. 35, part 1, p. 152.

51. Author interview with R. Lowenstein, November 1998. See also Eric Koch, *Deemed Suspect: A Wartime Blunder* (Toronto: Methuen, 1980) for the story of Canadian internees; and Wasserstein, *Britain and the Jews*, pp. 95–100.

52. Interview, Walter Kohn by Karin Hanta, *Kindertransport 60th Reunion*, p. 12.

53. Cyril Pearl, *The Dunera Scandal* (London: Angus & Robertson, 1983) pp. 153, 217.

54. Pearl, *The Dunera Scandal*, p. 41. See also Benzion Patkin, *The Dunera Internees* (Sydney: Cassell Australia Ltd, 1979).

55. Gottlieb, *Men of Vision*, p. 170; Koch, *Deemed Suspect*, pp. 72–3; Wasserstein, *Britain and the Jews*, p. 96.

56. Koch, *Deemed Suspect*, p. 68.

57. Pearl, *The Dunera Scandel*, pp. 22–3, 30–9.

58. Author interview with C. Wallenstein, December 1998.

59. Wasserstein, *Britain and the Jews*, p. 97.

60. Koch, *Deemed Suspect*, p. 250.

61. Chappell, *Island of Barbed Wire*, p. 49.

62. Bell Papers, vol. 35, part 1, p. 156.

63. Ibid., p. 182.

64. CBF, Reel 28, 153/35.

65. Schonfeld, Ms 183 90/2 folder 1. It is interesting to find that several names were suggested for this corps, including Judeans, Ariel Guards, Bar Cochba, Carmel Foresters and Gideon Fusiliers.

66. Bell Papers, vol. 35, part 1, p. 160.

67. Imperial War Museum, Colin Anson, interview 11883/5; London Metropolitan Archives, Acc 2793/01/01/03, 10 May 1945, Minutes of Council of the Central British Fund. The CBF's third annual report, March 1942, shows boys serving in the RAF, the Australian, Canadian and Polish forces and the Merchant Marine.

68. Turner, *And the Policeman Smiled*, pp. 203, 207. Turner's figures vary from those of the CBF. He writes, 'more than a thousand Kindertransport refugees served … among them 300 girls.' He goes on to list 800 in technical units, 650 in combat units, 450 in the intelligence and specialist units, 300 in the commandos, airborne and special forces, and 100 in the navy and RAF.

69. Hansard, HCD, vol. 343, 2 February 1939: 'The duty of a local education authority to enforce the law of school attendance is equally applicable to British and alien children resident in the area.'

70. Board of Deputies, Acc 3121/E3/525/1, 1.

71. See chapter on 'Bunce Court School' in Josephs, *Survivors*, pp. 71ff.

72. Imperial War Museum, Burkill, interview number 004588/18, p. 50.

73. Whitaker and Johnson, *Stoatley Rough School*, pp. 15–19.

74. 'The Child Estranging Movement', Schonfeld, Ms 183/344/10.

75. Bentwich, *They Found Refuge*, p. 72.

76. Ibid., p. 83.

77. Ronald Gorell Barnes, *One Man … Many Parts* (London: Odhams Press, 1956) p. 304; also quoted in Gopfert, *Der jüdische Kindertransport*, p. 174.

78. Schonfeld, Ms 183/234/folder 2.

5. Crises, Cries and Lamentations

1. Manchester Public Library/Archives, Children's Sub-Committee of Manchester Jewish Refugees Committee, September 1942.

2. Schonfeld to Cohen, Ms 183/53/2/folder 2.

3. *Jewish Chronicle*, 28 July 1939, p. 8.

4. Schonfeld, Ms 183/234/folder 3.

5. Schonfeld, Ms 183/90/2/folder 3.

6. Lambeth Palace Library, Geoffrey Fisher Papers, vol. 115.

7. Emanuel and Gissing, *Nicholas Winton and the Rescued Generation*, pp. 83–5.

8. Schonfeld, Ms 183/132/4. See also Gissing, *Pearls of Childhood*, pp. 100–1.

9. Archbishop Geoffrey Fisher, Papers, vol. 12, Lambeth Palace Library, London, p. 337.

10. Davidson and Ross, *For a Future and a Hope*, pp. 28, 16. See also Turner, *And the Policeman Smiled*, pp. 246–53.

11. Emanuel and Gissing, *Nicholas Winton and the Rescued Generation*, p. 83.

12. London Metropolitan Archives, Board of Deputies, Acc 3121/C2/1/6, 8 December 1942.

13. Fisher Papers, vol. 12, p. 337.

14. Bell Papers, vol. 35, part 1, p. 314.

15. Ibid., vol. 27, p. 116.

16. Ibid., vol. 35, part 1, p. 270b.

17. Fisher Papers, vol. 12.

18. Josephs with Bechhofer, *Rosa's Child*, p. 29.

19. Hartley Library University of Southampton, Hertz, Ms 175/139/1/folder 1, 26 September 1945.

20. Board of Deputies, Acc 3121/E2/53, 18 January 1945.

21. Author interview with J. Fieldsend, September 1994.

22. Fisher Papers, vol. 27, p. 124.

23. Chief Rabbi Hertz, Ms 175/139/1/folder 1, 1 November 1943; Hartley Library/Archives, University of Southampton; also, Ms 175/86/9, Neville Laski to C. Roth, 28 November 1941.

24. Blond, *Marks of Distinction*, p. 88.
25. Board of Deputies of British Jews, Acc 3121/E2/53, London Metropolitan Archives, p. 2.
26. *Jewish Chronicle*, 23 May 1941, p. 21.
27. *Jewish Chronicle*, 23 April 1948, p. 5.
28. *Jewish Chronicle*, 23 May 1941, p. 21.
29. Hertz, Ms 175/139/1/folder 1, 12 July 1943.
30. Olga Levy Drucker, *Kindertransport* (New York: Henry Holt, 1992) p. 144.
31. Irene Reti and Valerie Jean Chase (eds) *A Transported Life: Memories of Kindertransport. The Oral History of Thea Feliks Eden* (Santa Cruz, CA: HerBooks, 1995).
32. Board of Deputies, Acc 3121/E3/532/2, 22 November 1938.
33. Hertz, Ms 175/86/9, n.d.
34. Hertz, Ms 175/139/1/folder 1, 20 May 1943.
35. Quoted in Hertz, Ms 175/139/1, 3 December 1943.
36. Hertz, Ms 175/55/3, 18 May 1945.
37. Rabbi Solomon Schonfeld, Papers, Ms 183/382/folder 1, Hartley Library/ Archives, University of Southampton.
38. CBF, Reel 72/333/130.
39. Board of Deputies, Acc 3121/E3/532/2.
40. *Jewish Chronicle*, 26 May 1939, p. 13.
41. Board of Deputies, Acc 3121/E3/286/1; Acc 3121/E3/525/1; Acc 3121/E3/533/1.
42. *Jewish Chronicle*, 23 June 1939, p. 21; 2 June 1939, p. 8.
43. Schonfeld, Ms 183/382/folder 1.
44. Schonfeld, Ms 183/53/2/folder 2.
45. *Jewish Chronicle*, 23 December 1938, p. 26. The numbers of letters were to increase: Board of Deputies Acc 3121/E3/532/2, 21 April 1939, 'Notes of an Interview with Sir Benjamin Drage' notes that 17,000 letters per week were received in February and 13,000 in March.
46. *Jewish Chronicle*, 14 July 1939, p. 23.
47. Board of Deputies, Acc 3121/E3/532/2.
48. Gottlieb, *Men of Vision*, p. 121; *Jewish Chronicle*, 16 December 1938, p. 32.
49. Board of Deputies, Acc 3121/E3/532/3.
50. Schonfeld, Ms 183/117/1, Minutes, 13 December 1939.
51. Ibid., Ms 183/123/3.
52. Ibid., Ms 183/391/1/folder 1.
53. Ibid., Ms 183/391/1/folder 1.
54. Ibid., Ms 183/234/folder 3.
55. Board of Deputies, Acc 3121/E3/286.
56. Formerly the Council for German Jewry. See Gottlieb, *Men of Vision*,

pp. 146–60, for an excellent discussion of the financial crisis facing British refugee organizations. The figures in this section are based largely on Gottlieb.

57. Gottlieb, *Men of Vision*, p. 146.

58. Ibid., p. 153. Lord Bearsted's cable to Lewis Strauss asked for one million pounds, half as a loan if necessary. The Americans offered £50,000 as a contribution and £50,000 as a loan with strings attached. It was rejected out of hand. (CBF Reel 002, 6/32).

59. CBF, Reel 41/9. See also Minutes and Correspondence, CBF Reel 002/6.

60. CBF, Reel 002/6/63, Minutes of Emergency Meeting of the Executive Council, December 1939; also Minutes of the Executive, 12 December 1939 (CBF Reel 002, 6/67–8, also 6/73).

61. CBF, Reel 002, 6/58–60, 28 November 1939.

62. *Jewish Chronicle*, 28 April 1939, p. 34.

63. CBF, Reel 002, 6/61, 1 December 1939.

64. CBF, Reel 002, 6/61.

65. Gottlieb, *Men of Vision*, p. 157.

66. Ibid., p. 160; CBF, Reel 41, 'Introduction', p. 14.

67. CBF, Reel, 72, 333/18–19.

68. Bell Papers, vol. 35 part 1, p. 191.

69. CBF, Reel, 28/153/51.

70. CBF, Reel, 71/323/140.

71. Turner, *And the Policeman Smiled*, p. 201.

72. Schonfeld, Ms 183/264/folder 1, 'The Gas Light and Coke Company to the Jewish Secondary Schools'.

73. CBF, Reel, 71, 324/1–3.

74. Turner, *And the Policeman Smiled*, pp. 225–30.

75. Blond, *Marks of Distinction*, pp. 78–9; Schonfeld, Ms 183/264/folder 1; Ms 183/382/folder 1.

76. Turner, *And the Policeman Smiled*, pp. 225–30.

77. CBF, Reel, 68, 305/85–91.

6. The Orthodox Experience

1. *Jewish Chronicle*, 23 December 1938, p. 2; *Jewish Chronicle*, 28 July 1939, p. 11.

2. *AJR Information*, May 1949, p. 3.

3. David Kranzler, *Thy Brother's Blood*, p. 179; Schonfeld, Ms 183/264/folder 1, 28 December 1938; J. Schonfield to V. Fast, June 2002.

4. *The Times* (London), 8 February 1984.

5. Kranzler, *Thy Brother's Blood*, p. 14. See also *Jewish Chronicle*, 19 February 1982, p. 22.

6. Kranzler, *Thy Brother's Blood*, pp. 13, 15.
7. Ibid., pp. 14–16, 176–7; Dr Jeremy Schonfield to V. Fast, June, 2002.
8. Schonfeld married Judith Hertz in 1940.
9. Dr J. H. Hertz, Dr Schonfeld, Jacob Rosenheim and H. A. Goodman were present at the first meeting on 21 July (Schonfeld, Ms 183/132/3).
10. Schonfeld, Ms 183/576/1, Minutes, 12 December 1938.
11. *Jewish Chronicle*, 19 February 1982, p. 22.
12. Blond, *Marks of Distinction*, p. 74.
13. Schonfeld, Ms 183/53/2/folder 2, 12 March 1939, Chief Rabbi to Major Langdon.
14. Schonfeld, Ms 183/883/folder 3, 15 April 1942.
15. Schonfeld, Ms 183/883/folder 3, 2 December 1938, L. Baeck to Dr Hertz; Dr Hertz to Sir Robert Waley Cohen, 27 December 1938. 'Dr Baeck was overwhelmed with joy when he learned of my efforts to prevent the outrage,' this in spite of Dr Baeck's non-Orthodox orientation.
16. Kranzler, *Thy Brother's Blood*, p. 20.
17. Schonfeld, Ms 183/53/2/folder 2.
18. Schonfeld, Ms 183/53/2/folder 2, H. Nyman to Dr Hertz, 16 January 1939.
19. Schonfeld, Ms 183/53/2/folder 2, Grumpter to Schonfeld.
20. Sessi Jakovits quoted in Leverton and Lowensohn, *I Came Alone*, p. 157.
21. Revd Dr Grumpter to Dr Hertz, Hertz, Ms 175/139/1/folder 1.
22. Dr Grumpter to Chief Rabbi Hertz, 7 March 1939, Hertz, Ms 175/139/1/folder 1.
23. *AJR Information*, December 1949, p. 3.
24. Schonfeld, Ms 183/123/3, 5 October 1943.
25. Schonfeld, Ms 183/234/folder 3, 17 June 1941 to Ministry of Health.
26. Schonfeld, Ms 183/53/2/folder 1.
27. Schonfeld, Ms 183/997/3; these are Sabbath songs of welcome.
28. *Jewish Chronicle*, 6 December 1940, p. 13.
29. Schonfeld, Ms 183/391/1/folder 1.
30. Schonfeld, Ms 183/53/2/folder 2, 4 January, 1939 to H. Pels.
31. Imperial War Museum, Margareta Burkill, Interview 004588/08, p. 19.
32. Schonfeld, Ms 183/132/4.
33. M. Burkill, interview 4588/8, p. 60 of transcript; Davidson and Ross, *For a Future and a Hope*, pp. 29, 31, 49.
34. Imperial War Museum, M. Burkill, interview 4588/08.
35. Schonfeld, Ms 183/117/1, Minutes, 9 May 1939; Ms 183/382/folder 1.
36. Kranzler, *Thy Brother's Blood*, p. 24.
37. *The Times*, 25 June 1945, clipping also in Hertz, Ms 175/55/3.
38. *The Times*, 26 June 1945, letter by R. Waley-Cohen; another by W. M. Stern.
39. *The Times*, 10 July 1945.

40. Quoted in Turner, *And the Policeman Smiled*, p. 259.

41. *Jewish Chronicle*, April–September 1949.

42. Schonfeld, Ms 183/132/4, Schonfeld to I. Kestenbaum, Hartley Library University of Southampton, Rosenfelder Papers, Ms 116/157 (AJ 396/2) I. Kestenbaum from 'EM', 2 January 1939, among others; Minutes of Sub-committee for the Care of Children from Germany, 12 December 1938.

43. Hertz, Ms 175/139/1/folder 2.

44. Schonfeld, 183/53/2/folder 2; Hertz, Ms 175/139/2, 10 September 1943, when the disagreement with Sir Robert Waley Cohen is 'forced into open court'.

45. Schonfeld, Ms 183/883/folder 3, 23 April 1943.

46. Hartley Library University of Southampton, Greenberg Collection, Ms 150 (AJ/110/4), Brotman to Greenberg, 29 January 1943; Brodetsky to Greenberg, 2 February 1943.

47. Hartley Library, Greenberg Collection, Ms 150 (AJ/110/4), Brodetsky to Greenberg, 5 January, 1943.

48. CBF, Reel 16, 83/198, 201, 5 February 1948, 9 February 1948.

49. Schonfeld, Ms 183/234/folder 1.

50. Schonfeld, Ms 183/234/folder 2, Chief Rabbi's circular letter, 5704.

51. Schonfeld, Ms 183/883/folder 3, 6 June 1943.

52. Schonfeld, Ms 183/90/2/folder 1, 22 March 1939.

53. *Jewish Chronicle*, 21 April 1939, p. 21; see also Hertz, Ms 175/86/9 'Memorandum'.

54. London Metropolitan Archives, Board of Deputies, Acc 3121/C9/1/D2 May 1942.

55. Schonfeld, Ms 183/593/1, 'CRREC Report 1938–1948'; Ms 183/641/folder 2; *Jewish Chronicle*, 2 June 1939, p. 22, 'Orthodox children can best be accommodated in hostels'.

56. Hertz, Ms 175/139/5, 15 October 1939.

57. CBF, Reel 62, 287/546; these were hidden or concentration camp children.

58. *Jewish Chronicle*, 23 June 1939, p. 54, a letter to the editor from the chief rabbi.

59. Hartley Library University of Southampton, Rosenfelder Papers, Ms 116/157 (AJ 396/2), 2 January 1939.

60. Shabtai Teveth, *Ben-Gurion: The Burning Ground, 1886–1948* (Boston: Houghton Mifflin, 1987) p. 855.

61. Turner, *And the Policeman Smiled*, p. 250. See also Emanuel and Gissing, *Nicholas Winton and the Rescued Generation*, p. 85.

62. Aaron Haas, *In the Shadow of the Holocaust: The Second Generation* (Ithaca: Cornell University Press, 1990) p. 156.

63. Blond, *Marks of Distinction*, p. 86.

64. Emanuel and Gissing, *Nicholas Winton and the Rescued Generation*, p. 83.

65. Schonfeld, Ms 183/90/2/folder 1, Cohen to Schonfeld, 11 March 1941.
66. J. Schonfield to V. Fast, June, 2002.
67. Schonfeld, Ms 183/90/2/folder 1, 14 June 1940.
68. *Jewish Chronicle*, 13 February 1942, p. 10.
69. Schonfeld, Ms 183/227/1/folder 1.
70. Schonfeld, Ms 183/015, 'A Shaft of Light' by Ruben Katz.
71. *AJR Information* provides helpful data about the two-year effort to elect a new chief rabbi, believing 'the delay being due to a tug-of-war between Zionists and non-Zionists'. *AJR Information*, October 1947, p. 77; March 1948, p. 3; April 1948, p. 3; May 1948, p. 3.
72. Schonfeld, Ms 183/576/1, Executive Minutes, 24 May 1948.
73. CBF, Reel 62, 287/105.
74. Schonfeld, Ms 183/576/1/Part 2, 'Letter to Charity Commissioners', 7 November 1949.
75. Schonfeld, Ms 183/576/1/Part 2.
76. *Jewish Chronicle*, 23 September 1949, p. 14.
77. CBF, Reel 62, 287/107, Montefiore to Stephany, 18 April 1949.
78. CBF, Reel 62, 286/25–26, 17 September 1954.
79. Kranzler, *Thy Brother's Blood*, p. 177.
80. Hertz, Ms 175/141/1; see also Schonfeld, Ms 183/224/2, 'CRREC Report 1938–1944'.
81. Leverton and Lowensohn, *I Came Alone*, p. 295.
82. Schonfeld, Ms 183/576/1/Part 2, 'Final Letter of Arrangements'.
83. Schonfeld, Ms 183/576/1/Part 2, 'To the Chief Rabbi'.
84. Ibid.
85. Schonfeld, Ms 183/576/1/Part 2; Minutes, 5 February 1949. Deeds of Covenant were agreements of financial support.
86. Schonfeld, Ms 183/576/1/Part 2, 10 February 1949.
87. See for example, among others, R. Katz, 'A Shaft of Light' (Schonfeld, Ms 183/101/5); Leverton and Lowensohn, *I Came Alone*, pp. 187, 234, 295.
88. J. Schonfield to V. Fast, June 2002.
89. See for example, Esther Baumel, 'The Jewish Refugee Children', p. 105; Reeve R. Brenner, *The Faith and Doubt of Holocaust Survivors* (New York: Free Press, 1980).
90. Rosa M. Sacharin (compiler) *Recollections of Child Refugees from 1938 to the Present: Kindertransport Scotland's Child Refugees* (Glasgow: Scottish Annual Reunion of Kinder, 1999) p. 47.
91. Fred Dunstan, 'Jewish Refugee Youth in England 1938–1940', handwritten manuscript in Wiener Library, p. 5.
92. Anon, *Twenty-Five Years of Youth Aliyah* (London: Children and Youth Aliyah, 1959) 'Introduction'.

93. *AJR Information*, February 1946, p. 11.
94. Norman Bentwich, *Jewish Youth Comes Home: The Story of Youth Aliyah, 1933–1943* (London: Gollancz, 1944) p. 89.
95. Dunstan, 'Jewish Refugee Youth in England'. Youth Aliyah camps included Pinetrees Farm, Great Engeham Camp, Great Engeham Farm, and Llandoff and Gwrych castles in Wales. Not all were involved in the problems Dunstan cited.

7. Jewish Christian Children

1. As with many Nazi words, this term is untranslatable, but a closer rendering would be 'half-breed' or 'half-caste' (I wish to thank L. Steiman for this information). There was also an American Committee for 'Non-Aryan' Christians, headed by a Mr Ritchie. See Bodleian Library, Ms SPSL 114/2–3; also Hilberg, *Perpetrators, Victims, Bystanders*, pp. 150–5. The Church of England records always use a capital 'N' when referring to non-Aryans, while common usage indicates a small 'n'.
2. Kaplan, *Between Dignity and Despair*, pp. 74–93. See Kaplan's excellent study for more information related to Jewish and 'mixed' marriages.
3. Lambeth Palace Library, Bishop George Bell Papers, vol. 27, p. 35; vol.34, p. 155.
4. Author interview with H. Schramm, 1991.
5. Author interview with Henry K., 1994.
6. Kaplan, *Between Dignity and Despair*, p. 21. Kaplan points out that Quaker youth groups, in contrast to those of the mainline churches, accepted *Mischlinge* as members.
7. Gilbert, *Kristallnacht*, p. 262.
8. LeBor and Boyes, *Seduced by Hitler*, pp. 76–7. See also Nathan Stoltzfus, *Resistance of the Heart: Intermarraige and the Rosenstrasse Protest in Nazi Germany* (New York: W. W. Norton, 1996).
9. Gilbert, *Kristallnacht*, pp. 191–3.
10. Hecht, *Invisible Walls*, p. 65.
11. Ibid., p. 72.
12. Bodleian Library, Society for the Protection of Science and Learning. Ms SPSL 114/2–3, 'First Annual Report of the Inter-Faith Committee'.
13. Bell Papers, vol. 35, part 1, p. 135.
14. Ibid. This view is also recorded in the 'Inter-Faith Committee for Children from Germany' report, Bodleian Library, Ms SPSL 114/2–3.
15. Author interview with H. Schramm, 1991. For more information on the Hitler Youth, see Jennifer Keeley, *Life in the Hitler Youth* (San Diego, CA: Luent Books, 2000).

16. Author interview with H. Schramm, 1991; see also Kaplan, *Between Dignity and Despair*.

17. Bell Papers, vol. 27, p. 69, letter dated 12 October 1933.

18. Bell Papers, vol. 27, pp. 9–10. For more information on the life and work of Bishop Bell, see Chandler, *Brethren in Adversity*; and Edwin Robertson, *Unshakeable Friend: George Bell and the German Churches* (London: CCBI Publications, 1995).

19. Bell Papers, vol. 27, pp. 46, 48.

20. Ibid., pp. 17, 76.

21. Ibid., p. 82.

22. Bell Papers, vol. 6, pp. 452, 185.

23. Ibid., p. 185.

24. Bell Papers, vol. 34, p. 149.

25. Ibid., Interview on 'Non-Aryan Christians'.

26. Bell Papers, vol. 6, pp. 143–4, 181.

27. Karl Barth, *The German Church Conflict*, translated by P. T. A. Parker (Richmond: John Knox Press, 1965) p. 9.

28. Bell Papers, vol. 27, pp. 12–13.

29. Martin Gilbert, *The Righteous: The Unsung Heroes of the Holocaust* (Toronto: Key Porter Books, 2003) pp. 182, 184, 185. See also Richard L. Rubenstein, 'The Dean and the Chosen People', in John Roth and Michael Berenbaum (eds) *The Holocaust: Religious and Philosophical Implications* (New York: Paragon House, 1989).

30. Hecht, *Invisible Walls*, p. 24, quotes the confidential directive to local authorities stating that, 'to avoid jeopardizing the 1936 Olympic Games in Berlin, all anti-Jewish placards and posters in the vicinity of Garmisch-Parterkirchen, where the Winter Games will be held, are to be removed' (12 March 1935). The notices referred to 'Jews Unwelcome' signs and the like.

31. Mary Bosanquet, *The Life and Death of Dietrich Bonhoeffer* (London: Hodder & Stoughton, 1968) p. 178.

32. Bell Papers, vol. 35, p. 133, 'Church of England Committee for "Non-Aryan" Christians'. See, however, Gerlach, 'When the Witnesses were Silent', pp. 68–82. For a different opinion on the part the Confessing Church played, see Ludwig Heine, *Geschichte des Kirchenkampfes in der Grenzmark Posen-Westpreußen 1930–1940* (Göttingen: Vandenhoeck & Ruprecht, 1961); Horst Kater, *Die Deutsche Evangelische Kirche in den Jahren 1933 und 1934: Eine rechts- und verfassungsrechtliche Untersuchung zu Gründung und Zerfall einer Kirche im nationalsozialistischen Staat* (Göttingen: Vandenhoeck & Ruprecht, 1970); Baron Dieter von Lersner, *Die evangelischen Jugendverband Württembergs und die Hitler-Jugend 1933–1934* (Göttingen: Vandenhoeck & Ruprecht, 1958).

33. Bell Papers, vol. 34, p. 150.

34. Robertson, *Unshakeable Friend*, p. 47.

35. Bell Papers, vol. 27, p. 173.

36. Sir John Hope Simpson, *Refugees: A Review of the Situation since September 1938* (London: The Royal Institute of International Affairs, 1939).

37. J. Gorsky, 'Pius XII and the Holocaust', in Carol Rittner, Stephen D. Smith and Irene Steinfeldt (eds) *The Holocaust and the Christian World* (London: Kuperard, 2000) p. 36. See also Michael Phayer, 'The Response of the German Catholic Church to National Socialism', in Carol Rittner, Stephen D. Smith and Irene Steinfeldt (eds) *The Holocaust and the Christian World* (London: Kuperard, 2000) pp. 59–61; Michael Phayer, *The Catholic Church and the Holocaust, 1930–1965* (Bloomington: Indiana University Press, 2000).

38. E. Rosenblatt, 'Edith Stein's Canonization: Acknowledging Objections from Jews and Catholics', in Carol Rittner, Stephen D. Smith and Irene Steinfeldt (eds) *The Holocaust and the Christian World* (London: Kuperard, 2000) pp. 224–7. See also Patricia Hampl, 'Edith Stein – Poland, 1942: A Book Sealed with Seven Seals', in Susan Bergman (ed.) *Martyrs: Contemporary Writers on Modern Lives of Faith* (San Francisco: HarperSanFrancisco, 1996) pp. 197–215; Edith Stein, *Life in a Jewish Family (1891–1916): An Autobiography*, translated by Josephine Koppel, OCD (Washington, DC: ICS Publications, 1986).

39. Brenda Bailey, *A Quaker Couple in Nazi Germany: Leonard Friedrich Survives Buchenwald* (York: William Sessions UK, 1994) p. 65; Greenwood, *Quaker Encounters*, vol. 1, pp. 261–3.

40. Bailey, *A Quaker Couple in Nazi Germany*, p. 65.

41. Ibid., p. 7; Bell Papers, vol. 27, p. 332 refer to the Quakers' programme as 'a continuous and sustained effort'.

42. Greenwood, *Quaker Encounters*, pp. 262–3.

43. Bell Papers, vol. 27, pp. 9–10, 103, 108.

44. Ibid., p. 360.

45. Ibid., p. 412.

46. Hartley Library, Christian Council, Ms 65, 'Christian Council for Refugees from Germany and Central Europe: A Five Year Survey', pp. 3–6.

47. L. J. Bliss, *Christians and Ant-Semitism* (Birmingham: Council of Clergy & Ministers for Common Ownership, 1944) p. 3.

48. Friends House Library/Archives, Friends Committee for Refugees and Aliens, minutes, 27 June 1939.

49. Bodleian Library, Oxford, Ms SPSL 99/5, David C. Thompson to Fr Geraerts, 15 August 1938, Catholic Committee for Refugees from Germany.

50. Bell Papers, vol. 35, part 1.

51. Ibid., p. 134.

52. Ibid., 1 February 1938.

53. Hilberg, *Perpetrators, Victims, Bystanders*, p. 150.

54. CBF, Reel 71, 326/4.

55. Robertson, *Unshakeable Friend*, p. 53. Bishop and Mrs Bell personally took responsibility for ten of these children (Bodleian Library Ms SPSL 114/2–3).

56. Simpson, *Refugees: A Review of the Situation since September 1938*, p. 33.

57. Bell Papers, vol. 35, part 1, p. 135.

58. Bodleian Library Oxford, Ms SPSL 104/4, Greenwood to Cleghorn Thomson, 1 February 1939.

59. The figure varies between 10 and 30 per cent. Norman Bentwich, *The Refugees from Germany, April 1933 to December 1935* (London: George Allen & Unwin Ltd, 1936) p. 198, says approximately 20 per cent; CBF Reel 28, 53/35 uses 10 per cent; David Cesarani, 'Introduction to Children's Transport' in the Wiener Library records, says that '30 per cent were not Jewish'; Sir John Hope Simpson, *Refugees: A Review of the Situation since September 1938*, p. 31, believes that 'no certain figure is available'. CBF Reel 28, 153/20 cites the following figures: Jews 7482; Christians 1123; and undenominational 749. The 15 per cent used in the body of this manuscript has been chosen because the Christian Council for Refugees received 15 per cent of monies available for refugee work, with Jewish organizations receiving the other 85 per cent.

60. Baumel, 'The Jewish Refugee Children', p. 102.

61. Imperial War Museum, Margarete, interview 17542/2BX.

62. Despite urging by the British government, Canada did not as a rule open its doors to Jewish refugees until after the war. See Irving Abella and Harold Troper, *None Is Too Many: Canada and the Jews of Europe, 1933–1948* (Toronto: Lester & Orpen Denys, 1991) pp. 53, 70, 101f.

63. See Vera K. Fast (ed.) *Companions of the Peace: Diaries and Letters of Monica Storrs, 1931–1939* (Toronto: University of Toronto Press, 1999) pp. 199–200.

64. Bell Papers, vol. 35, part 1, p. 149.

65. Bell Papers, vol. 35, part 1, Minutes, Church of England Committee, 25 May 1943, pp. 197–8.

66. Bell Papers, vol. 35, p. 197.

67. Bell Papers, vol. 35, p. 196; CBF Reel 28, 153/49.

68. Bodleian Library Oxford, Ms SPSL 114/2–3.

69. Hansard, HCD, vol. 342, 8 December 1938.

70. Bell Papers, vol. 35, part 1, p. 134, correspondence with Sir Wyndham Deedes.

71. Bell Papers, vol. 35, p. 135.

72. Bell Papers, vol. 35, p. 242b.

73. Bell Papers, vol. 35, part 1, pp. 328–31.

74. CBF, reel 37, 198/30, 7 February 1946; 298/11; 198/15; 198/21.

75. Hartley Library University of Southampton, Christian Council Ms 65 (A755/1/1), Buesing to Carter, 25 April 1944.

76. Bell Papers, vol. 35, pp. 248, 258b, 284b, 331; Mrs Burkill of the Cambridge Refugee Committee, who complained bitterly about Orthodox Jewish activity among the children, also commented that 'the difficult people were the Catholic Committee' (Imperial War Museum, Interview 004588/08).

77. Hartley Library, Christian Council, Ms 65 (A755), pp. 3–5, Christian Council: Reports and Accounts, 30 September 1942.

78. Bell Papers, 'After Ten Years: A Letter from the Bishop of Chichester', vol. 35, p. 1.

79. Greenwood, *Quaker Encounters*, p. 273. The Friends Service Council, of which the refugee committee formed a component, was awarded the Nobel Peace Prize in 1947 (Bell Papers, vol.35, part 1, p. 337b).

80. Hartley Library, Christian Council, Ms 65 (A755/1/2), Christian Council, 18 March 1948.

81. Hartley Library, Christian Council, Ms 65 (A755/1/2), Christian Council Minutes Ledger.

82. Hartley Library, Christian Council, Ms 65 (A755/1/2), Christian Council Report, 30 September 1942, p. 4; Christian Council Final Report and Survey 1938–1951.

83. Bell Papers, vol. 34, p. 13.

84. Hartley Library, Christian Council, Ms 65(A755/1/2), Christian Council, July 1950.

8. Hidden Children and Camp Survivors: The Postwar Refugees

1. Martin Gilbert, *Kristallnacht*, p. 232.

2. For postwar use of 'children's transport', see Schonfeld Collection Ms 183/53/224/1 folder, letter 10, 10 May 1946, among many others.

3. The best published sources at present are Martin Gilbert, *The Boys: Triumph Over Adversity: The Story of 732 Young Concentration Camp Survivors* (Vancouver: Douglas & McIntyre, 1996); Gottlieb, *Men of Vision*, pp. 183–91; and Sarah Moskovitz, *Love Despite Hate: Child Survivors of the Holocaust and their Adult Lives* (New York: Schocken Books, 1983).

4. Michael Berenbaum, *The World Must Know: The History of the Holocaust as Told in the United States Holocaust Memorial Museum* (Boston: Little Brown & Company, 2006) p. 192.

5. Toby A. Axelrod, *In the Camps: Teens Who Survived the Nazi Concentration Camps* (New York: The Rosen Publishing Group Inc., 1999) pp. 23, 31, 32.

6. Donald L. Niewyk (ed.) *Fresh Wounds: Early Narratives of Holocaust Survival* (Chapel Hill: University of North Carolina Press, 1998) p. 20.

7. Axelrod, *In the Camps*, pp. 21, 38.

8. *Jewish Chronicle*, 17 August 1945, p. 5. Bailey, *A Quaker Couple in Nazi*

Germany, p. 221, writes: 'some 800 children had been found living among the prisoners at Buchenwald, many of them had been sexually abused.'

9. Schonfeld, Ms 183/234/folder 1: 'Council of British Societies for Relief Abroad: Report on Care of Children' 1943 (marked 'Strictly Confidential); 'Plans for European Reconstruction', and other documents.

10. CBF, Reel 003, 9/64, Minutes of CBF Council, 6 May 1945, 10 May 1945.

11. Rita Grunbaum, quoted in Brana Gurewitsch (ed.) *Mothers, Sisters, Resisters: Oral Histories of Women Who Survived the Holocaust* (Tuscaloosa: University of Alabama Press, 1998) pp. 21–3. Walter Laqueur, *The Terrible Secret: Suppression of the Truth about Hitler's Final Solution* (Boston: Little, Brown & Company, 1980) p. 2, says that Bergen-Belsen was not initially a concentration camp, but a Krankenlager (a 'sick camp') with death only by starvation and sickness.

12. Herman Langbein, *Against All Hope: Resistance in the Nazi Concentration Camps 1938–1945*, translated by Harry Zohn (New York: Paragon House, 1994) pp. 1–2, 359; Laqueur, *The Terrible Secret*.

13. *Jewish Chronicle*, 15 June 1945, p. 6.

14. Other members of the committee were Carmel Gilbert, Oscar Joseph, Anna Schwab and, later, Sir Keith Joseph and Major Edmund de Rothschild.

15. *Jewish Chronicle*, 15 June 1945, pp. 6, 10.

16. George Lauer quoted in Anita Brostoff and Sheila Chamovitz (eds) *Flares of Memory: Survivors Remember – Stories of Childhood during the Holocaust* (Oxford: Oxford University Press, 2001) pp. 265–6.

17. Moskovitz, *Love Despite Hate*, pp. 7–8.

18. Gilbert, *The Boys*, pp. 279ff; Gottlieb, *Men of Vision*, pp. 183ff. Of these children, only 50 were girls, 17 were aged three to seven, 20 were eight to twelve, 50 were thirteen to fourteen, and the rest were over 15 (*Jewish Chronicle*, 31 August 1945, p. 1). See also CBF, Reel 37, 202/1–2.

19. Bentwich, *They Found Refuge*, p. 75; also Gottlieb, *Men of Vision*, p. 186.

20. CBF, Reel 37, 198/14, 18 December 1945.

21. Rita Grunbaum, quoted in Gurewitsch, *Mothers, Sisters, Resisters*, pp. 21–3.

22. Hartley Library University of Southampton, Hertz, Ms 175/55/3, *Daily News Bulletin*, 29 August 1945.

23. Hertz, Ms 175/137/2/folder 1, Otto Schiff to Dr Hertz, 19 October 1945.

24. CBF, Reel 33, 198/4. *Jewish Chronicle*, 22 June 1945, 17 August 1945, p. 5, also reports difficulties between Leonard Cohen and Rabbi Vilenski of the CRREC regarding camp children.

25. Gottlieb, *Men of Vision*, p. 189.

26. Schonfeld, Ms 183/576/1, Ms 183/1015, 184.

27. Schonfeld, Executive Committee Minutes, 24 May 1948, Ms 183/576/1.

28. Schonfeld, Ms 183/385/2.

29. For a family in hiding, see Stacy Cretzmeyer, *Your Name is Renée: Ruth Kapp Hartz's Story as a Hidden Child in Nazi-Occupied France* (New York: Oxford University Press, 1999); also Jane Marks, *The Hidden Children: The Secret Survivors of the Holocaust* (Toronto: Bantam Books, 1995) p. 44; Wolf, *Beyond Anne Frank*.

30. Kathy Kacer, *Hiding Edith: A True Story* (Toronto: Second Story Press, 2006) p. 33.

31. See for example, André Stein, *Hidden Children: Forgotten Survivors of the Holocaust*, p. 137. Hynrik's story and similar ones are found in the Schonfeld papers, Ms 183/385/2.

32. Deborah Dwork, *Children with a Star: Jewish Youth in Nazi Europe* (New Haven, CT: Yale University Press, 1991) p. 76.

33. Schonfeld, Ms 183/385/2, Ms 183/1002/2.

34. See Dwork, *Children with a Star*, pp. 34ff.; Stein, *Hidden Children*, pp. 3ff.; and Wolf, *Beyond Anne Frank*, especially Chapter 4.

35. See Dwork, *Children with a Star*, p. 33; Wolf, *Beyond Anne Frank*. According to Dwork, the congregation of Franciscan Sisters of the Family of Mary, and the Grey Ursulines, were exceptionally courageous, being urged by their superiors to help Jewish children, altogether 'two-thirds of the 74 female religious communities in Poland took part in helping Jewish children and adults. It is estimated that 1500 children were saved in this way', p. 281, fn. 4, quoting Ewa Kurek-Leski's study. W. Choms is credited with bringing many children out of the Lvov ghetto and placing them in monasteries or orphanages, while Yvonne Nevejean of Belgium, Bishop Monsignor Guiseppe Nicolini in Italy, and Metropolitan Andreas Szeptycky of the Uniate Church brought hundreds more to convents and orphanages, to mention but a few outstanding examples. See Silver, *The Book of the Just*, pp. 94ff, 125ff.

36. Schonfeld, Ms 183/385/2.

37. Dwork, *Children with a Star*, pp. 36ff., 60ff.; Wolf, *Beyond Anne Frank*, pp. 11–54.

38. Dwork, *Children with a Star*, p. 35.

39. Silver, *The Book of the Just*, p. 11; Schonfeld also mentions payments by parents; see Ms 183/385/2.

40. Hertz, Ms 175/118/2/folder 2, Ferdman to Brodetsky, 10 November 1944.

41. Dwork, *Children with a Star*, p. 52.

42. Ibid., p. 65. Rabbi Schonfeld's papers also contain evidence of parents paying for their children's safety (Ms 183/385/2).

43. Vromen, *Hidden Children*, p. 36.

44. Ibid.

45. Dwork, *Children with a Star*, p. 105; Wolf, *Beyond Anne Frank*.

46. Quoted in Stein, *Hidden Children*, pp. 207–8.

47. Quoted in Vromen, *Hidden Children*, pp. 144–6.

48. Ibid., p. 17.

49. Kacer, *Hiding Edith*, pp. 113–15.

50. Quoted in Vromen, *Hidden Children*, p. 22.

51. *Jewish Chronicle*, 1 August 1947, p. 10.

52. *Jewish Chronicle*, 13 December 1946, p. 9.

53. *Jewish Chronicle*, 1 August 1947, p. 10; Silver, *The Book of the Just*, p. 161.

54. Gilbert, *Kristallnacht*, p. 200.

55. Ibid., p. 181.

56. Vromen, *Hidden Children*, p. 145.

57. Dwork, *Children with a Star*, pp. 281–2; Silver, *The Book of the Just*, pp. 13, 16.

58. Vromen, *Hidden Children*, p. 144.

59. See, among others, Berenbaum, *The World Must Know*, pp. 158–62; Janet Keith, *A Friend Among Enemies: The Incredible Story of Arie Van Mansum in the Holocaust* (Richmond Hill, Ontario: Fitzhenry & Whiteside, 1991); and Carol Rittner and Sondra Myers (eds) *The Courage to Care: Rescuers of the Jews during the Holocaust* (New York: New York University Press, 1986) for a discussion of those who hid Jewish adults and children.

60. Vromen, *Hidden Children*, p. 5.

61. Martin Gilbert, quoted in Krell, *Messages and Memories*, p. 72.

62. Dwork, *Children with a Star*, pp. 32–3; Jerzy Kosiński, *The Painted Bird* (London: Black Swan, 1965); Jack Kuper, *Child of the Holocaust* (Toronto: General Publishing Company, 1967); Yeduda Nir, *The Lost Childhood: A Memoir* (New York: Harcourt, Brace, Jovanovich, 1989).

63. Schonfeld, Ms 183/385/2.

64. CBF, Reel 026, 146, 'Letters from Children'.

65. Quoted in Charles Anflick, *Resistance: Teen Partisans and Resisters Who Fought Nazi Tyranny* (New York: Rosen Publishing Group, Inc., 1999) pp. 26, 27.

66. Silver, *The Book of the Just*, p. 142.

67. Schonfeld, Ms 183/385/2 contains many such stories.

68. Schonfeld, Ms 183/385/2.

69. Lena Kuchler-Silberman, *My 100 Children* (London: Souvenir Press, 1961) pp. 122–3; Faye Schulman, *A Partisan's Memoir: Woman of the Holocaust* (Toronto: Second Story Press, 1995).

70. Kuchler-Silberman, *My 100 Children*, p. 103; Nir, *The Lost Childhood*, p. 161.

71. Anflick, *Resistance*, p. 47.

72. *Jewish Chronicle*, 6 July 1945, p. 10.

73. *Jewish Chronicle*, 10 January 1947, p. 14; Kuchler-Silberman, *My Hundred Children*; Schonfeld, Ms 183/227/1 folder 2.

74. Schonfeld, Ms 183/227/1/folder 1, 'Arrived Warsaw 4th Nov. 1945'. The

Jewish Committee for Relief Abroad was set up in January 1943. By May of that year 400 volunteers were already in training to assist in the 'reconstruction of Europe', which included the gathering of Jewish children (Schonfeld, Ms 183/234/folder1). These documents are marked 'Strictly Confidential'.

75. Quoted in Gurewitsch, *Mothers, Sisters, Resisters*, p. 178.
76. Wolf, *Beyond Anne Frank*, p. 167.
77. Schonfeld, Ms 183/227/1/folder 2. Handwritten diary entry, November 1945.
78. Gilbert, *The Boys*, p. 275. See also Ruben Katz, 'A Shaft of Light', p. 179 in Schonfeld, Ms 183/1015; Kuchler-Silberman, *My Hundred Children*, pp. 145, 151. Led by Cardinal Jozef Glemp, 100 Roman Catholic bishops 'apologized to God' and to 'our Jewish brothers and sisters', referring with regret and repentance to the crimes that took place against the Jews in Poland (*Winnipeg Free Press*, 28 May 2001, B2).
79. Quoted in Michael C. Steinlauf, *Bondage to the Dead: Poland and the Memory of the Holocaust* (Syracuse: Syracuse University Press, 1997) pp. 52–6.
80. Martin Gilbert quoted in Krell, *Messages and Memories*, p. 73.
81. Schonfeld, Ms 183/1015, pp. 184–5.
82. As a safety precaution most hidden and hiding children had changed their names or assumed the name of their foster parents, and many of the younger ones could not remember their Jewish names. See Kuchler-Silberman, *My Hundred Children*, pp. 151, 176–7. Handwritten instructions n.d., Schonfeld, Ms 183/227/1 folder 2.
83. CBF Reel 37, 199/112.
84. Schonfeld, Ms 183/227/1 folder 2. Dr Schonfeld was very suspicious of the (Zionist) Central Committee for Displaced Persons, which had links with UNRRA and which would only agree to sending children to Palestine or occasionally South Africa. Schonfeld was afraid that children under their auspices would not receive adequate religious instruction and therefore was willing by any means, to 'liberate' children from their jurisdiction and send them to Britain. He goes so far as to suggest to his contacts in Poland, 'try to discover other Central Committee Orphanages e.g. Krakow' to get those children to Britain as well.
85. Schonfeld, Ms 183/227/1 folder 2; Ms 183/1002/1.
86. *Jewish Chronicle*, 16 February 1945, p. 8; see also Kuchler-Silberman, *My Hundred Children*, p. 125.
87. *Jewish Chronicle*, 21 September 1945, p. 5.
88. Hertz, Ms 175/55/3, 11 September 1945.
89. Vromen, *Hidden Children*, p. 135.
90. Krell, *Messages and Memories*, p. 59.

91. Hertz, Ms 175/55/3, 7 August 1945.

92. *Jewish Chronicle*, 11 January 1946, p. 9; 6 June 1947, p. 9; 5 September 1947, p. 5. A report from David Ferdman, a representative of Belgian Jewry, to Professor Bodetsky, 10 November 1944, describes in some detail the situation of hidden children in Belgium (Hertz, Ms 175/118/2/folder 2).

93. *Jewish Chronicle*, 22 March 1946, p. 9.

94. Vromen, *Hidden Children*, pp. 134–5, 137.

95. Hartley Library University of Southampton, Greenberg Papers, Ms 150 (AJ/110/7), Report of Arieh Handler.

96. Schonfeld, Ms 183/1001/2.

97. Schonfeld, Ms 183/576/1.

98. Schonfeld, Ms 183/234/folder 1, 23 October 1946.

99. Schonfeld, Ms 183/883/folder 1, 15 July 1945; *Jewish Chronicle*, 5 January 1945, p. 1, reports other instances: 'twelve French families who have flatly refused to restore to Jewish parents 18 children aged between three and seven years, whom they adopted and baptized'. Even the Chief Rabbi of Palestine, Dr Herzog, came to Europe on behalf of hidden children (*Jewish Chronicle*, 7 June 1946, p. 1; 27 September 1946, p. 10).

100. Schonfeld, Ms 183/227/1 folder 2. See also Kuchler-Silberman, *My Hundred Children*, p. 126.

101. Schonfeld, Ms 183/227/1 folder 1; also 8 July 1947. See also Ms 183/53/1 folders 1 and 2.

102. Schonfeld, Ms 183/385/2. In an autobiographical sketch, Ruben Katz claims to have assisted in kidnapping his friend's four-year-old niece when her Polish foster parents refused to give her up (Schonfeld, Ms 183/1015 'A Shaft of Light').

103. Schonfeld, Ms 183/224/2, where Schonfeld requests £30 per child for additional expenses.

104. Schonfeld, Ms 183/234/folder 1. The receipts are found in Ms 183/975/1.

105. Schonfeld, Ms 183/1015, 'A Shaft of Light', by Ruben Katz, unpublished manuscript.

106. Schonfeld, Ms 183/234/folder 1, March 1946; see also Ms 183/1015, p. 187.

107. Schonfeld, Ms 183/1015, pp. 187–8.

108. Schonfeld, Ms 183/1015, p. 190.

109. Author interview with J. Schonfield, June 2000.

110. Schonfeld, Ms 183/53/1 folder 1.

111. Schonfeld, Ms 183/234/folder 1, 28 October 1946.

112. CBF, Reel 37, 198/20, 18 December 1945; 198/7; 198/18; for lists and descriptions of the hostels see CBF, Reel 37, 198/15 to 198/26.

113. CBF, Reel 37, 315/90, 9 October 1945; see also *Jewish Chronicle*, 31 August 1945, p. 13.

114. The director of the Lingfield home, Alice Goldberger, was assisted by Anna Freud, daughter of the famed psychoanalyst, Sigmund Freud. For the story of Quare Mead, see Eva Kahn-Minden, *The Road Back: Quare Mead* (Jerusalem: Gefen Publishing House, 1991).

115. CBF, Reel 37, 199/110–11.

116. *Jewish Chronicle*, 18 October 1946, p. 14.

117. *Jewish Chronicle*, 3 January 1947, 10 January 1947, p. 1; 16 January 1947, p. 10.

118. CBF, Reel 37, 199/12.

119. Gilbert, *The Boys*, pp. 334, 335.

120. Ibid., p. 330.

121. CBF, Reel 37, 199/125–6, 13 June 1946.

122. London Metropolitan Archives, Acc 2793/01/01/03, L. Montefiore, 'Memorandum: The Committee for the Care of Children from Camps', 15 October 1945.

123. Quoted in Anton Gill, *The Journey Back from Hell: Conversations with Concentration Camp Survivors* (London: Grafton Books, 1988) pp. 141, 155.

124. Schonfeld, Ms 183/883/folder 1, 4 October 1945; see also CBF Reel 62, 286/136–7, 23 July 1950.

125. Letter by Henry Pels, Schonfeld's friend and supporter, *Jewish Chronicle*, 10 January 1947, p. 14.

126. Schonfeld, Ms 183/883 folder 1, 25 April 1945, a letter from a 'GI' to Moses Schonfeld, with which Solomon Schonfeld agreed wholeheartedly.

127. Schonfeld, Ms 183/234/folder 1/2; Ms 183/883/folder 3 among others.

128. *Jewish Chronicle*, 24 August 1945, p. 5; 17 August 1945, pp. 5, 10; 31 August 1945, p. 13.

129. Martin S. quoted in Joshua M. Greene and Shiva Kumar, *Witness: Voices from the Holocaust* (New York: The Free Press, 2000) p. xxv.

130. *Jewish Chronicle*, 18 October 1946, p. 14.

131. London Metropolitan Archives, CBF, Acc 2793/01/01/01/03, 'Memorandum: The Committee for the Care of Children from Camps', 15 October 1945.

132. CBF, Reel 37, 198/53, 3 July 1946.

133. Gilbert, *The Boys*, p. 413.

134. Quoted in Gill, *The Journey Back from Hell*, p. 154.

135. Imperial War Museum, Interview 17369/4. Many of the taped interviews housed in the archives of the IWM relate to hidden children. See especially Interview 15431 BX.

136. Krell, *Messages and Memories*, p. 68. See also Dominique Frischer, *Les Enfants du Silence et de la Reconstruction* (Paris: Grasset, 2008); and Maria Lachs, *From Paris to Sydney: A Chaotic Roller Coaster. An Autobiography of a 'Hidden Child Survivor of the Holocaust'* (Marrickville, NSW: Southwood, 2007).

137. Bentwich, *They Found Refuge*, p. 76.

138. CBF, Reel 37, 198/79.

139. CBF, Reel 37, 199/12.

140. CBF, Reel 37, 198/53, 198/55.

141. CBF, Reel 37, 198/55ff.

142. *Jewish Chronicle*, 17 October 1947, p. 9.

143. CBF, Reel 37, 202/1–2.

144. Gilbert, *The Boys*, p. 370.

145. CBF, Reel 37, 203/195. It is amazing that only three boys in more than 700 required long-term psychiatric care and in 1996 there was only one (Gilbert, *The Boys*, p. 388).

146. Moskovitz, *Love Despite Hate*, p. 231.

147. Gilbert, *The Boys*, p. 376.

148. Ibid., pp. 380–1.

149. Gilbert, *The Boys*, p. 388.

150. Moskovitz, *Love Despite Hate*, pp. 225, 227.

151. CBF, Reel 37, 200/76.

152. Quoted in Gilbert, *The Boys*, p. 364. Used by permission.

9. In Later Years

1. *Jewish Chronicle*, 3 January 1947, p. 1.

2. Krell, *Messages and Memories*, p. 57; see also Robert Krell's later work, *Child Holocaust Survivors: Memories and Reflections* (Victoria: Trafford Publishing, 2007).

3. Krell, *Messages and Memories*; Moskovitz, *Love Despite Hate*.

4. Gissing, *Pearls of Childhood*, pp. 174–5.

5. Susie Bradfield, *Kindertransport 60th Anniversary* (London: ROK, 1999) p. 85.

6. *Jewish Chronicle*, 9 May 1947, p. 17.

7. Quoted in pamphlet entitled *This is Our Life* (London: Free German Youth, n.d.) p. 11 (courtesy of Margaret Goldberger).

8. Harris and Oppenheimer, *Into the Arms of Strangers*, p. 224. Gissing returned to the UK in January 1949.

9. Gissing, *Pearls of Childhood*, pp. 132–3.

10. CBF, Reel 67, 316/139–40.

11. *AJR Information*, September 1947, p. 65; Gilbert, *The Boys*, p. 260.

12. Quoted in Harris and Oppenheimer, *Into the Arms of Strangers*, p. 241.

13. Anon, 'Lives Lived: Paul Felix (Sontheimer) Sutton', obituary in *Globe and Mail* (Toronto) 29 January 1998.

14. Schonfeld, Ms 183/1002/1. London Metropolitan Archives, Acc 2793/03/06/08: 32 boys from the 1938–39 *Kinder* applied for rabbinical studies.

15. Gissing, *Pearls of Childhood*, pp. 100–1.
16. CBF Reel 68, 304/169.
17. Schonfeld, Ms 183/25/1.
18. Dina Wardi, *Memorial Candle: Children of the Holocaust*, translated by Naomi Goldblum (London: Tavistock/Routledge, 1992) p. 40.
19. Quoted in Blond, *Marks of Distinction*, p. 79.
20. Whiteman, *The Uprooted*, pp. 266–7.
21. Gopfert, *Der jüdische Kindertransport*, p. 184.
22. CBF, Reel 018, records a letter dated 18 February 1946. 'Great anxiety is felt by the refugees in Shanghai. ... The Chinese authorities treat them as enemy aliens and apparently they have been warned officially that China intends to repatriate them forcibly to Germany and Austria.' It may have been for this reason that Hugh Schramm's mother and brother were allowed into the United States.
23. Author interview with Hugh Schramm, 1991.
24. Ibid.
25. Inge Sadan, quoted in Anon, *Kindertransport 60th Anniversary*, p. 117.
26. Quoted in Marion Berghahn, *German-Jewish Refugees in England: The Ambiguities of Assimilation* (New York: St Martin's Press, 1984) pp. 135–6.
27. London Museum of Jewish Life, Anonymous, in Kindertransport files.
28. Vromen, *Hidden Children*, p. 6.
29. Author interview with Bertha Leverton, 1994.
30. Quoted in Vromen, *Hidden Children*, p. 23.
31. Ibid., p. 135.
32. Quoted in Leverton and Lowensohn, *I Came Alone*, p. 286. See also Harris and Oppenheimer, *Into the Arms of Strangers*, pp. 229, 235ff.
33. Gill, *The Journey Back from Hell*, p. 167.
34. Harris and Oppenheimer, *Into the Arms of Strangers*, p. 225. See also Moskovitz, *Love Despite Hate*, pp. 96–7 and passim.
35. Gissing, *Pearls of Childhood*, pp. 155–6.
36. Max Dickson, 'My Jerusalem Diary', typescript, n.d., p. 5.
37. Franklin Littell, 'Christians in a World of Genocide', in Carol Ritter, Stephen D. Smith and Irena Steinfeldt (eds) *The Holocaust and the Christian World: Reflections on the Past Challenges for the Future* (New York: Continuum, 2000) p. 231.
38. William B. Helmreich, *Against All Odds: Holocaust Survivors and the Successful Lives they Made in America* (New York: Simon & Schuster, 1992) p. 137.
39. Ibid., p. 136. See also, Haas, *In the Shadow of the Holocaust*, pp. 29, 40, 110.
40. See, for example, CBF, Reel 28, 166; Harris, *Into the Arms of Strangers*.
41. Author interview with John Fieldsend, June 1994; and Emanuel and Gissing, *Nicholas Winton and the Rescued Generation*, pp. 150–3.

42. Helmreich, *Against All Odds*, p. 167.
43. Wolf, *Beyond Anne Frank*, p. 157.
44. Berghahn, *German-Jewish Refugees in England*, pp. 186–9, quoted by Haas, *In the Shadow of the Holocaust*, p. 45.
45. Helmreich, *Against All Odds*, p. 249. See also Nat Hentoff, *Black Anti-Semitism and Jewish Racism* (New York: Schocken, 1970) Introduction.
46. Moskovitz, *Love Despite Hate*, p. 233.
47. Helmreich, *Against All Odds*, p. 258.
48. Vromen, *Hidden Children*, p. 45.
49. Quoted in ibid., p. 13.
50. Berghahn, *German-Jewish Refugees in England*, pp. 231–4. Berghahn's study is comprehensive and provides the basis for much of this discussion; Kinder-transport seminar discussion period, University of Southampton, 17 May 2000.
51. Berghahn, *German Jewish Refugees in England*, p. 232.
52. Ibid., p. 234.
53. Ibid.
54. Author interview with Bertha Leverton, 1994.
55. Author interview with J. Schonfield, June 2000.
56. Hartley Library, Brodetsky, Ms 119 (AJ3/1–150, part 1), de Rothschild to Brodetsky, 16 December 1940.
57. Harris and Oppenheimer, *Into the Arms of Strangers*, p. 249.
58. Ibid., p. 250.
59. Berghahn, *German-Jewish Refugees in England*, pp. 176–7; Imperial War Museum, Colin Anson, Interview 11883/5A.
60. London Museum of Jewish Life, Anonymous, Kindertransport Collection.
61. Author interview with John Fieldsend, 1994. Fieldsend defines Messianic Jews as those who acknowledge Jesus as Messiah but who observe the Sabbath, read from the Torah, pray the Siddur, and sing the Shema. See John Fieldsend, *Messianic Jews: The Search for Identity* (Tunbridge Wells: Marc Olive Press, 1993).
62. Quoted in Gissing, *Pearls of Childhood*, p. 101.
63. Quoted in Moskovitz, *Love Despite Hate*, p. 232.
64. Vromen, *Hidden Children*, p. 26.
65. Vromen, *Hidden Children*, p. 26.
66. Ibid., p. 44.
67. Quoted in Harris and Oppenheimer, *Into the Arms of Strangers*, p. 221.
68. Imperial War Museum, Burkill, Interview 004588/08, pp. 50–1.
69. Emanuel and Gissing, *Nicholas Winton and the Rescued Generation*, pp. 110–11.
70. Quoted in Leverton and Lowensohn, *I Came Alone*, p. 242.
71. Interviews housed in the Imperial War Museum; *Kindertransport Reunion Book*

(London: J. E, Emanuel, 1989); *Kindertransport Reunion Book* (Jerusalem: Coll Print, 1994); *Kindertransport Reunion Book* (London: ROK, 1999); Leverton and Lowensohn, *I Came Alone*; list of occupations in the possession of M. Burkill, Cambridge.

72. For Joe Schlesinger's story see his autobiography, *Time Zones*; for a brief overview of Lord Alf Dubs's career, see Emanuel and Gissing, *Nicholas Winton and the Rescued Generation*, pp. 160–1.

73. Gilbert, *The Boys*, p. 326.

74. Helmreich, *Against All Odds*, pp. 267–8.

75. Author interviews with Henry K. 1994; B. Leverton, 1994; and R. Lowenstein, 1998. See also Gilbert, *The Boys*, footnote 111.

76. Quoted in Whiteman, *The Uprooted*, p. 386.

77. Author interviews with John Fieldsend, 1994; B. Leverton, 1994; David Lewinski, 1992; R. Lowenstein, 1998; Hugh Schramm, 1991; and S. Wasserman, 1998.

78. Quoted in David, *A Child's War*, pp. 2–5; Marks, *The Hidden* Children, p. 258.

79. *Souvenir Brochure, 1939–1989* (London: J. E, Emanuel, 1989).

80. Berghahn, *German-Jewish Refugees in England*, p. 143.

81. Imperial War Museum, Gertie, Interview 16505/2.

82. Quoted in Berghahn, *German-Jewish Refugees in England*, p. 142.

83. CBF, Reel 28, 166.

84. LeBor and Boyes, *Seduced by Hitler*, p. 14.

85. Matthew Hughes and Chris Mann, *Inside Hitler's Germany: Life under the Third Reich* (Dulles, VA: Brassey's Inc., 2000) pp. 194–5.

86. Ibid., p 101.

87. CBF, Reel 28, 193–9; quoted in Helmreich, *Against All Odds*, pp. 250–2.

88. David, *A Child's War*, p. 15. See also Gershon, *We Came as Children*, pp. 136–7.

89. Quoted in Harris and Oppenheimer, *Into the Arms of Strangers*, pp. 215–16.

90. Moskovitz, *Love Despite Hate*, p. 230.

91. Harris and Oppenheimer, *Into the Arms of Strangers*, p. 263.

92. Dippel, *Bound Upon a Wheel of Fire*, pp. 256, 257.

93. Author interview with D. Lewinski, 1992; Helmreich, *Against All Odds*, p. 167.

94. Berghahn, *German-Jewish Refugees in England*, pp. 218–19; Haas, *In the Shadow of the Holocaust*, pp. 119–29; interviews, Imperial War Museum; Whiteman, *The Uprooted*, p. 397.

95. Gopfert, *Der jüdische Kindertransport*, p. 152.

96. Author interview with J. Schonfield, June 2000; Haas, *In the Shadow of the Holocaust*, pp. 148–9; Whiteman, *The Uprooted*, p. 397.

97. J. Schonfield to V. Fast, June 2002. Dorothee Sölle, 'Introduction', in Carol

Rittner, Stephen D. Smith and Irene Steinfeldt (eds) *The Holocaust and the Christian World* (London: Kuperard, 2000), writes: 'I studied theology and for a long time I asked myself why God didn't intervene on behalf of his people. Quite a number of people have lost their faith over this, both Christians and Jews. Today I would say, God was very weak at that time, because he had no friends in Germany. ... Because of the lack of friends, God is indeed "in need of humans" as the Jewish teacher, Abraham Joshua Heschel, phrased it.'

98. Haas, *In the Shadow of the Holocaust*, pp. 152–3; Imperial War Museum, Rena, Interview 17369/4.

99. London Metropolitan Archives, CBF, Acc 2793/01/01/01/03, Leonard Montefiore, 'Memorandum from the Committee for the Care of Children from Camps', 15 October 1945.

100. Quoted in Helmreich, *Against All Odds*, p. 241.

101. Quoted in Helen Epstein, *Children of the Holocaust: Conversations with Sons and Daughters of Survivors* (Toronto: Longman Canada, 1979) p. 18.

102. Raul Hilberg, in Foreword to Claudia Cornwall, *Letter from Vienna: A Daughter Uncovers her Family's Jewish Past* (Vancouver: Douglas & McIntyre, 1995) p. ix. See also Helmreich, *Against All Odds*, pp. 237–41.

103. Author interview with John Fieldsend, September 1994.

104. See also Helmreich, *Against All Odds*, pp. 237–47.

105. Moskovitz, *Love Despite Hate*, p. 239.

106. Haas, *In the Shadow of the Holocaust*, p. 119; Whiteman, *The Uprooted*, pp. 382–7.

107. Haas, *In the Shadow of the Holocaust*, p. 4; Wardi, Memorial Candles, pp. 9–10.

108. Wardi, *Memorial Candles*, pp. 9–10. See also David, *A Child's War*, pp. 2–5, 14.

109. Haas, *In the Shadow of the Holocaust*, p. 13; see also Moskovitz, *Love Despite Hate*, pp. 226–7.

110. Berghahn, *German-Jewish Refugees in England*, p. 129, quotes reports showing the male suicide rate among refugees as 5.5 per 10,000 compared with the general population rate of 1.08. These statistics, of course, include all refugees, not only *Kinder*.

111. Moskovitz, *Love Despite Hate*, p. 231.

112. Quoted in ibid., p. 235.

113. *Guardian Weekly*, 15 August 2002, p. 15. See also, among others, Leverton and Lowensohn, *I Came Alone*, p. 147.

114. Krell, *Messages and Memories*, p. 24.

115. Lambeth Palace Library, Bell Papers, vol. 35, part l, November 1942.

116. Quoted in Epstein, *Children of the Holocaust*, p. 21.

117. Ibid., p. 305.

118. *Jewish Chronicle*, 26 June 1987; Josephs, *Survivors*, p. 207.

119. Dunstan, 'Jewish Refugee Youth in England', p. 2.

120. Ruth Michaelis, *Kindertransport 60th Anniversary* (London: ROK, 1999) p. 87.

121. See Anon, *Anniversary Books for Kindertransport Reunions* (1989, 1994, 1999); also Whiteman, *The Uprooted*, pp. 395–6.

122. Helmreich, *Against All Odds*, p. 135. Also author interview with Rudi Lowenstein, Winnipeg, 1996.

123. Author interview with Bertha Leverton, 1994; Haas, *In the Shadow of the Holocaust*, p. 166; one *Kind* refused to be interviewed in 1994 because she had never told her story, even to her own children.

124. Quoted in Gurewitsch, *Mothers, Sisters, Resisters*, pp. 172, 178.

125. Bertha Leverton, *Reunion of Kindertransport* (Jerusalem: Coll Print, 1994) p. 2.

126. Moskovitz, quoted in Krell, *Messages and Memories*, p.99. See also Moskovitz, *Love Despite Hate*, p. 231.

127. Helmreich, *Against All Odds*, p. 276. See also Gerhard Sonnert and Gerald Holton, *Was geschah mit den Kindern? Erfolg und Trauma junger Flüchtlinge, die von den Nationalsozialisten vertrieben wurden* (Vienna: Lit, 2008) for more information related to the later years.

10. Epilogue

1. CBF, Reel 67, 316/156–7.

2. CBF, Reel 68, 304/182.

3. CBF, Reel 65, 300/872, 874; Reel 67, 316/118.

4. CBF, Reel 67, 316/164.

5. *AJR Information*, August 1947, p. 59.

6. Moskovitz, *Love Despite Hate*, p. 231.

7. Berghahn, *German-Jewish Refugees in England*, p. 186.

8. Vromen, *Hidden Children*, p. 147.

9. Address by André Geulen, who escorted children to their hiding places, quoted in Vromen, *Hidden Children*, p. 103.

10. Author interview with David Lewinski, September 1995.

11. Wolf, *Beyond Anne Frank*, p. 17. Wolf offers a comprehensive analysis of the silence of hidden children in relation to their experiences.

12. Vromen, *Hidden Children*, p. 121.

13. Quoted in Gopfert, *Der jüdische Kindertransport*, p. 192, footnote 15. Whatever the definition of 'survivor', it should be noted that there is no scholarly consensus on exactly when the 'Holocaust' began. There is, accordingly, no consensus on a definition of 'survivor'. (My thanks to L. Steimen for this information.)

14. Baumel, 'The Jewish Refugee Children in Great Britain', p. 5.

15. Bentwich, letter to *The Times*, 15 April 1943.

16. Quoted in Harris and Oppenheimer, *Into the Arms of Strangers*, p. 182.

17. Quoted in Greenwood, *Quaker Encounters*, p. 329.
18. Gottlieb, *Men of Vision*, p. 195; Rabbi Schonfeld's teachers, for example, received £1.15 a week (Schonfeld, Ms 183/391/1/folder 1).
19. *Jewish Chronicle*, 23 April 1948, p. 48.
20. *Jewish Chronicle*, 23 April 1948, p. 5.
21. Bentwich to *The Times*, 15 April 1943.
22. Hertz, Ms 175/139/2, Hertz form letter, 31 May 1940.
23. *Jewish Chronicle*, 9 May 1947, p. 8. See also Esther Waterman (ed.) *Golden Jubilee: Canadian Hadassah-Wizo 1917–1967* (Montreal: The Eagle Publishing Co., 1967).
24. Gilbert, *The Righteous*, p. 114.
25. Schonfeld, Ms 183/576/1.
26. Vromen, *Hidden Children*, pp. 124–6ff.
27. See Gilbert, *The Righteous*; Milton Meltzer, *Rescue: The Story of How Gentiles Saved Jews in the Holocaust* (New York: Harper & Row, 1988); Samuel P. Oliner and Pearl M. Oliner, *The Altruistic Personality: Rescuers of Jews in Nazi Europe* (New York: The Free Press, 1988); Silver, *The Book of the Just*, among others.
28. Gilbert, *The Righteous*, pp. 437, 21.
29. Ibid., p. xvi.
30. Vromen, *Hidden Children*. See also Ewa Kurek, *Your Life is Worth Mine: How Polish Nuns Saved Hundreds of Jewish Children in German-Occupied Poland, 1939–1945* (New York: Hippocrene Books, 1997); Uriel Tal, 'Introduction', in Johan M. Snoek (ed.) *The Grey Book* (Assen: Van Corcum & Company, 1967).
31. Gilbert, *The Righteous*, p. 13.
32. Ibid., p. 443.
33. Ibid., p. 125.
34. London Metropolitan Archives, CBF, Acc 2793/01/01/01/03, Minutes 14 January 1946.
35. Hansard, HCD, vol. 341, 21 November 1938.
36. Abella and Troper, *None Is Too Many*; Feingold, *The Politics of Rescue*.
37. Quoted in Pross, *Paying for the Past*, p. 191. In all fairness, it must be recorded that the United States admitted approximately 200,000 Jews between 1937 and 1939 and, while this was fewer per capita of population than the United Kingdom, it was still substantial (thanks to D. Stone).
38. Quoted in Bailey, *A Quaker Couple in Nazi Germany*, p. 267.
39. CBF, Reel 67, 313/17, 12 May 1949, 'Report'.
40. Hartley Library University of Southampton, Greenberg Collection, Ms 150 (AJ 110/4), Laski to Greenberg, 14 December 1941. The dialogue continues with writers such as Peter Ochs, who is the Edgar Bronfman Professor of Modern Jewish Thought at the University of Virginia. An impressive list of publications with which he was associated includes, among others, Tikva

Frymer-Kensky, David Novak, Peter Ochs, David Fox Sandmel and Michael A. Signer (eds) *Christianity in Jewish Terms* (Boulder, CO: Westview Press, 2000); Peter Ochs, *The Return to Scripture in Judaism and Christianity: Essays in Postcritical Scriptural Interpretation* (Mahwah, NJ: Paulist Press, 1993); and John Howard Yoder, *The Jewish-Christian Schism Revisited: Theology in a Postcritical Key*, edited by Michael G. Cartright and Peter Ochs (London: SCM Press, 2003).

41.   Bell Papers, vol. 35, part 1, p. 336.

42.   Hartley Library, Christian Council, Ms 65(A755/1/2), July 1949.

43.   Chartock and Spencer, *Can It Happen Again?* p. 362.

44.   *Winnipeg Free Press*, 7 January 2002 and 29 April 2002, A6; Jörg Wollenberg (ed.) *The German Public and the Persecution of the Jews, 1933–1945* (Amherst, NY: Prometheus Books, 1996) p. xi.

45.   Sölle, 'Introduction', p. ii.

46.   Yehuda Bauer, '2000 International Forum Conference on the Holocaust', in Eva Freed (ed.) *Beyond the 'Never Agains'* (Värnamo, Sweden: Fälth & Hässler AB, 2005).

47.   Pross, *Paying for the Past*, p. 19.

48.   Ibid., p. 3.

49.   Schonfeld, Ms 183/108/3. The schools listed were Hasmonean Grammar School for Girls, Avigdor Primary School, and Menoah Primary School.

50.   Schonfeld, Ms 183/108/3: the date was 24 January 1958.

51.   M. Goldberger to V. Fast, 8 October 2009.

52.   Schonfeld, Ms 183/227/1/folder 2.

53.   Berenbaum, *The World Must Know*, p. xx.

54.   Nicholson, *Remember World War II*.

55.   Krell, *Messages and Memories*, p. 6.

56.   Presland, *A Great Adventure*, p. 16.

BIBLIOGRAPHY

Manuscript Collections

Bell, Bishop George, Papers, vols 6, 27, 28, 34, 35 (LPL)

Board of Deputies of British Jews (LMA)

Canadian National Committee on Refugees and Victims of Political Persecution (National Archives of Canada, Ottawa)

Central British Fund for World Jewish Relief (LMA)

Central British Fund for German Jewry/Central Council for Jewish Refugees/Central British Fund for Jewish Relief and Rehabilitation (Reports 1933–1943) (Wiener Library, London)

Fisher, Archbishop Geoffrey, Papers, vol. 12, 27 (LPL)

Friends Committee for Refugees and Aliens, 1933–1950 (FHLA)

German Jewish Aid Committee (later Jewish Refugees Committee) (Manchester Central Library/Archives)

Hertz, Chief Rabbi (Hartley Library, University of Southampton)

Kindertransport Files (London Museum of Jewish Life)

Parliamentary Debates, *Hansard* (British Library, London)

Schonfeld, Rabbi Solomon (Hartley Library, University of Southampton)

Society for the Protection of Science and Learning (Bodleian Library, Oxford)

Sound Archives

Imperial War Museum (IWM).

Other Sources

Abella, Irving (1990) *A Coat of Many Colours: Two Centuries of Jewish Life in Canada* (Toronto: Lester & Orpen Dennys)

Abella, Irving and Harold Troper (1991) *None is too Many: Canada and the Jews of Europe, 1933–1948* (Toronto: Lester & Orpen Dennys)

241

Adler, David A. (2002) *A Hero and the Holocaust: The Story of Janusz Koreczak and His Children* (New York: Holiday House)

Alma, Ann (2008) *Brave Deeds: How One Family Saved Many from the Nazis* (Toronto: Groundwood Books)

Anflick, Charles (1999) *Resistance: Teen Partisans and Resisters Who Fought Nazi Tyranny* (New York: Rosen Publishing Group, Inc.)

Anon (1959) *This is our Life* (pamphlet) (London: Free German Youth)

Anon (1959) *Twenty-Five Years of Youth Aliyah* (London: Children and Youth Aliyah)

Anon (1972) *Encyclopaedia Judaica* (New York: Macmillan) vol. 6

Anon (1998) 'Lives Lived: Paul Felix (Sontheimer) Sutton', obituary in *Globe and Mail* (Toronto) 29 January

Anon (1999) 'A Tribute to our Brother', in *Kindertransport 60th Anniversary* (London: ROK)

Anon (1989) *Anniversary Book for Kindertransport Reunions* (London: J. E. Emanuel)

Anon (1994) *Anniversary Book for Kindertransport Reunions* (Jerusalem: Coll Print)

Anon (1999) *Anniversary Book for Kindertransport Reunions* (London: ROK)

Axelrod, Toby A. (1999) *In the Camps: Teens Who Survived the Nazi Concentration Camps* (New York: The Rosen Publishing Group Inc.)

Bailey, Brenda (1994) *A Quaker Couple in Nazi Germany: Leonard Friedrich Survives Buchenwald* (York: William Sessions UK)

Bard, Mitchell G. (2008) *48 Hours of Kristallnacht: Night of Destruction/Dawn of the Holocaust: An Oral History* (Guilford, CT: The Lyons Press)

Bar-On, Dan (1989) *Legacy of Silence: Encounters with Children of the Third Reich* (Cambridge, MA: Harvard University Press)

Barth, Karl (1965) *The German Church Conflict*, translated by P. T. A. Parker (Richmond: John Knox Press)

Bauer, Yehuda (1981) *American Jewry and the Holocaust: The American Jewish Joint Distribution Committee, 1939–45* (Detroit: Wayne State University Press)

Bauer, Yehuda (2005) '2000 International Forum Conference on the Holocaust', in Eva Freed (ed.) *Beyond the 'Never Agains'* (Värnamo, Sweden: Fälth & Hässler AB)

Baum, Jeffrey and Barbara (1993) *Never Before, Never Again! Evacuation in the Edmonton Hundreds* (London: Heritage no. 4, Jewish Research Group of the Edmonton Hundred Historical Society)

Baumel, Esther Judith (1981) 'The Jewish Refugee Children in Great Britain, 1938–1945', unpublished MA thesis, Bar-Ilan University, Israel

Baumel, Judith Tydor (1983) *Twice a Refugee: The Jewish Refugee Children in Great Britain during Evacuation, 1939–1943* (Bloomington: Indiana University Press)

Baumel, Judith Tydor (1990) *Unfulfilled Promise: Rescue and Resettlement of Jewish Refugee Children in the United States 1934–1945* (Juneau Alaska: Denali Press)

Bentley, Elaine (1989) 'Reception in the United Kingdom of Jewish Refugees with Special Emphasis on the Role of the Kitchener Camp 1938–1939', MA thesis, Polytechnic of Central London (Wiener Library, London)

Bentwich, Norman (1936) *The Refugees from Germany, April 1933 to December 1935* (London: George Allen &Unwin Ltd)

Bentwich, Norman (1944) *Jewish Youth Comes Home: The Story of Youth Aliyah, 1933–1943* (London: Gollancz)

Bentwich, Norman (1956) *They Found Refuge: An Account of British Jewry's Work for Victims of Nazi Oppression* (London: The Cresset Press)

Berenbaum, Michael (2006) *The World Must Know: The History of the Holocaust as Told in the United States Holocaust Memorial Museum* (Boston: Little, Brown & Company)

Berger, Allan L. and Naomi Berger (2001) *Second Generation Voices: Reflections by Children of Holocaust Survivors and Perpetrators* (Syracuse: Syracuse University Press)

Berghahn, Marion (1984) *German-Jewish Refugees in England: The Ambiguities of Assimilation* (New York: St Martin's Press)

Besel, Richard (2001) *Life in the Third Reich* (Oxford: Oxford University Press)

Blend, Martha (1995) *A Child Alone* (London: Vallentine, Mitchell & Co.)

Bliss, L. J. (1944) *Christians and Anti-Semitism* (Birmingham: Council of Clergy & Ministers for Common Ownership)

Blond, Elaine (1988) *Marks of Distinction* (London: Vallentine, Mitchell & Company)

Bosanquet, Mary (1968) *The Life and Death of Dietrich Bonhoeffer* (London: Hodder and Stoughton)

Bowen-Jakabowitz, Edith (n.d.) 'Memories and Reflections', unpublished memoir, Wiener Library, London

Bradfield, Susie (1999) *Kindertransport 60th Anniversary* (London: ROK)

Brenner, Reeve R. (1980) *The Faith and Doubt of Holocaust Survivors* (New York: Free Press)

Brostoff, Anita and Sheila Chamovitz (eds) (2001) *Flares of Memory:*

Survivors Remember – Stories of Childhood during the Holocaust (Oxford: Oxford University Press)

Buber, Martin (1967) *On Judaism*, edited by Nahum N. Glatzer (New York: Schocken Books)

Bukey, Evan (2000) *Hitler's Austria; Popular Sentiment in the Nazi Era 1938–1945* (Chapel Hill: University of North Carolina Press)

Cesarani, David (1996) 'Great Britain', in David S. Wyman (ed.) *The World Reacts to the Holocaust* (Baltimore: Johns Hopkins University Press)

Chandler, Andrew (1997) *Brethren in Adversity: Bishop George Bell, the Church of England and the Crisis of German Protestantism 1933–1939* (London: Church of England Record Society)

Chappell, Connery (1984) *Island of Barbed Wire: The Remarkable Story of World War Two Internment on the Isle of Man* (London: Robert Hale)

Chartock, Roselle K. and Jack Spencer (eds) (1995) *Can It Happen Again? Chronicles of the Holocaust* (New York: Black Dog & Leventhal)

Cornwall, Claudia (1995) *Letter from Vienna: A Daughter Uncovers her Family's Jewish Past* (Vancouver: Douglas & McIntyre)

Crane, Cynthia (2000) *Divided Lives: The Untold Stories of Jewish–Christian Women in Nazi Germany* (New York: St Martin's Press)

Cretzmeyer, Stacy (1999) *Your Name is Renée: Ruth Kapp Hartz's Story as a Hidden Child in Nazi-Occupied France* (New York: Oxford University Press)

David, Kati (1989) *A Child's War: World War II through the Eyes of Children* (New York: Four Walls Eight Windows)

David, Ruth L. (2008) *Ein Kind unserer Zeit: Erinnerungen eines jüdischen Mädchens an Deutschland und an das Exil* (Wiesbaden: Thrun)

Davidson, Lucy V. and John S. Ross (eds) (1989) *For a Future and a Hope: The Story of the Houses of Refuge in Chislehurst* (Chislehurst: CWI Publications)

Dawidowicz, Lucy S. (1986) *The War Against the Jews 1933–1945: The Definitive Holocaust History* (New York: The Free Press/Seth Books)

Dickson, Max (n.d.) 'My Jerusalem Diary', typescript

Dippel, John V. H. (1996) *Bound upon a Wheel of Fire: Why So Many German Jews Made the Tragic Decision to Remain in Nazi Germany* (New York: Basic Books)

Drucker, Olga Levy (1992) *Kindertransport* (New York: Henry Holt)

Dunstan, Fred (alias Fritz Deutsch) (n.d.) 'How it all Started', unpublished memoir (Wiener Library)

Dunstan, Fred (n.d.) 'Jewish Refugee Youth in England, 1938–1940', handwritten manuscript (Wiener Library)

Dunstan, Fred (n.d.) 'The Great Engeham Farm Camp July–December 1939', handwritten account (Wiener Library)

Dwork, Deborah (1991) *Children with a Star: Jewish Youth in Nazi Europe* (New Haven, CT: Yale University Press)

Dwork, Deborah and Robert van Pelt (1996) *Auschwitz 1270 to the Present* (New York: W. W. Norton & Company)

Dwork, Deborah and Robert Jan van Pelt (2002) *Holocaust: A History* (London: John Murray)

Eisner, Gisela (n.d.) 'Cottage Pie on Tuesdays', typescript (Wiener Library)

Emanuel, Muriel and Vera Gissing (2001) *Nicholas Winton and the Rescued Generation: Save one Life, Save the World* (London: Mitchell Vallentine & Company)

Epstein, Helen (1979) *Children of the Holocaust: Conversations with Sons and Daughters of Survivors* (Toronto: Longman Canada)

Fast, Vera K. (ed.) (1999) *Companions of the Peace: Diaries and Letters of Monica Storrs, 1931–1939* (Toronto: University of Toronto Press)

Feingold, Henry L. (1970) *The Politics of Rescue: The Roosevelt Administration and the Holocaust, 1938–1945* (New Brunswick, NJ: Rutgers University Press)

Feldman, Alfred (2000) *One Step Ahead: A Jewish Fugitive in Hitler's Europe* (Carbondale: Southern Illinois University Press)

Fieldsend, John (1993) *Messianic Jews: The Search for Identity* (Tunbridge Wells: Marc Olive Press)

Figes, Eva (1978) *Little Eden: A Child at War* (New York: Persea Books)

Fleischner, Eva (ed.) (1974) *Auschwitz: Beginning of A New Era? Reflections on the Holocaust* (New York: KTAV Publishing House Inc.)

Fogelman, Eva (1994) *Conscience and Courage: Rescuers of Jews During the Holocaust* (NewYork: Anchor Books)

Fox, Anne L. (1996) *My Heart in a Suitcase* (London: The Library of Holocaust Testemonies)

Fox, Anne and Eva Abraham-Podietz (2008) *Ten Thousand Children: True Stories Told by Children who Escaped the Holocaust on the Kindertransport* (Campell, CA: Paw Prints)

Freeman, Kathleen (1965) *If any Man Build: The History of the Save the Children Fund* (London: Hodder & Stoughton)

Freud, Anna and Dorothy T. Burlingham (1944) *Infants Without Families* (New York: International Universities Incorporated)

Friedlander, Saul (1997) *Nazi Germany and the Jews*, vol 1, *The Years of Persecution 1933–1939* (New York: Harper Collins)

Friedmann, Walter F. (1941) 'Refugee Children in Great Britain: Some Notes on the Problems and Background of the Jewish Children's Transports 1938–1939', unpublished paper (Wiener Library)

Frischer, Dominique (2008) *Les Enfants du Silence et de la Reconstruction: la Shoah en Partage* (Paris: Grasset)

Frymer-Kensky, Tikva, David Novak, Peter Ochs, David Fox Sandmel and Michael A. Signer (eds) (2000) *Christianity in Jewish Terms* (Boulder, CO: Westview Press)

Furet, François (ed.) (1989) *Unanswered Questions: Nazi Germany and the Genocide of the Jews* (New York: Schocken Books)

Gelman, Charles (1989) *Do Not Go Gentle: A Memoir of Jewish Resistance in Poland 1941–45* (Hamden Court: Archon Books)

Gerlach, Wolfgang (1996) 'And the Witnesses were Silent: The Confessing Church and the Persecution of the Jews', in Jörg Wollenberg (ed.) *The German Public and the Persecution of the Jews, 1933–1945* (Amherst, NY: Prometheus Books)

Gershon, Karen (1985) *The Bread of Exile* (London: Victor Gollancz Ltd)

Gershon, Karen (ed.) (1989) *We Came as Children: A Collective Autobiography* (London: Papermac)

Gilbert, Martin (1996) *The Boys: Triumph Over Adversity: The Story of 732 Young Concentration Camp Survivors* (Vancouver: Douglas & McIntyre)

Gilbert, Martin (2003) *The Righteous: The Unsung Heroes of the Holocaust* (Toronto: Key Porter Books)

Gilbert, Martin (2006) *Kristallnacht: Prelude to Destruction* (New York: HarperCollins)

Gill, Anton (1988) *The Journey Back from Hell: Conversations with Concentration Camp Survivors* (London: Grafton Books)

Gillespie, V. M. (1992) 'Kindertransports', A talk given at the University of Sussex (Wiener Library)

Gissing, Vera (1988) *Pearls of Childhood* (London: Robson Books)

Gopfert, Rebekka (1997) *Der jüdische Kindertransport von Deutschland nach England, 1938–39* (Frankfurt: Campus Verlag)

Gorell Barnes, Ronald (1956) *One Man … Many Parts* (London: Odhams Press)

Gorsky, J. (2000) 'Pius XII and the Holocaust, in Carol Rittner, Stephen D. Smith and Irene Steinfeldt (eds) *The Holocaust and the Christian World* (London: Kuperard)

Gottlieb, Amy Zahl (1998) *Men Of Vision: Anglo-Jewry's Aid to Victims of the Nazi Regime, 1933–1945* (London: Weidenfeld & Nicholson)

Gottlieb, Erika (2008) *Becoming My Mother's Daughter* (Waterloo: Wilfrid Laurier University Press)

Greene, Joshua M. and Shiva Kumar (2000) *Witness: Voices from the Holocaust* (New York: The Free Press)

Greenwood, John Ormerod (1975) *Quaker Encounters: Friends and Relief Work*, vol. 1 (York, UK: Friends & Relief)

Gregor, Neil (ed.) (2008) *Nazism, War and Genocide* (Exeter: University of Exeter Press)

Gruber, Ruth (1983) *Haven: The Unknown Story of One Thousand World War Two Refugees* (New York: Coward-McCann Inc.)

Grynberg, Henryk (1997) *Children of Zion*, translated by Jacqueline Mitchell (Evanston, IL: Northwestern University Press)

Gurewitsch, Brana (ed.) (1998) *Mothers, Sisters, Resisters: Oral Histories of Women Who Survived the Holocaust* (Tuscaloosa: University of Alabama Press)

Haas, Aaron (1990) *In the Shadow of the Holocaust: The Second Generation* (Ithaca: Cornell University Press)

Haas, Ilse (1993) 'Ilse Haas', in Bertha Leverton and Shmuel Lowensohn (eds) *I Came Alone: The Stories of the Kindertransports* (Sussex: The Book Guild Ltd) pp. 133–5

Halleck, Elaine (ed.) (2004) *Living in Nazi Germany* (San Diego: Greenhaven Press)

Hampl, Patricia (1998) 'Edith Stein', in Susan Bergman (ed.) *Martyrs: Contemporary Writers on Modern Lives of Faith* (Maryknoll, NY: Orbis Books) pp. 197–215

Harris, Mark Jonathan (2000) *Into the Arms of Strangers: Stories of the Kindertransport*, documentary film written and directed by Mark Jonathan Harris, released 24 November

Harris, Mark Jonathan and Deborah Oppenheimer (2000) *Into the Arms of Strangers: Stories of the Kindertransport* (London: Bloomsbury)

Hecht, Ingeborg (1999) *Invisible Walls and to Remember is to Heal*, translated from German by J. Brownjohn and J. Broadwin (Evanston: Northwestern University Press)

Heine, Ludwig (1961) *Geschichte des Kirchenkampfes in der Grenzmark Posen-Westpreußen 1930–1940* (Göttingen: Vandenhoeck & Ruprecht)

Helmreich, William B. (1992) *Against All Odds: Holocaust Survivors and the Successful Lives they Made in America* (New York: Simon & Schuster)

Henderson, Sir Nevile (1940) *Failure of a Mission* (London: Hodder & Stoughton)

CHILDREN'S EXODUS

Hentoff, Nat (1970) *Black Anti-Semitism and Jewish Racism* (New York: Schocken)

Hilberg, Raul (1985) *The Holocaust: The Destruction of the European Jews*, 3 vols (New York: Holmes & Meier)

Hilberg, Raul (1992) *Perpetrators, Victims, Bystanders: The Jewish Catastrophe 1933–1945* (New York: HarperCollins Publishers)

Hillman, Laura (2005) *I will Plant you a Lilac Tree: A Memoir of a Schindler's List Survivor* (New York: Simon Pulse)

Hitler, Adolf (1969) *Mein Kampf*, translated from the German by Ralph Manheim (London: Hutchinson)

Hofreiter, Gerda (2008) *You Must Go Alone: The Rescue of Viennese Jewish Children on Kindertransporte during the Nazi Era: A Historical Enquiry with Particular Reference to the United States* (Morrisville: G. Hofreiter)

Horowitz, Gordon (1990) *In the Shadow of Death: Living Outside the Gates of Mauthausen* (New York: The Free Press)

Housden, Martyn (1997) *Resistance and Conformity in the Third Reich* (London: Routledge)

Hughes, Matthew and Chris Mann (2000) *Inside Hitler's Germany: Life under the Third Reich* (Dulles, VA: Brassey's Inc.)

Inglis, Ruth (1989) *The Children's War: Evacuation 1939–1945* (London: Collins)

Jasper, Ronald C. D. (1967) *George Bell: Bishop of Chichester* (London: Oxford University Press)

Josephs, Jeremy and Susi Bechhofer (1996) *Rosa's Child: The True Story of One Woman's Quest for a Lost Mother and a Vanished Past* (London: I.B.Tauris)

Josephs, Zoe (1988) *Survivors: Jewish Refugees in Birmingham 1933–1945* (London: Institute of Jewish Affairs)

Kacer, Kathy (2006) *Hiding Edith: A True Story* (Toronto: Second Story Press)

Kahn-Minden, Eva (1991) *The Road Back: Quare Mead* (Jerusalem: Gefen Publishing House)

Kaplan, Marion A. (1998) *Between Dignity and Despair: Jewish Life in Nazi Germany* (New York: Oxford University Press)

Kapp, Yvonne and Margaret Mynatt (1997) *British Policy and the Refugees, 1933–1941* (London: Frank Cass)

Kater, Horst (1970) *Die Deutsche Evangelische Kirche in den Jahren 1933 und 1934: Eine rechts- und verfassungsrechtliche Untersuchung zur Gründung und Zerfall einer Kirche im nationalsozialistischen Staat* (Göttingen: Vandenhoeck & Ruprecht)

Keeley, Jennifer (2000) *Life in the Hitler Youth* (San Diego, CA: Luent Books)

Keith, Janet (1991) *A Friend Among Enemies: The Incredible Story of Arie Van Mansum in the Holocaust* (Richmond Hill, Ontario: Fitzhenry and Whiteside)

Klemperer, Victor (1998) *I Will Bear Witness: A Diary of the Nazi Years*, translated by Martin Chalmers (New York: Random House)

Koch, Eric (1980) *Deemed Suspect: A Wartime Blunder* (Toronto: Methuen)

Kosiński, Jerzy (1965) *The Painted Bird: Autobiographical Fiction* (London: Black Swan)

Kranzler, David (1987) *Thy Brother's Blood: The Orthodox Jewish Response During the Holocaust* (New York: Mesorah Publications Ltd)

Krell, Robert (ed.) (1999) *Messages and Memories: Reflections on Child Survivors of the Holocaust* (Vancouver, Deskside Publishing)

Krell, Robert (2007) *Child Holocaust Survivors: Memories and Reflections* (Victoria: Trafford Publishing)

Kuchler-Silberman, Lena (1961) *My Hundred Children* (London: Souvenir Press)

Kugel, James (1990) *On Being a Jew* (Baltimore: The Johns Hopkins University Press)

Kuper, Jack (1967) *Child of the Holocaust* (Toronto: General Publishing Company)

Kurek, Ewa (1997) *Your Life is Worth Mine: How Polish Nuns Saved Hundreds of Jewish Children in German-Occupied Poland 1939–1945* (New York: Hippocrene Books)

Lachs, Maria (2007) *From Paris to Sydney: A Chaotic Roller Coaster. An Autobiography of a 'Hidden Child Survivor of the Holocaust'* (Marrickville, NSW: Southwood)

Langbein, Herman (1994) *Against All Hope: Resistance in the Nazi Concentration Camps 1938–1945*, translated by Harry Zohn (New York: Paragon House)

Lappin, Ben (1963) *The Redeemed Children: The Story of the Rescue of War Orphans by the Jewish Community of Canada* (Toronto: University of Toronto Press)

Laqueur, Walter (1980) *The Terrible Secret: Suppression of the Truth about Hitler's Final Solution* (Boston: Little, Brown & Company)

LeBor, Adam and Roger Boyes (2000) *Seduced by Hitler: The Choices of a Nation and the Ethics of Survival* (Naperville, IL: Sourcebooks, Inc.).

Lersner, Baron Dieter von (1958) *Die evangelische Jugendverband Württembergs und die Hitler-Jugend 1933–1934* (Göttingen: Vandenhoeck & Ruprecht)

Leuner, H. D. (1966) *When Compassion Was a Crime: Germany's Silent Heroes* (London: Oswald Wolff)

Leverton, Bertha (1994) *Reunion of Kindertransport* (Jerusalem: : Coll Print)

Leverton, Bertha and Shmuel Lowensohn (eds) (1993) *I Came Alone: The Stories of the Kindertransports* (Sussex: The Book Guild Ltd)

Levin, Nora (1968) *The Holocaust: The Destruction of European Jewry 1933–1945* (New York: Schocken Books)

Levine, Karen (2002) *Hana's Suitcase: A True Story* (Toronto: Second Story Press)

Levy, Herbert (1995) *Voices from the Past* (Lewes, Sussex: Book Guild Ltd)

Lipman, Vivian (1959) *A Century of Social Service, 1859–1959: A History of the Jewish Board of Guardians* (London: Routledge & Kegan Paul)

Littell, Franklin (2000) 'Christians in a World of Genocide', in Carol Ritter, Stephen D. Smith and Irena Steinfeldt (eds) *The Holocaust and the Christian World: Reflections on the Past Challenges for the Future* (New York: Continuum)

Lukas, Richard C. (1994) *Did the Children Cry? Hitler's War Against Jewish and Polish Children 1939–45* (New York: Hippocrene Books)

Marks, Jane (1995) *The Hidden Children: The Secret Survivors of the Holocaust* (Toronto: Bantam Books)

Martz, Fraidie (1996) *Open Your Hearts: The Story of the Jewish War Orphans in Canada* (Montreal: Vehicule Press)

Meltzer, Milton (1988) *Rescue: The Story of How Gentiles Saved Jews in the Holocaust* (New York: Harper & Row)

Michaelis, Ruth (1999) *Kindertransport 60th Anniversary* (London: ROK)

Millman, Isaac (2005) *Hidden Child* (New York: Francis Foster Books)

Moskovitz, Sarah (1983) *Love Despite Hate: Child Survivors of the Holocaust and their Adult Lives* (New York: Schocken Books)

Moskovitz, Sarah (1999) 'Making Sense of Survival: A Journey with Child Survivors of the Holocaust', in R. Krell (ed.) *Messages and Memories: Reflections on Child Survivors of the Holocaust* (Vancouver, Deskside Publishing) pp. 11–19

Nicholson, D. (2005) *Remember World War II: Kids Who Survived Tell Their Stories* (Washington: National Geographic)

Niewyk, Donald L. (ed.) (1998) *Fresh Wounds: Early Narratives of Holocaust Survival* (Chapel Hill: University of North Carolina Press)

Nir, Yehuda (1989) *The Lost Childhood: A Memoir* (New York: Harcourt, Brace, Jovanovich)

Ochs, Peter (1993) *The Return to Scripture in Judaism and Christianity: Essays in Postcritical Scriptural Interpretation* (Mahwah, NJ: Paulist Press)

Oliner, Samuel P. and Pearl M. Oliner (1988) *The Altruistic Personality: Rescuers of Jews in Nazi Europe* (New York: The Free Press)

Paldiel, Mordecai (2000) *Saving the Jews: Amazing Stories of Persons who Defied the 'Final Solution'* (Rockville: Schrieber Publishing)

Papanek, Ernest and Edward Linn (1975) *Out of the Fire* (New York: William Morrow & Co.)

Patkin, Benzion (1979) *The Dunera Internees* (Sydney: Casell Australia Ltd)

Pearl, Cyril (1983) *The Dunera Scandal* (London: Angus & Robertson)

Phayer, Michael (2000) *The Catholic Church and the Holocaust 1930–1965* (Bloomington: Indiana University Press)

Phayer, Michael (2000) 'The Response of the German Catholic Church to National Socialism', in Carol Rittner, Stephen D. Smith and Irene Steinfeldt (eds) *The Holocaust and the Christian World* (London: Kuperard)

Pick, Hella (2000) *Guilty Victim: Austria from the Holocaust to Haider* (London: I.B.Tauris)

Pilch, Judah (1995) 'Jewish Life in Europe between the Two World Wars (1919–1939)', in Roselle Chartock and Jack Spencer (eds) *Can It Happen Again? Chronicles of the Holocaust* (New York: Black Dog & Leventhal) pp. 88–96

Pollak, Ernest (n.d.) 'Departure to Freedom Curtailed', unpublished memoir (Wiener Library, London)

Presland, John (1944) *A Great Adventure: The Story of the Refugee Children's Movement* (London: Bloomsbury House)

Pross, Christian (1998) *Paying for the Past: The Struggle Over Reparations for Surviving Victims of the Nazi Terror*, translated by Belinda Cooper (Baltimore: The Johns Hopkins Press)

Rempel, Gerhard (1989) *Hitler's Children: The Hitler Youth and the SS* (Chapel Hill: The University of North Carolina Press)

Reti, Irene and Valerie Jean Chase (eds) (1995) *A Transported Life: Memories of Kindertransport. The Oral History of Thea Feliks Eden* (Santa Cruz, CA: HerBooks)

Rittner, Carol and Sondra Myers (eds) (1986) *The Courage to Care: Rescuers of the Jews during the Holocaust* (New York: New York University Press)

Rittner, Carol, Stephen D. Smith and Irene Steinfeldt (eds) (2000) *The Holocaust and the Christian World* (London: Kuperard)

Robertson, Edwin (1995) *Unshakeable Friend: George Bell and the German Churches* (London: CCBI Publications)

Rosenberg, Roy A. (1990) *The Concise Guide to Judaism: History, Practice and Faith* (New York: NAL Books)

Rosenblatt, E. (2000) 'Edith Stein's Canonization: Acknowledging Objections from Jews and Catholics', in Carol Rittner, Stephen D. Smith and Irene Steinfeldt (eds) *The Holocaust and the Christian World* (London: Kuperard) pp. 224–7

Rubenstein, Richard L. (1989) 'The Dean and the Chosen People', in John Roth and Michael Berenbaum (eds) *The Holocaust: Religious and Philosophical Implications* (New York: Paragon House)

Russo, Marisabina (2005) *Always Remember Me: How One Family Survived World War II*, unpaginated booklet (New York: Atheneum Books)

Sacharin, Rosa M. (compiler) (1999) *Recollections of Child Refugees from 1938 to the Present: Kindertransport Scotland's Child Refugees* (Glasgow: Scottish Annual Reunion of Kinder)

Satloff, Robert (2006) *Among the Righteous* (New York: Public Affairs)

Schlesinger, Joe (1990) *Time Zones: A Journalist in the World* (Toronto: Random House)

Schleunes, Karl (1970) *The Twisted Road to Auschwitz: Nazi Policy toward German Jews, 1933–1939* (Chicago: University of Illinois Press)

Schulman, Faye (1995) *A Partisan's Memoir: Woman of the Holocaust* (Toronto: Second Story Press)

Seligman, Matthew, John Davidon and John McDonald (2003) *Daily Life in Hitler's Germany* (New York: Thomas Dunn Books)

Seltzer, Robert M. (1980) *Jewish People, Jewish Thought: The Jewish Experience in History* (New York: Macmillan Publishing Co., Inc.)

Sherman, A. J. (1994) *Island Refuge: Britain and Refugees from the Third Reich, 1933–1939* (London: Frank Cass & Co. Ltd)

Silver, Eric (1992) *The Book of the Just: The Silent Heroes Who Saved Jews from Hitler* (London: Weidenfeld & Nicolson)

Simpson, Sir John Hope (1938) *Refugees: A Preliminary Report of a Survey* (London: Royal Institute of International Affairs)

Simpson, Sir John Hope (1939) *Refugees: A Review of the Situation since September 1938* (London: The Royal Institute of International Affairs)

Sölle, Dorothee (2000) 'Introduction', in Carol Rittner, Stephen D. Smith and Irene Steinfeldt (eds) *The Holocaust and the Christian World* (London: Kuperard)

Sonnert, Gerhard and Gerald Holton (2008) *Was geschah mit den Kindern? Erfolg und Trauma junger Flüchtlinge, die von den Nationalsozialisten vertrieben wurden* (Vienna: Lit)

Stein, André (1993) *Hidden Children: Forgotten Survivors of the Holocaust* (New York: Viking)

Stein, Edith (1986) *Life in a Jewish Family (1891–1916): An Autobiography*, translated by Josephine Koppel, OCD (Washington, DC: ICS Publications)

Stevens, Austin (1975) *The Dispossessed* (London: Barrie and Jenkins)

Steinlauf, Michael C. (1997) *Bondage to the Dead: Poland and the Memory of the Holocaust* (Syracuse: Syracuse University Press)

Stoltzfus, Nathan (1996) *Resistance of the Heart: Intermarraige and the Rosenstrasse Protest in Nazi Germany* (New York: W. W. Norton)

Supple, Carrie (1993) *From Prejudice to Genocide: Learning about the Holocaust* (Stoke-on-Trent: Trentham Books Ltd)

Tal, Uriel (1967) 'Introduction', in Johan M. Snoek (ed.) *The Grey Book* (Assen: Van Corcum & Company)

Teveth, Shabtal (1987) *Ben-Gurion: The Burning Ground, 1886–1948* (Boston: Houghton Mifflin)

Tierney, Brian, Donald Kagan and Pearce Williams (eds) (1976) *Great Issues in Western Civilization*, vol. 2 (New York: Random House)

Tokayer, Marvin and Mary Swartz (1979) *The Fugu Plan: The Untold Story of the Japanese and the Jews During World War II* (New York: Paddington Press)

Turner, Barry (1990) *And the Policeman Smiled* (London: Bloomsbury)

Turner, Barry (n.d.) *The Long Horizon: Sixty Years of CBF World Jewish Relief* (London: CBF World Jewish Relief)

Vromen, Suzanne (2008) *Hidden Children of the Holocaust: Belgian Nuns and their Daring Rescue of Young Jews from the Nazis* (New York: Oxford University Press)

Wardi, Dina (1992) *Memorial Candle: Children of the Holocaust*, translated by Naomi Goldblum (London: Tavistock/Routledge)

Wasserstein, Bernard (1979) *Britain and the Jews of Europe, 1939–1945* (Oxford: Clarendon Press)

Waterman, Esther (ed.) (1967) *Golden Jubilee: Canadian Hadassah-Wizo 1917–1967* (Montreal: The Eagle Publishing Co.)

Westall, Robert M. (1985) *Children of the Blitz: Memories of Wartime Childhood* (Harmondsworth: Viking)

Whitaker, Katherine and Michael Johnson (1995) *Stoatley Rough School 1934–1960*, booklet produced for the school's sixtieth anniversary reunion in May 1994 (Watford: Archives of the Jewish Museum)

Whiteman, Dorit Bader (1993) *The Uprooted: A Hitler Legacy: Voices of those who Escaped before the 'Final Solution'* (New York: Insight Books)

Wicks, Ben (1988) *No Time to Wave Goodbye* (Toronto: Stoddart)

Wicks, Ben (1989) *The Day they Took the Children* (Toronto: Stoddart)

Winton, Nicholas (n.d.) 'Saving the Children: Czechoslovakia 1939', 2 vols of notes, clippings and reports in Wiener Library, London

Wistrich, Robert S. (1991) *Antisemitism: The Longest Hatred* (New York: Pantheon Books)

Wolf, Diane L. (2007) *Beyond Anne Frank: Hidden Children and Postwar Families in Holland* (Berkeley: University of California Press)

Wolfenden, Barbara (2008) *Little Holocaust Survivors and the English School that Saved Them* (Westport, CT: Greenwood World Publications)

Wollenberg, Jörg (1996) 'The Expropriation of the "Rapacious" Capital by "Productive Capital"', in Jorg Wollenberg (ed.) *The German Public and the Persecution of the Jews, 1933–1945*, English edition translated and edited by Rado Pribic: (Amherst, NY: Prometheus Books)

Wollenberg, Jörg (ed.) (1996) *The German Public and the Persecution of the Jews, 1933–1945* (Amherst, NY: Prometheus Books)

Wyman, David S. (1968) *Paper Walls: America and the Refugee Crisis, 1938–1941* (Amherst, MA: University of Massachusetts Press)

Wyman, D. (ed.) (1996) *The World Reacts to the Holocaust* (Baltimore: Johns Hopkins University Press)

Yackin, Hannah (n.d.) 'Of Tortoises and Other Jews', typescript (Wiener Library)

Yoder, John Howard (2003) *The Jewish–Christian Schism Revisited: Theology in a Postcritical Key*, edited by Michael G. Cartright and Peter Ochs (London: SCM Press)

INDEX

A

Abramowicz, Myriam, 187
Adas Yisroel, 98
Africa, 9, 166
Aguda, 156, 157
Agudas, 99, 105, 147
Agudas Yisroel Organization, 105
Ahlwardt, Herr, 3
Albert, Dr, 124
Albright, Madeleine, 197
Allard, Lorraine, 7, 48
American Gathering of Jewish Holocaust Survivors, 187
Amir, Shulamit, 31
Amsterdam, 133
Anglicans, 15, 83, 130
Anglo-Jewish Association, 147
Anschluss, 8
Anson, Colin, 33, 74
anti-Semitism, 3–5, 7, 9, 48, 64, 92, 120, 123, 147, 169–70, 181, 192–4
Argentina, 72

Army Transport Service (ATS), 130
Aryan, 5–6, 26, 116–18, 124, 146
Ashby, Mr, 67
assimilation, 2, 4, 55–7, 74, 115, 171–2, 174, 179
Attenborough, Lord, 49
Auschwitz, 121, 152, 167, 177
Australia, 69, 72–3
Austria, 3, 8, 10, 14, 18, 20, 25, 35, 50, 68, 124, 178, 189
Avigdor House, 42, 53

B

B'nai B'rith, 13, 46, 88, 99, 105, 108, 190
Baal Shem Tov, 198
Bachad, 152
Bader, Adolf, 149
Baeck, Rabbi Dr Leo, 12, 99
Baldwin, Stanley, 47
Balfour, Lord, 43
Bamber, Helen, 158
Bannister, Jean, 23